Creative Hands

Creative HANDS

AN INTRODUCTION TO CRAFT TECHNIQUES

DORIS COX AND BARBARA WARREN

SECOND EDITION

JOHN WILEY & SONS, INC. · NEW YORK
CHAPMAN & HALL, LIMITED · LONDON

to
HARRIET and VETTA
GOLDSTEIN ————
in acknowledgment of an
inspirational association

Preface

THIS SECOND EDITION OF *Creative Hands* IS OUR RESPONSE TO the many requests and helpful suggestions that have come from readers of the original edition. Certain crafts that were included in the first manuscript have been condensed or generalized, and new techniques have been introduced. Every effort has been made to adhere to the primary purpose of *Creative Hands* as it was originally conceived—that of assembling under one cover directions sufficient to the enjoyable completion of useful and attractive craft articles that could be made with minimum equipment and at low cost.

Frequently, in connection with our teaching, we have been asked to recommend books or other material dealing with the problems that make up the practical activities experienced by our students in craft work. Since class projects are keyed to the abilities of individuals who have little or no pre-training in either the fine arts or craft techniques, the good books available are often beyond the range of such students. This book is our answer to the need voiced by many of these beginners. The group such people represent can be divided into the following classifications:

1. The person who lacks training.
   The individual who has developed a keen interest but because of circumstances has never received formal art training.

The person who does not know whether he possesses ability because he has never attempted creative work in this field.

2. The person lacking self-assurance.

The individual who has no confidence in his originality.

The individual who has had a taste of art training but who, because of his limited background, feels insecure in going ahead in this field.

The individual who thinks he "cannot even draw a straight line."

3. The person who is budget-conscious.

The individual whose eyes are bigger than his purse.

The individual who appreciates and yearns for beautiful surroundings but who has felt he cannot afford them.

4. The person who lives in cramped quarters.

The individual who is making an effort to create an attractive home in a single room.

5. The person who desires a creative hobby.

6. The person who needs therapeutic handicraft.

7. The person engaged in teaching or in camp, social center, or club work, such as 4-H or county extension groups.

The individual who needs a manual of craft technique based upon sound design principles and purposes (life situations) for use in educational pursuits.

The person who has minimum equipment for craft work.

In this compilation of numerous craft techniques we have attempted to explain the principles and techniques simply and directly in order not to overwhelm the beginner. Most books limit themselves to the development of one craft; this book offers condensed methods of procedure in a wide variety of crafts in order that one may experience many, select the few best adapted to his interests, then specialize with the aid of books dealing with more advanced technique.

The techniques added to this second edition and the new articles included in the photographs represent our work and research for the past five years. It is our sincere hope that the reader will find that these additions will broaden his knowledge and appreciation of craft work.

Making an article without any thought of relating it to the individual who is to use it, or to the room in which it is to be used, is a frequent practice. We do not hold with the theory "Art for Art's sake." Any well designed, beautifully made object merits a suitable setting, which ordinarily is most surely achieved if considered when the craft project is begun.

For the crafts discussed in this book, the average home would provide all the needed equipment; if not, less than a dollar would suffice to cover the cost of needed tools for one or more of the problems. The cost of the actual materials used would be governed by the choice of the individual.

We wish to acknowledge with all sincerity the encouragement given us by members of the faculty of the University of Minnesota; the assistance with photography given us by Miss Helen Ludwig, Mr. Lloyd Matterson, and Mr. George H. Thomas; the generosity of students and friends who permitted us to photograph their handiwork; the cooperation of the Milwaukee and Minneapolis WPA Handicraft Projects; and the patience and kindness of our friends and families while this book was in preparation.

We hope that this edition will answer the needs of the many who generously sent their suggestions to us. And we trust that, for those to whom the book is new, it will prove a source of stimulation which will lead to the many rewards attendant upon interested participation in craft activities.

Doris Cox (Mrs. George H. Thomas)
Barbara Warren

May 1, 1951

Contents

Chapter I · A Word to the Wise   1

Chapter II · Design   3
   Tools of the Trade (*Structural and Decorative Design*)   3
   Intelligent Integration (*Principles of Design*)   9
   Nothing New under the Sun (*Design Adaptation*)   14

Chapter III · The Rainbow, Not the Gold (Some Notes on Color)   37
   Theory Is Easy   37
   Rainbows Within Reach   42
   Color at Work   43

Chapter IV · A Good Judge of Character (Selective Taste)   45

Chapter V · Ways and Means (Unit Designs and Repeat Methods)   60
   The Way Around (*Border Designs*)   60
   Repeat with Reason (*Allover Designs*)   66
   Unusual Units (*Unit Designs*)   74

Chapter VI · Figure Flattery (Dress Accessories)   81
   As the Indians Did It (*Finger Weaving*)   83
   From the Egyptians (*Card Weaving*)   91

Grandmother Did This (*Embroidery*)   100
Stitchery for Style (*More Embroidery*)   113

Chapter VII · Traveling Companions (Handbags)   117
Strictly Business (*Tailored Bags*)   120
Conversation Piece (*Afternoon Bags*)   132
Glamorous Gadgets (*Evening Bags*)   134

Chapter VIII · "Rich Man, Poor Man" (Buttons)   140
Leather Buttons   140
Wooden Buttons   141
Fabric Buttons   143
Metal Buttons   144

Chapter IX · Mix or Match (Mittens and Hoods)   149
For Frosty Fingers (*Mittens*)   149
To Top It Off (*Hoods*)   158

Chapter X · Leather Is Versatile   165
The Leather Itself   168
Design and Construction   172
Tooling Leather   179
Metal Decoration for Leather Articles   197
Coloring or Dyeing Leather   199
Preparing the Leather for Construction   201
Construction Processes   204
Buckles, Fasteners, and Buttons   223
Reinforcement Materials   227
Lining Materials   228
Assembling   229
Final Surface Care   231

Chapter XI · *Paint and Wood (Household Accessories)*   234
     Plates and Bowls   236
     Tea Tiles   244
     Painted Boxes   247

Chapter XII · *Fanciful Fabrics*   251
     Old Art into New   253
     Stenciling   269

Chapter XIII · *Decorative Needlework (Household Accessories)*   280
     Pretty as Pictures (*Wall Hangings*)   284
     More Stitches and Time (*More Accessories*)   289
     Always Under Foot (*Hooked Rugs*)   295
     Priority on Patches (*Appliqué*)   300

Chapter XIV · *Practical Portfolios*   305

Chapter XV · *Metal, Solder, and Acid*   321
     Vessels, Deep or Shallow   324
     Metal Etching   330
     Serving Pieces   333
     Pretty and Practical (*More Table Accessories*)   338

Chapter XVI · *Festive Ways (Holiday Trimmings)*   343
     To Anyone's Heart (*Decorative Food*)   343
     Eggs in One Basket (*Batik Process*)   350

Now You Know   356

Bibliography   359

Index   375

Chapter I

A Word to the Wise

IT IS DIFFICULT TO DEFINE THE INTANGIBLE QUALITIES OF SO elusive a heritage as taste in anything incorporating artistic principles. Taste is influenced by our cultural heritage and is based upon certain principles. The application of those principles tends to fluctuate slightly with fashion changes in any generation. It has always been the tendency of the current generation to judge most harshly those who lived just prior to themselves because it sees an unselected array of material evidences by which these people expressed themselves. This lack of selection embraces both the temporary aspects of fashion and the more sound phases of good taste. Such a situation arises because there has not been a sufficient lapse of time between the two generations for the development of an unbiased appraisal of their creative works.

With a well developed understanding of the principles of design one is better able to eliminate the superficial fashion traits from the more meritorious works of the generation before his, as well as from contemporary creative expression.

With the rapid development of industrial production methods and widespread advertising techniques one is faced with the necessity of selecting from a seemingly unlimited array of merchandise those comparatively few articles with which he associates. Since one judges his fathers by the things with which they associated, must one not realize that in like manner his neighbors evaluate his character? The things with which one surrounds himself are usually of his own selection and therefore indicate the stage to which one's taste has been developed as well as being reflections of one's personality.

Cost is no indication of the artistic worth of the object under consideration, and a realization or knowledge of the principles of design will destroy the smugness which is often an outgrowth of price consciousness. This knowledge will help one, therefore, to become an intelligent consumer of all objects whether their appearance or function is the prime consideration. A low cost article which meets all of the principles of design has just as high an artistic value as a higher priced article that fulfills the same principles. A realization of this will aid in the development of a more intelligent consumption of present day industrial products. It likewise will aid in forming a keener appreciation for well designed and executed craft products. It will lead to the realization of the futility of spending large amounts of time in producing by hand poorly designed articles.

Since there are no absolute or exact measurements by which a design may be catalogued as good or poor, it will be necessary to develop one's taste or appreciation to the point where the recognition of the beautiful in design becomes second nature. This is a long, slow process which may be hastened by constant and close association with objects of recognized aesthetic quality. Unless one has had adequate training by competent instructors in the appreciation of the beautiful, one should not depend solely upon one's own likes and dislikes, since these are often based upon childhood associations and may have been colored by false standards and sentimentality.

Chapter II

Design

DESIGN IS ANY CONTRIVANCE OR PLAN INTENDED FOR SOME DEFI-
nite purpose. A design may be for some actual object such as
a chair, a transport plane, a textile; or it may be a plan for a course
of action.

Design is anything to which man has put his mind and his
talents to alter or reorganize natural materials and forms. A crude
piece of wood which has been carved into a sensitive object of art
is representative of its creator's concept of design. The plan in the
mind of the artist-craftsman has determined whether that piece of
wood became the leg of a chair, a salad fork, or a piece of sculpture.
Any of these objects has its uses, and all may be important to both
the physical and aesthetic requirements of man. Whether the final
result is good or poor is dependent upon the intrinsic worth of the
plan—the design—as it was originally conceived by the creating
artist and upon the quality of craftsmanship employed in the construction of the object.

Tools of the Trade

STRUCTURAL DESIGN

*Structural design is that part of design which is represented
by an object visualized as stripped of all surface decoration.* In other

[3]

SCULPTURED HEAD
by Barbara Warren

The plan in the mind of the artist-craftsman will determine whether a piece of wood shall become the leg of a chair, a salad fork, or a piece of sculpture.

THOMAS

words, it is the contour by which that object is distinguished from others. Structural design is one of the most important means of identification. It represents the fundamental character of the article under consideration. This basic quality is extremely important in determining whether the article is considered good or poor in design. Structural design also includes color and texture of the material or materials from which the article has been formed.

The first consideration in the construction of any article is function. The use to which any object is to be put should be the determining factor in the selection: first, of the materials from which it is to be made; second, of the shape and proportions it will assume; and third, the color or surface treatment it will be given. Every material has inherent characteristics that make it suitable for certain uses and entirely unsuitable for others. A heavy tweed will serve admirably as a coating fabric but is quite inappropriate for a ruffled party frock. Pewter may be shaped into serving utensils, plates, and bowls, but it cannot be used for articles that might be placed over a stove burner since the melting point of the metal is low. Each construction material has its own personality. The interested craftsman will experiment with a new material to discover just what its characteristics seem to be. Materials should be analyzed for their qualities, should be manipulated in many ways to determine working methods, and should be tried in relation to other materials in order to discover every possibility that might be suggested through such experiment. Metal and wood may be beautifully combined, but certain metals seem to have a greater affinity for certain woods. There are no set rules which can be followed—new materials are being introduced every day, and old materials are constantly being put to new uses. Whatever the material used in the construction of an object, the fact of function cannot be considered lightly.

To make the consideration of function more concrete, reference will be made to the mittens shown in the accompanying photograph. Since the purpose of mittens is that of protection for the hands, the material from which they should be made must have certain qualities; namely, warmth, flexibility, durability, surface quality pleasing to the touch, workability in accordance with the method of construction, and harmony with such other garments as are worn with mittens. For the mittens in the photograph, a good quality of fleece coating was found satisfactory on all these points.

In order that mittens may be truly functional, it is necessary that they be made to conform to the contour of the hands closely enough to retain warmth yet freely enough to permit ease of movement. These factors contribute to the final shape of the hand-covering. The body of the mitten encases the four fingers together, which increases the heat-retaining qualities. The thumb is enclosed

EMBROIDERED MITTENS

THOMAS

in a separate unit in order that the hand can be used more easily. The opening must be large enough to allow the hand to be slipped into the mitten.

Normally, such detailed analysis of the steps involved in any part of construction would be somewhat telescoped because of familiarity with an object which has been gained through previous

[6]

experiences. The foregoing reasoning is illustrative of a *way of thinking* in the evolution of any idea from the abstract to the concrete. Objects other than a pair of mittens will present different requirements to be met and solved during the designing process. Some are more simple, perhaps, but others are far more complex. Careful and thoughtful consideration of every aspect of function is important in the planning stages, for oversights in these early steps may cause some article on which time and material have been spent to fulfill more or less unsatisfactorily the purpose for which it was intended.

Though the structure of an object is limited by its function, it is composed of proportionate relationships which one should endeavor to keep as pleasing as possible. Beauty in space relationships should never be achieved at the expense of proper function, but it is an important contributing factor to the ultimate appearance of an object. It may seem strange, but the more closely an object reaches perfection of function, usually the more beautiful the relationship of its parts one to the other. An airplane is a fine example of this. The early planes of Wilbur and Orville Wright seem misshapen when compared to present day airplanes. And today our planes have far outstripped the performance of that first flight at Kittyhawk. Function has a beauty of its own.

The color of the structural materials was mentioned as being important to the design of the object. There may be, of course, objects made in which this is a negligible consideration. With many things, however, it becomes an important factor. Any dress accessories or household accessories should be planned to harmonize with their setting. In reference to the mittens, which were used as an example in this discussion, it is necessary to consider the occasions upon which they would be worn, for these occasions will determine the types of garments with which they are to be combined. Color should be considered, in this case, in relation to the texture of the fabric, the occasion, and the colors of other garments of the ensemble.

The foregoing discussion has been devoted exclusively to those factors which comprise the structural design of an object. If the principles as outlined have been successfully realized, the object —whatever it be—will already have a beauty and character of its own. Sometimes this object may be enhanced further by the addition of a decorative design which is also governed by the principles stated for structural design. It should be borne well in mind that decorative enrichment should not only be in harmony with, but should also complement, the structure supporting it.

DECORATIVE DESIGN

Decorative design is surface treatment that is not necessary to the functional aspects of an object but which is intended to enhance the underlying structure.

Any attempt to create a beautiful object, regardless of its magnitude, involves a thoughtful consideration of the structural and decorative designs and their relation to the purpose for which the object is intended. An extremely delicate little spray of leaves would be inappropriate as a design to be applied to a severely tailored daytime handbag. The gay informal nature of a peasant-like design does not suit it to articles of formal characteristics.

The application of decorative design to an object should be so planned as to not interfere with the function of that object. Decorative design stimulates a person's interest in an object. If it is good, it causes one to look again. A delectable-appearing frosting on a cake whets one's appetite, increases one's desire to taste the cake beneath. In the same manner, a suitable decorative design will increase appreciation for the article which it enhances. It must be remembered, however, that the structure beneath any such design must bear up under close inspection. No amount of decorative design—no matter how good it may be—will be able to camouflage weak structural design. In like manner, many a fine example of structural design has been quite ruined by the application of poor or excessive decorative design. The artist and teacher Robert Henri has been credited with the well known statement, "Simplicity is the soul of art," a statement which may be used to advantage in evaluating a decorative design.

Intelligent Integration

One might reasonably say that there exists only one standard for the evaluation of a design. For the purposes of simplification it is possible to consider all the usual principles of design—harmony, unity, proportion, emphasis, rhythm, balance—as being merely ramifications of this one major maxim, ORDER. This is a term that implies absolute accord, not in a narrow sense but with a broad consideration for all its related aspects. To many, order may mean nothing more than neatness. Although neatness is a quality seen in all good craftwork, it is here understood as only one of the attributes of order in its larger meaning.

To make the discussion of the related aspects of order as concrete as possible let us refer again to the mittens.

In as much as mittens are primarily informal in nature, since they are usually made of sturdy materials and are intended for sports wear, the design should be informal and not too delicate. A design

[9]

of bold and simple character is most appropriate. This implies *harmony of idea*. Further thought should be directed toward the relationship of the textures which are used together. Yarn is an obvious selection as a material to be used for the application of decorative stitchery since it is by nature adapted to use on woolen fabrics and is of a *harmonious texture*. Shetland yarn is an excellent choice with regard to its scale or size, which is in harmony with the fabric on which it is used, and because it manipulates easily.

Another step in planning a design concerns itself with *shape harmony*. The shape or contour of the design should complement the structure which it decorates and should lead the eye pleasingly over the surface of the object. The shape of the design should be so related to the surface to which it is applied that the design becomes an integral part of the whole.

A study of the photograph of the mittens will indicate that there are three major places where decorative design might be placed to complement their structure: the cuff, the back of the hand, and the thumb. The entire surface might be covered with a quiet all-over design, or unit designs might be planned for any of the structural points listed. Since a mitten is normally longer than it is wide, a design applied to the back of the hand naturally tends to take a lengthwise direction instead of cutting across the area from side to side. Should the design be applied to the cuff which encircles the wrist, it should be planned to follow the cuff in a corresponding direction. This manner of reasoning should be used when decoration is being planned for the enhancement of any structural form. One should always start with the question, Where might the decorative design best be placed to complement the underlying structural design? The factor of shape harmony is of utmost importance, for design applied without regard for this principle is apt to destroy the very shape that it is intended to enhance.

If unit designs are used, they should be planned with regard to their size in relation to the particular part of the object they are to decorate: that is, they should be neither too large nor too small for that area. This *harmony of consistent sizes* is closely related to the principle of *proportion*. The term *scale* is used to cover this phase of design.

The fifth and last feature of *harmony* is *color*. This implies coördination of the color with the design, the texture, and the purpose of the object. In the mittens, the fabric selected determines the basic color and is a factor in the selection of colors to be used in their decoration. Of course, this basic color is first selected with regard to the other colors with which it is to be worn. The colors selected should be suited to the type of design used and to the purpose for which the mittens are intended. One would not expect to use colors that are usually most suited to sheer summery fabrics for the heavy wool used in the body of the mitten. The color as applied to the design of any surface should be so distributed as to produce pleasing *balance*. This implies, however, that the arrangement of the design parts has already been well balanced in preliminary planning.

The Greek standard for good *proportion* might aid in planning satisfying space relationships. This is based on the *golden oblong*, which consists of two units of measurement on one side to three units on the other. This standard of good proportion may be used as a guide both for the units of the design and for the proportion of the design in relation to the area to which it is being applied. However, any standard of this sort should be used with imagination since too rigid an adherence to a formula is apt to deaden a design.

Scale is also an aspect of proportion. It is a factor whenever shapes or objects are combined and refers to the appropriateness of the combinations of objects or areas of various dimensions. Scale must be considered with regard to the area allotted to the decorative design as compared with the entire area on which the design is placed. The units within the design itself must also be in pleasing proportion to one another—leaf to flower, line to dot, and so forth.

Balance is obtained by having an equal amount of interest on either side of an imaginary center line. There are three types of balance:

> *Symmetrical balance:* the normal human figure as seen from the front, each side being identical or nearly so with the other. Any design that is the same on one side of the center as it is on the other is an example of symmetrical balance. Symmetrical balance is always formal, but:

> *Formal balance* is not always symmetrical; for example, two objects or units will balance each other formally if they attract an equal amount of attention, yet the objects need not be identical. A leaf and a flower may balance one another formally in a design if they are both the same size and if they are both in the same position on either side of the imaginary center line.

> *Informal balance* is achieved when the larger of two objects is placed near the center line and the smaller of the two objects is placed proportionately farther away from the axis of the arrangement.

Rhythm is that quality within a design which leads the eye from one unit to another. This may be an easy flowing movement established by continuous lines or an accented movement achieved through a repetition of like units. Another form of movement may be obtained through the use of a broken line which so strongly suggests direction that the eye bridges the gaps between sections. The rhythm within a design should be in accordance with the structure on which the design is placed, or the design will not seem to belong to that particular structure. This implies that rhythm is a contributing factor to shape harmony. By shape harmony is meant the satisfaction one experiences when one sees a horizontal area enhanced with a horizontal design. This is much more pleasing than an area which is confusedly decorated with conflicting directional lines of equal attraction.

If all parts of a design are of equal interest, the eye involuntarily jumps from one of the units to another in quick succession. This results in confusion. In order to avoid such a feeling of restlessness, certain areas within a design should be stressed more than other areas. This is the principle of *emphasis* or *subordination*. The types of units used in planning a design will suggest which part of the design should receive the greatest emphasis. A design, the parts of which are successfully emphasized and subordinated, will produce a feeling of rest or repose, a feeling of rightness, which is also a by-product of good balance.

When all the foregoing factors have been considered in the planning and application of a design to an object, the result should produce a satisfactory whole; *an object of beauty suitable to its use, an expression of* ORDER.

Nothing New under the Sun

Up to this time the abstract qualities of structural and decorative design have been treated without consideration for the concrete problem of planning an actual design for a given purpose. Before entering more specifically into the methods of designing, it is necessary to point out the two categories into which most designing falls.

The ideal way of working is one of absolute originality. The original designer is so familiar with the techniques of breaking up spaces into pleasing shapes and is so sensitive to such divisions and their possibilities that he is not forced, nor does he wish, to lean upon the work of others. Ideas seem to flow from the end of his pencil and bear no semblance to designs previously created by other artists. Unfortunately, such facility usually demands a considerable amount of native ability or much training and experience in the field of creative effort. Few of us feel that we have such ability, nor have we been able to provide ourselves with such thorough background experiences.

There is another method of working. This is one that can be learned easily, and it is well suited to the average individual who has not been able to avail himself of much or any art training. This method permits the adapting of designs already in existence to some particular purpose. It does not infer outright copying, but rather it involves the alteration and adjustment of some motif to another shape or character. In a certain sense, it consists of using an already created design as a springboard to the creation of a new design. For example, a small, subordinate unit from a complex design might be enlarged to become the dominant unit in a new setting. Thus the unit itself might not be original, but through adaptation it has been given a new personality. Similarly, a number of small units, each taken from a separate source, might be combined to form a handsome new design. Thus one's lack of originality need not be a hindrance to the designing and execution of fine craftwork. The beginner may feel a certain awkwardness when first trying out these expedients, but with a few practice attempts he should be able to design with ease, confidence, and competence.

The act of adapting a design, even though cleverly done, is no guarantee of quality. The ability to select good source material is of as much importance as the adapting of that design to a particular purpose. It is wise to be ever on the alert for motifs which would lend themselves to decorative adaptation. A file of such source material goes far in stimulating the imagination. Currently popular and faddish designs are frequently of dubious quality and are best avoided. Often they are intended to catch the fancy of an insensitive public, and usually they are imitative to the extreme and wholly without tasteful decorative quality.

Photographs or actual examples of craft products from the Old World, such as needlework, wood carving, and ceramics, provide a wealth of good, sound material for the purposes of adaptation. Mexican and American Indian designs are almost always of excellent quality. *The Index of American Design,* as compiled by the WPA, much of which has been reproduced in magazines from time to time, is a treasure trove for inspiration. Numerous other examples of this nature will be discovered by the observant craftsman. The wise and interested person will collect these as they come to his attention. For the person who has no such files, a bibliography of source material is provided at the end of this book. It is sufficiently comprehensive to enable one to find abundant inspiration for any design problem.

The Process of Adapting a Design

In order to make the process of adapting a design more understandable, a brief outline giving the steps involved may be found helpful. If the points in the outline are conscientiously kept in mind, a design is much more apt to be successful than if the form is carelessly followed.

The points to be remembered are:

1. Familiarity with the size and shape of the object to be decorated.

2. Realization of the ultimate purpose of the object.

3. Consideration of the materials involved in the process of construction and decoration of the object.

4. Selection of source material best suited to the idea, materials, and process.

5. Analysis of source material to determine the motif, or motifs, best adapted to the problems involved.

6. Adjustment of the motif, or motifs, to the areas to be enriched by design.

7. Formulation of the idea on paper.

8. Careful checking of the design for adherence to the principles of design and good taste.

9. Completion of the drawing of the design.

10. Planning the color combination and distribution.

11. Application of the design to the object in the chosen medium.

As the beginning craftsman follows the above steps, he will be learning design and will be developing the security which will enable him to create original designs later. The familiarity with the principles of design which will be gained through this process of adapting designs to specific purposes will become greater with each new experience. Taste and judgment will grow along with the necessary technical facility, which will improve with careful use.

Perhaps the best advice that can be given to the inexperienced person is that, when he is planning a design, he must not be wholly satisfied with the product of his pencil until it incorporates all the principles outlined in the preceding material. The design must also satisfy and please the person creating it. If this is not true, the craftsman will be unable to work with the enthusiasm and delight that are always part of a good piece of work. The process of adapting a design for a specific piece of work is an exacting one, yet it is somewhat simpler than the process of creating an original design. For this reason it can give the beginner the confidence so necessary to many before they can begin to design with the originality and ease of the more advanced worker.

These points should be followed carefully when one is adapting a design for any craft product, whether the design be elaborate or extremely simple. The following pages will present a series of crafts representative of those included in this volume. They have all been adapted from the same source. It is hoped that from them the reader will be able to arrive at some understanding of the process of adapting a design and some awareness of the almost endless possibilities inherent in this method for planning decorative units.

DESIGN FROM MEXICAN LACQUER TRAY

This example of lacquer work is an excellent source for a number of varied forms which lend themselves well to new and interesting combinations. There is a refreshing spontaneity to the rhythmic movement of the design which is beautifully illustrative of a creative integration of dominant and subordinate motifs.

The above units were selected from the design on the opposite page as the motifs that were used in the craftwork of the following pages.

EMBROIDERED BELT

Satin and chain stitch used on two tones of wool.

The first problem selected was that of designing a belt which might be embroidered in wool upon a colored backing. Since it was desirable that the belt be fairly wide, and since it was to be made of scrap material, it was decided that two colors of fabric be combined for the body of the belt. This made it necessary to plan a design that would link the two fabrics together in some pleasing fashion.

The width and length of the belt suggested a border design as being the best choice for the problem. Thus, the size and shape of the article to be made dictated to some extent the nature of the design to be applied to it. The person for whom the belt was to be made desired that it be quite decorative so as to be the outstanding note in an otherwise simple costume. For this reason, the design could be bold and of brilliant color. The problem then became that of designing a border of strong decorative quality which could be embroidered over two colors of fabric to make an attractive and wearable belt. Shetland yarn was to be used for the stitchery.

[20]

The drawing at the upper left shows the preliminary plotting of the running border design against the divided background. The simple yet rhythmic motif of the two-colored leaf was superimposed on the background to tie the two fabrics together. The movement produced by the repetition of the leaf unit automatically created the continuous movement desirable in a border design. A sweeping curve was tentatively added at the top of each leaf to accent the movement and to give some variation in scale. The dot was added at the base for much the same reason. In the lower drawing, the details of the border have become somewhat more refined with the dot developing into a spiral form adapted from the lacquer motifs and the curve becoming a series of teardrop shapes taken from the same source. The final drawing shows the design as completed before the actual craftwork was begun. Color is indicated, and all the lines have been drawn carefully for transfer to the fabric for embroidery.

[21]

CORDUROY PILLOW

The units are appliquéd to a three-toned background.

As with the belt on the preceding page, this pillow cover was made from scrap material. Three colors of corduroy were combined by using appliqué. The colors picked up the scheme of the room in which the pillow was to be used. In as much as the room and the fabric to be used were both informal in nature, the design was held to one of quiet simplicity without any suggestion of the elaborate or ornate. The weight and texture of the fabric necessitated a simple design also, since corduroy does not lend itself to complicated or delicate manipulation. This consideration of the material involved in the process of construction is an important factor in the planning of any design. The three colors of corduroy harmonized so well that it seemed unnecessary to add further color. The texture of the material was such that large areas of the fabric were most pleasing to the eye and did not need to be broken with smaller units.

[22]

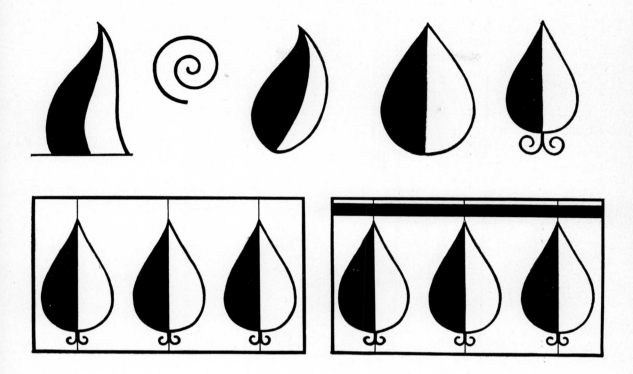

The same leaf unit that was used for the belt was used for this pillow design. In this instance, the leaf was altered in shape to give it a more solid form better adapted to the material used. The background area was plotted to make best possible use of the various colors available to the designer. The upper row of units in the diagram illustrates the evolution of the leaf shape as it changed from the curving to the more static form. Though the design is based upon repetition, as was the belt, the movement within the design has become far more restrained. The simple border above the leaves in the last drawing was added to stop the movement up and away from the design which seemed to be caused by the tapering points of the leaves.

[23]

THOMAS

STENCILED APRON *and*
some of the stencils used.

A border design to run along the lower edge of a pretty apron was selected as a simple first problem in stenciling. Because the stencil design could be tried out on paper or cloth scraps before being applied to the apron fabric, various colors could be experimented with until a satisfactory combination was obtained. Stenciling permits a controlled shaded effect, so the technique played an important part in the completed design.

[24]

The drawing at the upper left groups the units that were selected from the source design of Mexican lacquer work. These were combined, with little care for immediate accuracy, to produce a rough border design as a preliminary step to working out the repeat motif more in detail. The straight line above and below the decorative units served merely as a temporary guide. Since the design was based upon a flowing curved unit, a freely drawn wavy line at the base was found to be more in keeping with the spirit of the border. No line was put at the upper part of the design in as much as it was to have a large area of plain fabric above it. The technique of stenciling is a flexible one, so various combinations of position were worked out before the design was applied to the little apron.

BLOCK-PRINTED FABRIC

Two arrangements of the design unit are shown in the photograph.

When a design is being planned for a fabric which is to fall in folds, as does any drapery fabric, it is essential that this be considered in the initial stages of the designing process. Sometimes it is sufficient to repeat the motif over the surface of some soft paper which can be draped to simulate cloth. When one is working with block printing, various arrangements of the blocks can be printed upon scrap material to determine the best effect.

[26]

The scallop, teardrop, leaf, and heavy scroll were selected from the Mexican design for adaptation to a design for the block-printed fabric. Several rough sketches were made, one of which appears in the diagram. The sketches were done freely in order that a number of different arrangements could be created quickly. This method is usually best when one is just beginning to plan a design. From the quick sketches, the one which appeared to have the greatest possibilities was worked on further. The hasty lines of brush-work were refined into the shapes originally selected from the Mexican motif. Proportions were altered to produce an integrated unit suitable for repetition in an allover pattern.

PEWTER NAPKIN RING

The two metal layers are sweat together with lead foil.

The designing of this pewter napkin ring was a problem of structural design more than one of decorative design. The diameter of the ring had to be planned to slip easily over a rolled napkin, yet it could not be so great as to be awkwardly loose. The correct measurement was determined by taking the dimensions directly from a rolled napkin of standard size. Because table linens are frequently of floral or plaid design, it seemed wise to plan a napkin ring which would not be so decorative as to compete with any such pattern. However, the craftsman desired to make a ring that would have a distinct character of its own, a character which would adapt itself to both informal and somewhat more elegant table settings.

A wooden curtain rod of the correct diameter was used as a form around which the design was developed. Paper was taped to the rod and several sketches were made. Finally the leaf was tried and found to have possibilities for this design. Since the tapered ends of the leaf unit were too pointed to be practical for a napkin ring, the scroll was added to both ends of the leaf to give greater strength to the form. The design was drawn on paper which was spiraled around the wooden rod. The two-color division of the leaf unit in the source design suggested a double layer of metal for the napkin ring. When the ring was made, the pewter was cut, soldered, filed, and finished before being bent to the spiraled shape.

TOOLED LEATHER BELT CLOSING

The belt is made of three tones of rug binding stitched to buckram and is fastened with hooks and eyes.

Occasionally a small scrap of leather which seems useless because of its size may be converted into an interesting fastening for a belt made from some material other than leather. The photograph above shows just such a creative use of a waste piece of leather. A problem like the one in the picture might make a very good "first" for leather tooling. It is simple, effective, and something so easy to do that the results may be seen quickly. If errors are made on a small piece such as this, the waste of material is not great. New techniques in tooling might be tried to advantage on little articles of this nature.

The belt itself was inexpensively made from three strips of rug binding selected to harmonize with the color of the costume with which it was to be worn. These were stitched together, and the buckle was sewn to one end to form the fastening for the belt. Thus, quickly and at small cost, a very handsome wardrobe accessory was created.

[30]

The belt buckle was to be made from heavy tooling leather shaped slightly at the open end. Since it was planned as a decorative closing only, it was not necessary for the leather to be shaped for a prong closing. The fastening was to be done with snaps or hooks sewed to the underside of the buckle and to the end of the belt.

The scroll, because it immediately suggested the rounded form of the end of the buckle, was selected as the main motif of the design. To contrast with it in scale, the stamen forms were chosen to combine with it. The central drawing indicates the first arrangement of the forms that were used. The flared arrangement of the stamens did not seem to harmonize with the straight edges of the buckle shape so they were redrawn in a more rigid order which paralleled the outer edges of the buckle. The scroll was enlarged to become the rounded tip of the form, and the scallops were used to give emphasis to the stamens and to repeat, on a smaller scale, the curve of the large scroll.

[31]

THOMAS

NEEDLE POINT AFTER-NOON BAG

The felt body is completely interlined with canvas for additional strength. There is cardboard reinforcement in the flap, and the body is further stiffened with buckram. The bag has a button and loop closing.

This exceedingly handsome needle point bag is beautifully suited as an afternoon bag for dressy occasions. The design on the page opposite was worked out to be applied to the large flap of the bag as an *important* decorative note. Quite a few of the units from the Mexican tray were combined in a design that was balanced symmetrically to give it a formal air. With the shape of the flap to be decorated well in mind, the first sketches were worked out. When a sketch was made which seemed satisfactory, it was reworked on squared paper to indicate the stitches of the needle point.

[32]

Structural design, preliminary sketch, and diagram for stitchery for an afternoon bag of yarn-embroidered needle point.

ENAMELED WOODEN PLATE

This design preserves more of the characteristics of the original source material than does any of the foregoing craft problems. But a comparison of this with the Mexican tray at the beginning of this section will show that there have been a number of changes made in adapting a design which was applied to the oval shape of the tray for the round shape of this painted plate. The most important consideration in planning a design for a round area such as the center of this turned-wood plate is that of preserving the feeling of the circular form. Though there is a "top" and a "bottom" to the design, it is effective from any position from which the plate might be seen. The top sketches on the opposite page show the first steps in achieving the circular movement in the design.

Steps in adapting the Mexican design to the circular center of a turned-wood plate.

In the selection of crafts that have been pictured in the preceding section, every effort has been made to include examples of the major techniques covered in this book. However, though only a single example of each of the techniques is pictured, any number of designs might have been made for each of the objects, and all of them might have been derived from the same source, the Mexican tray. It should be obvious to the reader that a design as rich in detail as that selected for this series of adaptations offers almost unlimited suggestions if viewed with imagination. It is this quality of imagination which would assure as many different designs as there were craftsmen in a group even though all might be creating designs adapted from the same source material. It is hoped that no reader will attempt to reproduce one of the finished designs illustrated here, but rather that every reader will derive from the many examples an insight into the process of designing which will encourage him to follow for himself the steps of adaptation.

Chapter III

The Rainbow, Not the Gold

MANY AND LONG ARE THE TREATISES WRITTEN ON THE SUBJECT of color. A thorough understanding of the theories involved in the subject of color is highly desirable, but not absolutely necessary since a feeling for the use of color can be developed with the aid of just a few very important principles. Should a more technical knowledge of color theory be desired than is offered here, any library or encyclopedia will provide such information. We are purposely omitting technical discussion here, since it is often apt to confuse and discourage the inexperienced.

Theory Is Easy

There are three distinguishing elements of color with which even the beginner must familiarize himself. The most readily understood of these is the property of *hue*. It is the *name* of the color and simply designates the family to which the color belongs: i.e., red, blue, blue-green, green, etc. When dealing with pigments or dyes there exist only three fundamental colors, excluding black and white, which we will not here recognize as color. These basic or *primary* colors are red, yellow, and blue. A further division results from combining any two of these colors in *equal* amounts. These are known as *secondary* colors and include orange, green, and violet (purple). *Intermediate* colors such as blue-green, red-orange, and blue-violet are obtained by mixing any two of the primary colors in *unequal* amounts. This permits one of the colors to predominate. It is the predominating or outstanding color which gives the intermediate color its name. Another way of obtaining intermediate colors is through the combining of a primary color and its adjacent secondary color; i.e., blue, a primary, and a larger amount of its adjacent color green, a secondary, when combined, will produce blue-green. Reference to a color wheel will aid in the understanding of hue. An appreciation of the fact that an almost unlimited number of hues exist, will develop the potential ability of the beginner in his use of color.

The position of the hues on the color wheel is an important factor when changing hue and intensity of color. A color may be thought of in relation to its *adjacent* colors, the colors which successively follow one another around the color wheel; or it may be thought of in relation to its *complementary* color, the color which is found directly opposite to it on the color wheel. These positions are important to know when one is mixing colors to create new colors of full intensity, as yellow and blue to produce green; or when mixing colors to neutralize them, as blue and orange to produce brown.

Colors may be thought of in two groups; those that tend to be *cool* and those which are *warm*. In the first group would fall the greens, blues, and violets, and in the second group, the red, orange, and yellow hues. Intermediate colors which contain a mixture of a warm and a cool color will fall into the warm or the cool group according to the proportions of the warm or cool colors used in producing that hue.

Value is the second property of color. To many designers

this is the most important quality a color possesses. It is the *lightness* or *darkness* of a color. This is determined by the variation of a color from *normal* toward pure white or black. The normal value of a color is that value it assumes in its pure state as seen on the color wheel. It is obvious from reference to a color wheel that the normal value of colors is not constant. Yellow has the lightest normal value, and purple the darkest. Values which are lighter than normal are referred to as *tints*. When using paint or dye, tints are obtained by the addition of white pigment or water to the pure color, depending upon the medium with which one is working. Values darker than normal are known as *shades* and are obtained by the addition of black pigment to the normal value.

Intensity, the third property of color, is often confused with value. It is the *brightness* or *dullness* of a color. A simple example may lead to better understanding of this difference. Early morning, full daylight, and night may be thought of as three different values —middle value, light, and dark. But day, itself, has varying qualities of brightness; for example, sunshine with its brilliant color, and rain with its dull, subdued color, give a typical range of intensities. A color which does not have its fullest intensity is called a grayed color. Other terms which are frequently used but which have the same meaning are *neutralized, subdued*, and *dulled*. A color of full intensity is a pure color. It may be neutralized by adding some of its complementary color: i.e., add green to bright red to make a dull or neutralized red. The amount of the complementary color added will determine the extent to which the color has been grayed. If approximately equal amounts of both colors are mixed, the result will be a neutral gray. If the amount of warm color used is larger than the amount of cool color used, the result will be a warm gray or brown. If the amount varies the other way, the neutralized color will assume a cool tone such as is found in a steel gray.

Whether or not one is conscious of color combinations when using color, there are existing schemes which tend to act as suggestions, the knowledge of which will give the beginner greater confidence in color selection. These color schemes are rigid, rather mechanical patterns and should not be adhered to in all applications of color.

The first and probably the most simple of these color schemes is the *monochromatic* or one color scheme. It consists of the use of one color in various values. In order to create an interesting effect when using this scheme, the values must differ considerably or the design will appear very bland and unsatisfactory. A color scheme which uses black, white, and gray, plus one color is also known as monochromatic and is frequently more successful than a scheme built entirely around values of one color.

A second color plan is the *analogous* scheme, sometimes called an *adjacent* scheme. This involves the use of colors that are related to one another by their position on the color wheel. The relationship of such adjacent colors is strengthened by the fact that any two neighboring colors on the wheel always share a common hue: i.e., blue and blue-green have blue as a common color. Again, when this scheme is used, value is an important consideration. Failure to observe an interesting value pattern will make a color scheme lose all of its personality. This and the monochromatic scheme are known as *related* color schemes.

The third and perhaps the most difficult scheme to use is the *complementary* color scheme. This plan consists in the use of a color and its opposite on the color wheel. Interesting variations of the complementary scheme which are easier and more satisfying to use are: the *adjacent complementary* scheme, in which the color, its adjacent color, and its complementary color are used; the *split complementary* scheme, in which a color and the immediate neighbors of its complement are used. In this scheme, however, the complement itself is not used. This color scheme is usually more subtle than a straight complementary color plan. The third variation is termed the *double complementary* color scheme, and consists of the use of two complementary color schemes in the same design.

Frequently when complementary colors of the same value are used in juxtaposition, an illusion of movement or vibration appears which may be very disturbing. This is one of the factors which make a complementary scheme difficult to use. Such colors also often produce a harsh, jarring effect which tends to cheapen a design.

Not only is it important to have a good range of values in a scheme, but it is also helpful to vary the intensities of the colors. Often two colors which do not ordinarily appear well together may be used very successfully if one or both of the colors are grayed. Red and green might serve as an example in this instance.

The last important classification is the *triad* color scheme. It is composed of three colors equidistant from one another on the color wheel. The three primary colors, red, yellow, and blue, belong to this scheme. A triad scheme in its pure state is very difficult to use, but if one of the colors is somewhat neutralized, the scheme may be very pleasing. The triad scheme and all phases of the complementary scheme are known as *contrasting* color schemes.

Many people are so sensitive to the possibilities of color that they create what may be called color harmonies. These may be differentiated from color schemes in that they involve a more individual color pattern and do not strictly conform to the color schemes as listed above. This freer use of color is a mark of individuality and should be cultivated by constant association with fine examples of color usage.

Rainbows Within Reach

It is a fallacy to believe that the monetary value of an article is an assurance of good taste in the use of color or design. Simple, everyday things often have color harmonies superior to those found in more costly objects. One need only turn to nature for captivating suggestions for the selection of color. Such things as flowers, autumn leaves, birds with their colorful feathers, the soft subdued colors found in the furs of animals, the rainbow colors of fish, and the jewel-like colors of insects provide endless inspiration. If one cannot study the actual object itself, the *National Geographic* or *Audubon prints* will furnish reliable source material. The reader will doubtless be familiar with other publications of like nature.

Nature does not provide the only source for color suggestions. Many examples of good craft work from other countries as well as from our own country will offer stimulation. Fabrics, both printed and embroidered, will furnish further ideas. Other possibilities are ceramics with their colorful glazes.

An especially rich field for color suggestion is that of paintings of good quality. Usually there will be more colors in the painting than one would choose to use in a design, but by careful selection one can select an interesting scheme. To insure a truly satisfactory color harmony when using this source of inspiration, the painting should be analyzed to determine the relative proportions of the colors used. Failure to do this often results in a color harmony apparently completely different from the original source. Aside from offering a suggestion for a complete color harmony, a painting will sometimes suggest just one beautiful color to an appreciative student. This color the designer may select and combine with other colors of his own choosing.

Since it is not always possible to have these source materials at hand, one may build a file of good color suggestions clipped from magazine illustrations, advertisements, or covers. An expedient method to use in choosing the particular areas of the color reproductions is that of using a finder which eliminates undesirable portions of the picture. This method also removes the distraction of subject matter. A finder may be made of a four by six inch filing card which has a two inch square cut from its center. This "window" or frame may be moved over the surface of the illustration until the most satisfying combination of colors is found. That area may then be clipped and mounted on a filing card for future reference. A single illustration or advertisement often provides several different and interesting combinations.

Color at Work

The same principles which apply to the making of a design, apply equally to the use of color in that design. Probably the most important of these is *color proportion*. A successful color plan for a design maintains a pleasing relationship of the areas allotted to each color. The color areas should be so proportioned as to permit the dominance of one of the colors. The color covering the largest amount of space in a design determines the general color impression given by that design. There may be few or many subordinate colors depending upon the nature of the design and these should likewise be beautifully proportioned to one another.

When planning the distribution of color areas, one must also consider the *balance* of the design as it is affected by color. Size alone does not determine balance, but intensity and value are also important factors. A spot of intense color may be used to balance a large area of a dull color, since the attention focuses more quickly on the brighter area. Likewise a small amount of black in a light design will catch the eye quickly and will balance a large, light shape in the design. It is necessary to maintain a good color balance not only for the design itself but also to preserve the structural quality of the object which that design decorates.

The principle of balance in color overlaps that of *color emphasis*, which deals with the power of attraction of any unit of a design. Thoughtful arrangement of size, shape, placement, and color will determine the center of interest in a design. Color is important here because of its power to gather attention to itself and hence to the most important part of the design.

Since the principle of *rhythm* is that of movement, the eye may be led from one part of a design to another through the use of color gradations both in hue and value and/or repeated color. This rhythm may be very pleasing and musiclike or it may be so active as to be distracting and out of tune with the design.

If one mistrusts one's own judgment, a thoughtful study of fine examples of the use of color will aid in the development of an understanding and a feeling for these principles as applied to color.

Chapter IV

A Good Judge of Character

WHETHER SELECTING A DESIGN FOR ADAPTATION OR CREATING an original design, one must consider the quality of that design. Frequently a person who cannot himself draw feels that any unit reasonably resembling an object in actuality must be a good design. This is wholly untrue. Were it so, the camera would be used as a universal substitute for the hands and the head of the artist. The differences between a photograph of an object and an artistic drawing of the same object are many. The drawing usually represents a simplified version, a minimized detail here, an emphasized detail there; in short, an individualized interpretation of the unit in question. How well the arranging of details is done rests with the ability of the artist to select the salient characteristics of the actual object as he needs them for the particular effects he desires to achieve.

Consider, for the moment, the many designs used in printed textiles. Probably the most common unit used is the daisy. There are over fifty thousand copyrighted designs registered in Washington which make use of this motif. Many of them are excellent, many commonplace. One should learn to distinguish between the designs exhibiting definite character and those which are merely weak attempts at a photographic reproduction of the flower [or object] used as the predominating unit around which the design is based.

One of the prime factors in the evaluation of a design is the quality of its drawing—the care used in recording the individual interpretation of the unit onto the paper when the preliminary planning is done. This is not entirely a matter of skill or facility with the pencil or brush but rests often upon the patience and intellectual action of the person creating the design. The line of a stem or the curve of the edge of a leaf may first be put down as it is seen and then carefully corrected so that it becomes a graceful easy curve over which the eye travels smoothly. By way of demonstration, the reader might draw a simple spiral line. Look at it thoughtfully and try to determine whether the eye follows the line easily and freely or whether it must move around squared corners and clumsy curves which tend to give a sensation akin to that of riding over a bumpy country road. Now redraw the same spiral, endeavoring to correct any errors uncovered in the preliminary study of the original drawing. When the spiral is finally completed as perfectly as is possible with the freehand method, one can better appreciate the meaning of the term "good drawing."

Whether a person is a fount of originality, or one of the average group who finds it necessary to search for inspiration, the design being worked upon may fall far short of beauty and personality if it lacks this quality of good drawing. The term does not apply to photographic accuracy, speed, or the ease with which it was done. It pertains to that extra care necessary to the fineness in character of a design. A dozen people may use the same floral form in a design, yet the results will be varied and of numerous degrees of quality. One person will record every detail of line, every serration of petal and leaf, every tiny section of the flower itself; in short, he will attempt to draw everything he sees. By dint of much hard and painstaking work he may achieve a drawing which is startling in its accuracy of reproduction. However, as he labored to do what the camera could do more easily in but a fraction of a second, he has been entirely unaware of the principles of design which, like sign posts on a highway, would have guided him to a more fortunate result. Another person might incorporate a simplified silhouette of the flower into a stunning allover pattern; while yet another might find inspiration in the serrated line of a petal tip and the star-shaped stamens for a bold striped design of zigzag lines punctuated with starlike units. Good drawing requires more than good sight. It demands a consciousness and sensitivity to the purpose of the design being drawn; to the intelligent use of the principles of design; and an awareness of the possibilities of the material at hand and of one's own abilities. More than that, good drawing implies care and craftsmanship in the planning of a design; it does not tolerate sloppy workmanship.

The foregoing material applies to designing even though one's abilities may be limited to the extent that it seems necessary to trace part of a design from the work of another. While the authors recognize this as a minor larceny, they cannot overlook the fact that it is a crime committed daily by many people who would not be participating in any form of art work were this crutch removed. Even in the tracing of units, the same accuracy is essential, for the very character of the design being traced may depend on minor, seemingly insignificant, details for its charm. And for the person who leans thus upon the work of another, the foregoing discussion will be an aid to the selection of well planned designs from which to work.

Good drawing has further implications. The human eye is repulsed by impossibilities or clumsy distortions. For example, a horse may be carved from wood in the simplest manner with no attention paid to leg joints, nostrils, and so on. It might be made even less like a horse by being painted a brilliant orange; and to remove it further from actuality, be decorated with a few bright colored flowers painted on its back. The peasants of Sweden are skilled at producing these simple toys. They are completely satisfying in design, but if leg joints were indicated and done incorrectly the character of the toy would be destroyed; the human instincts would be repulsed.

Many people find that the use of flowers in a design is somewhat difficult. Perhaps it is because flowers are familiar to everyone and the designer becomes confused in his drawing through knowing too much about them. Photographic accuracy, as stated before, is not the answer; neither are abstractions or conventionalizations if done without a feeling for the fundamental principles of design. The attractive peasant flowers most of us admire are certainly unlike the real flowers themselves; yet, as flowers, they are still possible and quite recognizable. The petals radiate from a given point; often the stamens are represented, the serrations of a petal, sometimes thorns on the stems, sometimes seedpods, even though the flower is still in full bloom. Some of these things are not likely in nature but they do not offend our sensibilities because they show intelligent organization and drawing on the part of the artist. It might be said that the artist seeks to symbolize, to reduce to simple terms or lines, the flower as we know it in nature. To some extent this might be compared to the drawing of children. The child, in reproducing a figure, or an animal, or flower will do so by putting on the paper only the parts of the object which, in his limited observations, he deems important. A human figure may be reduced to a creature with a large head, straight arms and legs, and very little in the way of body. We have all seen drawings like that; we all recognize them for attempts at drawing the figure. These drawings are in reality symbolized versions of the child's ideas of the human form. His limited knowledge has not yet been confused with the addition of details of anatomy. On the other hand, the adult, knowing much more of how things really appear, frequently cannot bring himself to the point where he can simplify or cast aside detail in order to achieve the symbolic representation of the object or figure that he is using in a design. The problem must be approached with intelligence, observation, and experimentation. When the preliminary drawing is made one should study it and then seek to simplify, correct, and/or eliminate nonessential lines and forms. This should be done with all consideration for the principles of design as previously explained, and the final result is quite bound to bear the characteristics of a well drawn, well planned design.

Whether or not a design is original to the individual making the craft project, that person is bound to inject his knowledge and personality into the arrangement of the units within the design or into the use to which the design is put. Perhaps the most inclusive generalization one might make concerning character in design is that there is virtue and strength in simplicity and weakness in complexity and hazy overstatement. This does not imply that any design made of a few simple lines will be a strong, sincere artistic expression, for it may be a monotonous repetition of dull uninteresting shapes. However, the most effective patterns usually incorporate strong rhythmic lines forming contrasting shapes which are interesting without being overly complex. A design should be so planned that to remove any one part of it would be to rob it of its effectiveness. While preparing a design for some particular purpose, it is often advisable to remove uncertain shapes and lines until the final result bears not one irrelevant detail or form. This will insure a solid, well knit unit which in line and proportion will carry the stamp of sincere and vital character. With such scrupulous care one can create or select a design which will always be interesting and which will not lean upon some sentimental interpretation to hold attention.

The selection of units or motifs for a particular problem involves the consideration of harmonious kinship with their component parts and with the intended use of the article itself. The underlying quality which creates a certain effect within a design might be labeled the *spirit of the design*. Just as certain patterns in textiles seem to reflect a dainty feminine quality while others assume a sturdy or vigorous mood, so may any design for whatsoever purpose be designated as possessing certain definite tendencies in nature or spirit. It is essential that this spirit be identified and coordinated with the craft problem. It is quite conceivable that an excellent design will lose much, if not all, of its character should it be applied to an object of an alien nature. *The need for harmonious combination of design and finished product cannot be overstressed.*

Lines and areas within a design should possess this same kinship. A grouping of rather realistic floral forms with absolutely geometric or abstract shapes would tend to be distressing, while the same abstract shapes might keep pleasant company with very conventionalized flower units. A similarity of feeling between one line or shape and all of the others used within the design is part of the problem of planning that design. This harmonious adjustment of forms will allow the eye to travel over the design without being rudely stopped by some line or unit that appears not to belong with the rest. It assumes that every part of the design has been

[50]

carefully gone over and checked; yet that the result is not one which looks labored, but instead is one which sparkles with an artistic life not confused by superfluities or incongruities.

Color is another important element in the character of a design. Most of us have a limited color vocabulary; we recognize and enjoy pleasing colors when we see them, but when called upon to produce an original scheme using more than one color we fail to do so imaginatively. Our thinking usually follows a stereotyped pattern of accepted and frequently seen color combinations. We are familiar, for instance, with the unquestionable but trite schemes of peach, or orchid, and green; pink and blue; turquoise and wine to name but a few. It is advisable, therefore, that one cultivate greater sensitivity to the possibilities of color and its myriad variations of value and intensity. Anyone who has tried to match a swatch of plain fabric knows that there are many blues, or reds, or browns, as the case may be. To realize this and then learn to use color intelligently and with feeling takes time and imagination. In another chapter where color is discussed more fully, some of the scientific aspects of color and its mixing have been considered in greater detail. It is suggested there that a color file of interesting schemes be kept for reference.

When adapting a design for a particular purpose, it is not unusual to find that the colors used in the original design are unsuited to its new personality or are not especially attractive at the outset. If this be the case, substitutes may be used. However, it is well to bear in mind the fact that not only the color, but the value, or dark and light quality, of the color is an important factor in the balancing of the design. Hence, in changing a color scheme, one must consider the dark and light distribution of the original colors and attempt to keep that quality, at least, in order to retain a pleasingly balanced pattern.

Color should also identify itself with the subject matter providing the foundation for the design. A unit composed of flowerlets and a delicate tracery of leaves and stems would be harmonious with a soft pastel scheme; but the robust character of a sturdy peasant design of conventionalized flowers, leaves, and perhaps figures and animals demands brighter or more earthy colors to enhance it. Because a certain combination of colors is beautiful and pleasing in one design is no indication that it may be used indiscriminately for any design with the same satisfactory results. The color used in a design should look like the design, should so complement it that its removal or change would take away some of the character of the design itself.

Unless a unit is composed entirely of abstract shapes or lines, there is some subject matter from which it has been evolved. Probably nature with its flowers, leaves, grasses, and countless other forms is the source most drawn upon. Often an event, a world situation, literature, or a period in history will be popularized commercially by manufacturers and advertisers and this will be reflected in the designs used to decorate any number of contemporary items. The designs of Mexico and South America have been appearing in one form or another since the publicized drive for inter-American solidarity saw its inception.

Sometimes the results of such a drive are worth while for they bring to light many unfamiliar and highly artistic examples of the work done by artists and craftsmen of another civilization. Frequently and unfortunately, however, the true character and qualities of the designs of the country are overlooked or supplanted by an Americanized concept of what Americans believe to be characteristic of the native design. These results are seen in biased and unaesthetic designs on china, linens, textiles, book-ends, and similar products which are dependent in no degree upon basic quality but rather upon commercial appeal. It is wise to be wary of any design which appears too often upon manufactured articles. In considering a design, try to discover whether it is the subject matter used or the use to which the subject matter is put that has the greater appeal. Interesting or unusual subject matter is no guarantee of quality in a design; it is the arrangement, the drawing, the color, and the interpretation in general which determine whether a design is good or poor.

There are a great many sources from which one may seek inspiration for a design to be used in the decorating of a craft project. Roughly, these sources might be divided into two classifications: those from which the design alone is used for inspirational purposes, and those which lend themselves completely, design and material, to the making of some object. It is primarily this latter group with which we are concerned here, for it will serve as a stepping-stone for the beginner into the realm of more creative design. A wide range of materials, already bearing some design motifs, are easily available to everyone. Much of this can be used in one way or another to enhance what might otherwise be an unadorned structural unit. Wallpapers, yard goods, ranging from dress fabrics to drapery fabrics; printed handkerchiefs, wrapping papers, decorative ribbons, and belting, to name just a few, often incorporate designs which lend themselves to use in a way quite different from that for which they were originally designed. An unusual fabric which one might not consider at all suitable for a garment could be used to cover a portfolio or book. A wallpaper of pleasing design and color might renew a marred or ugly wastebasket. Many materials such as those mentioned are limited in their use only by the scope of one's imagination and ingenuity.

Sometimes the design in a paper or fabric will be completely satisfactory for the use to which one wishes to put it. Occasionally it may seem advisable to alter the design or color in some respect in order that it take on some quality not found in the original. For example, a wallpaper of the desired background color, texture, and design that one wished to use for covering a box might harmonize more completely with other objects in a room if one of the colors in the pattern were heightened. This might be done with water color since the paper takes this medium very well. A pale yellow could be made more brilliant, or a dark outline around a group of flowers might give more sophistication to that design unit. Perhaps just part of the design in the paper would answer some particular purpose. In that case, it might be cut out and applied to the object in mind.

There are two ways for considering materials of this nature. One might, given a length of beautiful fabric or a few yards of decorative wallpaper, try to think of all the possible uses to which the material could be put. How many variations are possible in converting the fabric or paper into useful and artistic objects? Or if one wished to decorate some particular article with a certain type of design, one might search about for a suitable material. Either method is entirely practicable since, on the one hand, the material is serving to stimulate constructive imagination and on the other hand it is being used to satisfy an already prescribed need.

Whether the material should be used in either of these two ways, however, rests with the quality of the design it embodies. Every design should be judged according to the standards previously outlined, for commercial reproduction and sale on the market does not signify that it is one which is worthy of being preserved in any permanent form.

To illustrate more clearly the premise that wallpaper or fabric of good design can be used to stimulate creative and constructive imagination, a volume of wallpaper samples was secured from a co-operative dealer. From these sample sheets a variety of articles were constructed; all of them were suggested by the papers themselves. These examples are in no way intended to include everything to which this material might lend itself but are reproduced to show just a few of the possibilities.

NEEDED MATERIALS

Besides the containers and wallpaper, paste, and scissors, India ink and water colors are useful for accenting the designs.

FINISHING MATERIALS

Wallpaper lacquer, spar varnish, and shellac are all useful for protecting the surfaces of various craft products. Rubbing down with number 3/0 steel wool improves the finished surface.

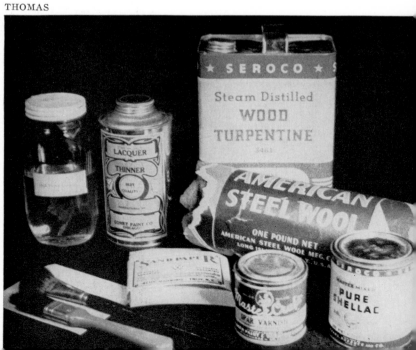

A LAMP SHADE OF WALLPAPER

A sheet from a sample book was large enough for a ten inch shade. The wallpaper should be mounted on heavy white paper before sewing it to the frame. Bias tape or gimp conceals the stitches.

THOMAS

THOMAS

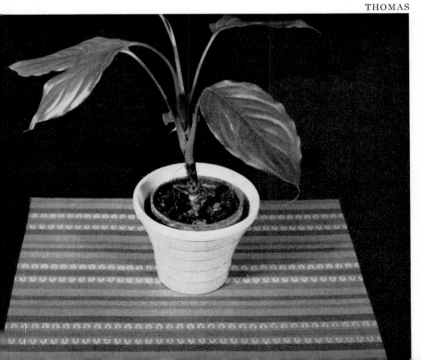

A TABLE MAT

A piece of wallpaper was mounted on cardboard, bound with bias tape applied with vegetable glue, then lacquered several times.

DESK SET

The motifs from a single piece of wallpaper may be used to make a matched set.

A SHORTENING CAN AND CLOSE RELATIVES

Two coats of enamel and wallpaper motifs saved these containers from the junk pile. A coat of shellac protects them.

EMBELLISHED BOXES

A quaint rooster camouflages a pill box.

THOMAS

THOMAS

WOODEN TILES

The square tile boasts the use of motifs cut from several different pieces of wallpaper.

Chapter V

Ways and Means

The Way Around

IT IS USUALLY EASIER FOR THE NOVICE TO BEGIN WITH A BORDER design or a unit design. This may be because a narrow bounded area is readily visualized as completed with the addition of some simple lines or forms. Actually just as soon as a top and a bottom boundary line have been drawn, the design might be considered as finished for it already answers its primary purpose, i.e., an edge or margin. However, for most purposes a border is used to add a decorative note. Consequently it is essential to know just what the possibilities and limitations of this type of design are.

Most border designs are composed of a unit or series of units or lines repeated at intervals over the length of the enclosed area. With this in mind, it can be seen that a design used as a border should be one which permits the eye to travel its length easily without serious interruption. Any line, form, or color which breaks this rhythmic movement does not rightly belong in a border design. Sometimes a design which does not seem to lead the eye easily over its length would be very successful if the units used within it were brought together more closely. Spacing the units forming a border too widely necessitates a jump in vision from one to another rather than suggesting a well planned, transitional movement.

Frequently the rhythmic effect is achieved through the use of an unbroken, though not always straight, line running the length of the border. The line may be unbroken or it may be so cut at regular intervals that the eye automatically bridges the gaps and sees it as a continuous line. It is important that this continuous rhythm be felt within a border design even though it may not be there as a definite line. It is well to take cognizance of the fact that the eye travels normally from left to right; recognition of this fact will lead the wise designer to plan a line movement in that direction. In so doing, the natural movement of the eye is facilitated. However, it is not essential that every line or object within the prescribed area lead in the direction indicated. While the main movement may be from left to right, minor lines or units may move in the opposite direction. Sometimes this is necessary, especially if the dominant movement is very strong and directs the eye too quickly down its length.

For one who has never designed a border there are numerous expedient tricks which will be of help. First, of course, the width should be decided upon and this in view of the particular area to which the border is to be applied. Since a border is a running design made up of repeated units, the length is not quite so important a consideration. Draw the top and bottom boundary lines the desired distance apart. Between these two lines at regular intervals (the distance should be proportioned to the height of the border and may be arbitrarily decided upon for this purpose) draw vertical or slightly diagonal lines to connect the boundary lines. Already there exists a somewhat more complicated design than that created by the first lines drawn; already there is a certain movement created by the repetition of these lines. Through the center and down the length of the border draw another line preferably not continuously straight but wavy, zigzag, scalloped, or broken. Between the first set

WARREN

of verticals and above the center line draw some simple geometric unit: a circle, triangle, or square. Between the adjoining verticals draw the same unit below the center line; the next above, then below, and so on. While the border is still quite simple, it has taken on new interest with each addition. Further additions may be made at will, but these additions should be so placed as to give dominance to either the vertical movement in the repetition or to the horizontal movement.

This same method with a few variations can lay the groundwork for any number of original border designs. The central line might be raised above dead center or placed somewhat lower on the band, or omitted entirely. The vertical lines might be curved in various ways, or they could be zigzagged, or scalloped. The vertical lines might be omitted and the center line given greater importance and interest. The abstract forms need not retain their abstract qualities entirely but might be turned into conventionalized flowers, leaves, or animals. If the border is a compact and complete unit the upper and lower boundary lines may be omitted entirely.

Another method which may be followed successfully to produce an attractive border design is equally simple. From colored paper cut a number of geometric forms of various sizes. Several units of each form are necessary, and it is well to cut each form from a different color of paper. One might, for example, cut six red triangles, six yellow circles somewhat smaller than the triangles, and six dark green squares either larger than the triangles or smaller than the circles. By arranging these or similar units on a piece of paper cut to the width desired for a border an interesting effect may be achieved. One will find that there are many variations possible in the arranging and rearranging of the shapes being used. When the design is interesting and satisfies the requirements for a good border, the cut pieces should be pasted to the paper to be used as a pattern for the final border if it is to be transferred to some particular object. Here again the shapes need not retain their abstract personalities but may be converted into recognizable forms. A triangle could become a leaf, a circle, a flower.

Line and form are not the only elements which establish the rhythm of a border design. Judicious use of color will also define or increase the rhythmic quality. Since color has several characteristics —hue, darkness and lightness, brightness and dullness—these should be used with an understanding of the effects they produce. A good border will be predominantly dark or light in value, and the light and dark arrangement will give strength to the movement within the design. An equal amount of dark and light color would make the border monotonous or broken owing to the lack of emphasis on any one part. The value which catches the eye first is the one to be used in playing up the important movement of line or form within the design. If the border is predominantly dark, probably the lightest value will command the attention first. This, then, would be the one to use in singling out the essential rhythmic quality of the border.

Since a bright color has the power to focus attention upon itself more readily than a dull color, the rhythmic order of a design may be further strengthened through the proper application of such color. A small area of brilliant color may become more powerful in a design than a larger area of a dull color. The eye will move over the design from one such bright spot to the next, and these spots or areas should be so placed as to complement the intended movement within the border. As with the apportionment of the amounts of light and dark used in the design, so should unequal amounts of bright and dull color be used in order that a disorganized or monotonous effect be avoided.

When one is planning a border which is to go around a square or rectangular area such as might occur in a tablecloth or wall hanging, certain problems arise where the design is to turn the corner. There are a number of methods for solving such problems which are as much a part of designing the border as is the border itself. One method which has been proved very satisfactory is that of placing a small mirror upright on the border and across it at a forty-five degree angle. It will reflect the design at right angles to itself, and by moving the mirror slowly back and forth one can discover the most effective treatment for the drawing of the design at that angle. While the mirror is held in position, a small sketch should be made of the corner design as reflected in it; when the mirror is removed, the design can be worked out in detail with the remainder of the border. Or if desired, a light pencil line can be drawn along the edge of the mirror as it rests on the border. A tracing of the first half can then be made, the tracing paper folded at the center edge of the tracing (the line upon which the mirror rested) and the complete unit drawn by going over the pencil lines seen through the thin paper.

Some border designs lend themselves to quite another treatment wherein an entirely separate but related unit is designed to fit into the corner square. The border design will lead up to this unit on either side. Such a method when used may be so planned as to give emphasis to the corner itself. This is sometimes desirable in certain designs. It should always be remembered, however, that the corner unit should be kept in harmony with the other portions of the border. There should be some existing relationship between the lines, forms, and colors used in that motif which will cause it to appear as part of the rest of the design and not as a wholly alien unit.

Not all border designs need special care at the corner area. If a design is repeated regularly within a square area, then it will fit naturally into the square formed at the corner. Or if the design is composed simply with the lines which run the length of the border, the lines will almost of themselves turn at the designated place It is only with the more complex designs that the corner area presents any particular problem, but since this problem is so easily solved by either one of the two methods described, one need have no fear when planning such a design.

Repeat with Reason

An allover design is one which is composed of a unit or series of units repeated according to some definite method whereby the entire surface of a given area is decoratively covered. In certain respects this type of design may seem somewhat more difficult to produce than a border design, since it involves an area not necessarily bounded on any particular side. Because allover designs range from the exceedingly simple to the very complex, and because there exist certain prescribed methods with which the repeat plan of the motif can be worked out, the beginner need have no more qualms over this phase of design than over that of border design.

Before attempting to create an allover pattern, it is essential that the characteristics of a good design of this sort be understood. If the purpose of an allover design is to cover a surface with a repeated unit, that repeated unit should make a pattern which will decorate but not destroy the surface that it covers. In other words, the structural base to which the design is applied should be optically preserved. A flat surface should remain a flat surface; a nicely shaped wooden bowl, if covered with an allover design, should still retain its beauty of contour. Any design which gives the illusion of depth within itself will tend to destroy the structure to which it is applied. In view of this, a flower drawn too realistically or a series of objects shown in all the accuracy of perspective are generally considered poor choices for surface patterns. While it is not necessary to dispense with forms based upon nature when selecting subject matter for a design, it is advisable that those forms be treated in a flat, decorative manner.

Occasionally a design composed entirely of abstract lines or shapes brings such lines or shapes together in a way which gives a three-dimensional quality quite unintentionally. This is the result of optical illusion and should be remedied either through changes made in the design itself or in the colors or values used, since often the last named are the elements producing the unwanted effect.

A successful surface design is one which is seen as a pleasing whole without a spotty or broken appearance. Whether the design is quiet or dramatic in its entirety, it should be one over which the eye can move rhythmically and easily without uncomfortable interruption. Lines and forms used in the pattern should adhere to the principles of good design; should be harmoniously related in scale and spirit. A loose, bold, free treatment of one portion of a design would scarcely harmonize with a small, detailed, and carefully drawn companion motif.

The ultimate use to which the design is to be put also has considerable bearing upon its nature. If the area it is to cover is small, the motifs and spacing of units within the design should be scaled to that area. A large design would lose much of its charac-

WARREN

WARREN

BASIC REPEAT PATTERNS

The diagrams to the left in the preceding designs are shown to indicate the patterns into which the designs fall. They may be used as guides in creating new designs. Often a unit will appear to greater advantage in some other arrangement than that in which it is first tried. Thus it would be wise to become familiar with all the methods shown here.

ter and charm when applied to a small surface. Scale is not the only consideration, for the nature or spirit of the design has equal bearing upon its final purpose. A delicately feminine allover pattern would not be at all suitable for the lamp shade of a sturdy pottery lamp used in a masculine room. Thus harmony of idea is another primary factor in the success of an allover pattern.

The nature of the design and the technique used in its drawing will do much to determine the kind of colors to be used. A bold handling of line and form will often gain added strength with an equally bold use of color; whereas a small, dainty pattern will usually seem to suggest a soft, feminine color scheme. The color is also controlled somewhat by the texture of the surface to which the design is applied. It would not be advisable to put a tiny tracery of design in pastel color onto a coarse heavy fabric.

The colors should be carried through a design in order to preserve the intended rhythmic pattern rather than to break it into spotty, disorganized points of interest. One is reminded again of the fact that color has two important properties, value and intensity, and that both of these will produce certain definite effects when the color is applied to the desired areas.

One may begin an allover design in several different ways. The most simple method and the one which is advisable for a beginner, is that of first designing a unit which can be repeated in the final design. By carefully working out a single unit, both in design and in color, and then tracing it according to the repeat pattern desired, the final effect is usually satisfactory. Occasionally when the unit is seen as a repeated pattern, it may seem necessary to adjust or omit some of its details in order to increase the rhythmic pattern or to bring it into closer organization. The beginner will keep his first motif simple in color and design, but as his knowl-

ABSTRACT ALLOVER DESIGN

by Esther Otte

Cut paper is an expedient method by which to work out designs.

THOMAS

edge increases, more complex patterns may be worked out. Frequently a unit repeated according to one of the simpler methods given will produce an altogether different effect than when it is repeated according to one of the more complicated methods.

Another means of designing an allover pattern is much like that discussed for border designs. Numerous units of varying shapes and sizes may be cut from colored paper and adjusted into an allover design. A piece of ruled or graph paper will serve as an ade-

CUT PAPER ALL-OVER DESIGN

by Josephine Brownlow

Designs of this type are excellent to use for block printing or stenciling.

THOMAS

quate background and will facilitate the regular placing of the units. This piece of work, then, may be used as a preliminary plan for the final design which may be worked out in another medium. It should be remembered that while the colored paper units will probably be essentially geometric, the final design may incorporate such shapes and cast them into more realistic or more recognizable forms. For example, a circle might become a flower. Free, totally abstract forms can be cut or torn from paper just as well if one is

[73]

inventive. It is said that one of our foremost textile designers lays out many of her designs in this way.

The foregoing material has dealt chiefly with allover designs consisting of definite units. It must be remembered that striped and/or plaid designs also fall into the classification of allover designs. In both of these types, the point of primary importance is the interest created by the variation in width and color of the background spaces as well as the lines which make the design. A design composed of stripes of equal width is quite apt to be monotonous, whereas one of stripes of unequal but pleasingly related widths will be interesting.

Unusual Units

When a design is being planned to decorate the surface of some particular object and it seems desirable to keep it as a single unit, the problem presents complications not encountered in the planning of an allover or border design. The first factor to be considered is the shape of the surface to be decorated. Whether it is round, square, or rectangular, the design should be so planned as to conform to, and become a part of, that shape. A unit planned for the top of a round box would not appear to advantage on a box with a rectangular cover. One might say that a good unit design, though not necessarily bordered by a definite line, so suggests the shape it is being planned for that when seen apart from it, the shape would still be felt strongly. To accomplish this successfully, any lines or forms which are so forceful as to break the given space into unharmonious shapes should be scrupulously avoided. A square broken into two triangles by the use of a definite diagonal line moving from one corner to the opposite corner would not be as useful a foundation for a design as would be a like square divided into

A symmetrical unit of design is one which is arranged in perfect balance on both sides of the center. It is a formal design arrangement.

WARREN

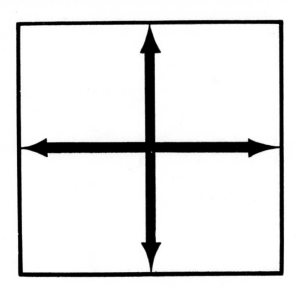

A bisymmetric unit of design is one which is arranged in perfect balance on all of its sides. It is a formal design arrangement.

WARREN

An *asymmetric unit of design* is one which differs on all sides but which still retains a balanced arrangement. It is an informal design arrangement.

WARREN

ABSTRACT DESIGN
by Marilyn Sincox

This cut paper design might very well be used for a patch-work pillow top.

four triangles through the use of two diagonal lines. In the second case, one line would tend to nullify the other since it moved in the opposite direction; and the attention would be drawn to the intersection of the two lines. Thus the center of interest remains within the unit rather than being drawn away from it, as would happen in the first example.

The designing of a unit for some particular shape means simply that the shape in question is broken up interestingly with lines and forms integrated into a pleasing relationship. These lines and forms may be very abstract with no representational qualities, or they may resolve themselves into conventionalized realistic objects such as flowers, leaves, animals, or figures. Usually, when working with abstract or geometric forms, it is well to use line and shape contrasts. A design composed entirely of straight lines is apt to

STYLIZED FLOWER
by Audrey White

*Strength is gained by omit-
ting realistic details.*

THOMAS

look sharp and brittle, whereas the introduction of some relief in
the form of curved lines will soften the design and afford pleasing
contrasts. If realistic objects are desired within the unit, they should
be selected and composed with every thought given to the design
itself. It is usually the tendency for the beginner to become so involved with accurate representation as to overlook the quality of
the form as it relates itself to the design. This can be avoided somewhat if the designer can coach himself to forget the actual flower,
bird, or other object which he may first have had in mind. Then
he may use a combination of geometric forms which, when assembled into a design unit, suggest an object of nature, without
being so specific as to portray an exact type at the expense of good

[79]

design. Too often a beginner will allow himself to be so strongly held by an idea that it becomes very difficult to give full play to the imagination. Good designing needs an imaginative approach.

No matter what comprises a unit design, it will follow one of several basic layouts. These layouts apply to a unit design intended for almost any shape, and a working knowledge of them will greatly aid the beginner when he first plans such a design. As has been suggested previously in another section, after the preliminary pattern has been decided upon, colored paper cut into various shapes might be used and arranged against a background of the correct dimensions until a satisfactory combination of foundation forms is arrived at. This arrangement could then serve its turn as an outline for a complete and detailed drawing of the design as it was first visualized or as it grew in the mind of the designer during the preliminary experimenting. The same principles of design that were described in more detail at the beginning of this chapter must be applied to any unit design. Contrasts in line, form, and value are essential to the well planned design in order that its nature will be one which will hold the interest over a long period of time. Such contrasts should be organized, of course, with care being devoted to the relationships of curved and straight lines, large and small forms, and dark and light values. The association of the unit of design and the shape onto which it is to be placed should not be forgotten at any time; each should and must complement the other.

Chapter VI

Figure Flattery

WOMAN, THY NAME IS VANITY IS PROVED EACH DAY THAT ONE lies abed in the morning suffering from wardrobe boredom. This may be just an excuse to stay in bed a little longer, but too often it's the truth. Perhaps one's closet does contain more costumes than the average; or perhaps it contains just one or two which must do duty day after day, and for every sort of occasion. Whichever the case, the psychological reaction is the same since everyone tires of the clothes he wears.

A wardrobe may be compared to a meal which lacks the proper variety or seasoning. Just as spices can stimulate an appetite, so can accessories lift a wardrobe from the commonplace, and add to a general feeling of well-being.

Not only is one's mental setup important to the way he starts the day, but it is important to the effect he makes upon others. Many do not admit dressing to impress others, but can it be denied? Refusal to admit this would mean that one took no precautions as to appearance before superiors, that one never gave a shiny nose an extra dusting of powder before going to a tea. The social responsibility of neatness and grooming is well understood, and since it is not the province of this book to instruct in that direction, this section will deal explicitly with the adjuncts of the wardrobe.

Most budgets cannot stand the strain of high style, though hearts may yearn for the newest expression of some creative stylist. Many take refuge behind a "don't care anyway" attitude which is expressed by complete disregard for the matter of wardrobe planning in any respect. Should consideration be given the economic factors here involved, it would be realized that no matter what talents one may possess, or how much of a success one may have achieved, ultimate attainments are often dependent upon the impression made upon others.

Frequently one hears of otherwise successful women who are kept from advancement or who lose their positions because of poor taste in personal clothing selection. Good taste does not mean an absolute acceptance of current style, but, rather, wise selections from the garments and accessories available at the time. This involves understanding of personal figure problems, personality, and financial standing.

Even though one may be cognizant of his particular problems, he may give the impression of being correctly but unimaginatively clothed. Why not strive for individualism? It takes so little time, effort, and ability to achieve distinction after one has the knack for selecting and combining accouterments with imagination. Do not bend over backward to be different; do not try to be conspicuous in a bizarre way! Such attempts usually bespeak poor taste and may mark one as an individual but not as an individual that one would wish to meet. Do not be sensational! To freshen up that wardrobe, or to add an unusual note, try a decorative accessory.

What is an accessory? It is something which is added to the wardrobe but which is not essentially a part of it. It is designed to heighten the effect of the wardrobe. One has often noticed how the effect of a basically plain dress is intensified by a beautiful clip or by some unusual buttons. In like manner, two or three different belts may be used to make one frock appear to be several. Embroidery might be added to a year-old dress to beguile one's friends into believing that there has been a new addition to the wardrobe.

Doubtless all will agree that accessories are valuable additions to any wardrobe, but perhaps many are already computing the cost of these articles as it would figure in their personal budgets. Consider making them. One may have a preconceived notion that making his own accessories would take a great deal of talent, or that if one did make them that they would look "home made." A little patience, very little money, visualization of the many possibilities, and a few spare moments will teach one that this is a fallacy. The following pages are filled with suggestions and directions for accessories which will add fillip to everyday existence. With these for suggestions plus a little personal imagination, countless other ideas will present themselves to the creative thinker.

As the Indians Did It

Fashion recurrently selects belts as her favorite point of emphasis, and the fashion-wise woman is ever alert to suggestions which will enable her to add to her own collection. Whether a wide belt or a narrow belt is the more becoming to one's own figure, it may be a distinctive note in a wardrobe. A belt need not be of leather or of the same material as one's dress or skirt to be attractive. There are any number of methods and materials suitable to the making of an unusual and interesting belt.

Because there has been a great deal of material published on the art of leather tooling, it is being purposely omitted in this chapter. We mention it only as a possibility and as a suggestion to those who might be interested in this craft. Less familiar techniques will be discussed here. Not only are these techniques less familiar, and therefore more unusual, but they also require less equipment and less expensive material.

FINGER WEAVING is a technique, really a many strand braiding process, that was developed by the North American Indians. Many tribes are credited with its development and preservation, but research has shown that similar techniques have been used from north to south on the American continent.

Originally this craft was probably done with leather thongs and it may still be so done. However, for the purposes of adaptability and convenience, yarn has proved itself very satisfactory. Heavy weights of yarn are best. Germantown, knitting worsted, tapestry, and peasant yarns may all be used. Fast color cotton yarns, such as moss yarn, the lighter weight rug fillers, and perle cottons, sizes three or five, are also suitable and attractive.

For the beginner, two of the more simple of the possible variations of this technique are most easily comprehended. One produces a chevron stripe if more than one color is used; the other, a diagonal stripe moving from one side of the belt to the other. The number of colors used is left to the discretion of the weaver. It should be borne in mind when selecting the colors that they be harmonious in combination and pleasing with the dress with which the belt is to be worn. One way of insuring this is through the use of one color that repeats

FINGER WOVEN BELT
by Barbara Bentson

Chevron stripe.

that of the dress. Both the hue and the value of the color are very important. The design of the belt will be most pleasing if there is an adequate value contrast.

The greatest problem in designing a belt of this kind is that of determining the relative width of the stripes. Each area or color should be considered as an individual stripe, so that both the dark and the light areas have pleasing variation. The relative proportions of the stripes are set by the number of strands of yarn used for each stripe; for example, if three times as many strands are used for one stripe as are used for another, the first stripe will be three times as wide as the other. When planning the sizes of the stripes the principles for obtaining good proportions should be applied.

One of the characteristic qualities of a belt of this kind is its flexibility, a factor which permits looping or tying into a soft knot. Calculation of the length of the strands of yarn to be cut for weaving involves consideration of the following: the woven length, which includes the waist measurement; the amount needed for the knot; and the length desired for sash ends; the sum of which must be doubled, because about that much is taken up in the process of weaving. To this add the length desired for fringe on each end of the belt.

Cut the desired number of strands of each color to the necessary length. The greater the number of strands used, the wider will be the belt. Sixty-two lengths of knitting worsted will produce a braid approximately three inches wide.

FINGER WEAVING

Diagonal stripe.

THE CHEVRON PATTERN

Arrange the same number of strands of each color on either side of the center in the same relative positions. In other words, duplicate one side of the center in reverse on the other. There should be not only an equal number on each side of the center, but also an even number on each side, such as ten and ten, twelve and twelve, twenty and twenty, etc. Thus your plan might read from the left, six brown, nine green, five tan, center, five tan, nine green, six brown. Starting at the left, wrap each thread in its proper order once around a pencil or short stick. Permit a length of yarn extending beyond the pencil in one direction to equal the length allowed for the fringe on one end of the belt. This divides the original length of yarn into long and short parts. After each yarn has been looped about the pencil in its correct position, the short or fringe end of the yarns should be tied together in one knot close to the pencil or stick.

Take a short piece of scrap yarn, about 18 inches long, double it and put the first left-hand strand of yarn in the loop thus formed. Twist this short length of yarn once, and place the second strand of yarn between the short ends against the twist. Twist the short piece again in the same direction as before, and place the third strand up against this twist. Repeat until all the strands of yarn are held firmly in place, one next to the other, and in their proper positions. This *stay* should be put as close to the pencil as possible.

The material is now ready for weaving. Tie the fringe end securely to some stable object at a height convenient for working. Divide the group of yarns in the center. *It is essential that this center division be constantly maintained.* Grasp one group firmly in each hand. Take the first thread from the center of the left-hand

[86]

PREPARING YARN FOR FINGERWEAVING

Wrap each strand firmly around a small stick or pencil allowing sufficient yarn above the stick to form a fringe of the desired length.

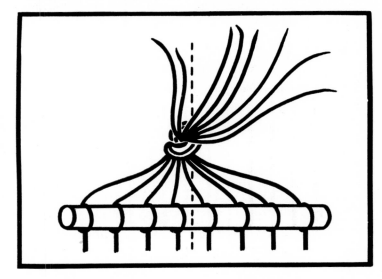

Tie the fringe end in a knot and fasten this knot to some secure object such as the back of a chair.

Secure the order of the yarn by twisting an extra length of yarn between and around each strand. The material is now ready for weaving.

WARREN

FINGER WEAVING

The chevron design.

WARREN

FINGER WEAVING

The diagonal stripe.

group and pass it over the first thread from the center of the right-hand group, under the second, over the third, under the fourth, etc., until it emerges at the opposite side of the group from where it started. Permit this thread to dangle free. Start again at the center with the first thread to the right of the center. Weave to the left until this thread emerges at the outside edge to the left; permit it to dangle free. Start again at the left-center and weave to the right as before. Bring the first dangling yarn into the group and weave over or under it as though it were a part of the group. This process is basically like that of any simple weaving; i.e., the weft thread passes alternately over and under the warp threads. Repeat the process, again using the right-center yarn and weaving left, being sure to include the dangling yarn on this side. Always leave the yarn last woven dangling free on the side until a new strand replaces it. Continue in this manner, left and right, until the desired length of fabric has been woven. The tension of the yarn and the width of the belt are controlled by adjusting the dangling thread as it is finally taken into the group of threads when it is replaced. Good technique is a necessity to the belt's beauty.

THE DIAGONAL STRIPE PATTERN

The length of yarns to be used is figured in the same way as for the chevron pattern but the weaving process differs slightly. Tie the yarn to the pencil in an arrangement that forms a pleasing striped pattern. It does not have to be arranged the same on both sides of the center. For weaving, instead of beginning at the center and weaving alternately right and left, begin with the first thread at the extreme left (or right) and, beginning over the first yarn, weave over and under across the entire group of yarns. Leave this

[90]

yarn dangling as before. Start at the original side with the second yarn and weave it across the entire group. When the new weaver emerges at the far side, be sure to include in the group the old one left dangling before. Continue weaving, always from the same side, always alternately over and under, until a sufficient length of woven fabric has been obtained.

From the Egyptians

CARD WEAVING, a method developed centuries ago by the Egyptians, is another process by which belts, hat bands, purses (strips sewed together), suspenders, and dress trimming, as well as braids for household purposes, can be made. The cards with which the weaving is done really comprise a simple loom; hence the fabric that results is actually woven, in contrast to finger weaving, which is basically a braiding technique.

The materials required for card weaving are simple. A number of cards two and one-half to three inches square, cut from stiff, smooth cardboard which does not fray easily, are needed. Trunk board, heavy poster board, or the cardboard used for bookbinding is excellent. Each card should have a hole one-eighth to one-fourth inch in diameter punched in each corner. These must be very accurately placed about one-half inch from the corner, exactly in the same positions on each card.

The holes should be labeled A, B, C, and D respectively in clockwise fashion. Corners A should be marked in some way so as to be easily observed when looking at the cards from the side. Clipping the corner or coloring it with a crayon or ink are suggested methods. Number each card successively 1, 2, 3, etc.

The number of cards needed depends upon the width of the fabric desired. Twenty cards will be sufficient to make a piece of material approximately one and one-half inches wide if woven with Shetland yarn. Narrower or wider widths may be made by using fewer or more cards. Germantown or knitting worsted will make a wider belt per number of cards than will the Shetland yarn. The use of carpet warp results in material of approximately the same width as that produced by Shetland yarn.

Warp and weft threads are needed for this craft. The warp threads may be of a good quality Shetland yarn, Germantown or knitting worsted, carpet warp, string or perle cotton in sizes three or five. The weft thread may be the same as the warp thread and is less conspicuous when chosen in the same color as that of the outside warp threads.

The warp threads will need to be considerably longer than the length desired for the finished woven band. Thirty-one inches of warp works up into about twenty-seven inches of woven material. This does not allow for fringing, finishing, or for the play of the cards when weaving. An extra eighteen inches of warp should be ample unless long fringe is desired. All warp threads must be exactly the same length.

The procedure followed when designing the pattern will be more easily understood if the accompanying diagrams are studied carefully. If there is no squared paper at hand, rule off a piece of paper so that there are four rows of squares, one above another. The number

CARD WOVEN BELT
by Virginia Nelson

The cards were threaded from one direction only. The cards were reversed every fourth step.

of squares in each row should be identical with the number of cards prepared for use. There are four rows of these squares, each row representing a corner of the cards; label them at one side of the diagram: A, B, C, and D. Above each square in the top row place a number beginning with 1 above the left-hand square and continuing in order until the right-hand square receives the same number that appears on the last card to be used in the weaving.

Decide how many colors are going to be used for the belt. As many or as few colors as one wishes may be used. Moderation, however, is always a good rule. A pleasing value contrast is helpful in bringing out a clean cut pattern. A colored pencil or crayon to indicate the color of each warp thread to be used will facilitate the designing of the pattern.

Study the group of squares to visualize the many possibilities obtainable if the squares were filled in solidly with the various crayons to form simple mosaiclike designs. Very young children often amuse themselves in this manner for hours at a time and many adults still find it a fascinating bit of seatwork. Try a number of the best ideas by actually filling in the squares. The proportion of each color used and the distribution of each should be checked carefully. The designs need not be symmetrical, but simple designs made up of fairly large areas usually weave up into the most attractive patterns. It may help to remember that each colored block represents only one "stitch," and appears very small indeed in the finished product.

CARD WOVEN BELT
by Edith Nelson

The cards were threaded from one direction only. The cards were turned in one direction.

Card for weaving.

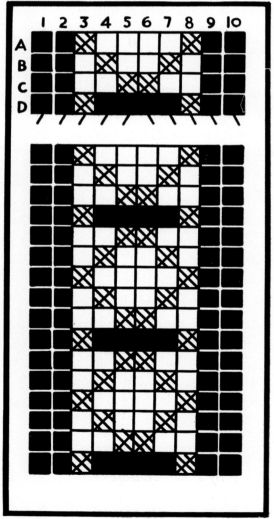

Preparing the design.

WARREN

Choose the best of the paper patterns. This pattern represents the design across the entire width of the belt to be woven, but only four weft threads of its length. This colored chart merely shows the areas in which the various colors will appear. The actual design takes on interest brought about by the direction the threads twist as the material is being woven, and by the manipulation as controlled by the craftsman.

The cards are warped according to the pattern chosen. This is a simple process if one always bears in mind the fact that each letter on the diagram represents a hole in the card and that each number represents a single card. To warp cards for the design shown in the accompanying diagram, the following order is indicated:

Card 1—A black, B black, C black, D black
Card 2—A black, B black, C black, D black
Card 3—A gray, B white, C white, D gray
Card 4—A white, B gray, C white, D black
Card 5—A white, B white, C gray, D black
Card 6—A white, B white, C gray, D black
Card 7—A white, B gray, C white, D black
Card 8—A gray, B white, C white, D gray
Card 9—A black, B black, C black, D black
Card 10—A black, B black, C black, D black

It will be seen from a study of this chart that in order to weave this pattern forty strands of yarn are needed—four for each card. Of these forty strands, twenty are black, eight are gray, and twelve are white. Each strand of yarn is drawn through its proper hole, with care being taken that the strands are all drawn through the proper side of the card. At the bottom of the pattern diagram or draft are small lines slanting up or down to indicate whether the threads are to be put through the holes in the cards from face

Warping the cards.

Preparing the warped cards for weaving.

to back or from back to face. Usually the direction of threading changes at the center of the pattern. Many patterns may be threaded all in one direction without destroying the design; in fact, the twisting of the threads is responsible for some interesting variations. The accompanying photographs show the effect of the two methods of threading. After each card is warped, it is well to tie the ends of the four strands into a loose knot to prevent their slipping free of the card.

The directions for weaving are as follows: Gather together all the warp ends from holes A, B, C, and D on one side of the cards, which have been stacked one upon the other in order of number, corresponding corners one over the other. Tie these ends securely into a knot. Fasten the knot firmly to some stationary object. This is important. Straighten out the warp from the other end and tie another knot about twenty-four inches from the first knot, keeping the cards between the two knots. Tie this knot to a chair (or to one's waist) so that the tension may be kept steady. After pulling the threads fairly taut, grasp the cards firmly in both hands and turn so that the lettered sides are perpendicular to the floor, with corner A closest to the weaver.

Push the cards along the warp threads toward the body so that one may grasp them comfortably without arm strain. It will be noticed that the threads have divided themselves into two groups forming a shed. Slip a one-fourth inch strip of thin cardboard into the shed nearest one's body. Turn the cards away from their original position in a counterclockwise direction so that the corner

CARD WOVEN SAMPLER

The cards were threaded both ways; the change of direction was made in the center.

lettered B takes the position just held by letter A. Put another strip of cardboard through this shed, pushing this cardboard close to the first piece. Continue turning the cards in this fashion until corner A is again in its original position. Using cardboard strips or a one-inch strip of rag for the first few turns instead of a regular weft thread gives a firm foundation for the rest of the weaving.

The regular weft thread is usually the same as the warp thread, and preferably the same color as the outside warp threads. Cut a piece a little less than two yards long and insert it in the new shed. Have an equal length extend on each side. Turn the cards again, and through the shed formed insert both ends of the weft thread, pulling them firmly but not tightly to the opposite sides of the warp from which they were first placed. The use of a double weft such as this produces a firm web, and it is easier to keep the edges of the belt even and free from loops. The weft threads should be pushed into place with the side of the hand, a ruler, or any other contrivance the weaver finds handy. Continue weaving until the warp on the other side of the cards is twisted so tightly that weaving is difficult. Then one may do one of two things: either start turning the cards in the opposite direction, which automatically unwinds the warp, or untie the warp end and untwist it by hand. Tie the warp into position again and continue weaving as before, turning the cards counterclockwise.

Pattern changes are obtained by changing the direction in which the cards are turned at regular intervals. For example, if the cards are turned four times counterclockwise, then four times clockwise a symmetrical unit is formed. It is fun to experiment with this procedure, for many original effects can be obtained. The edges of

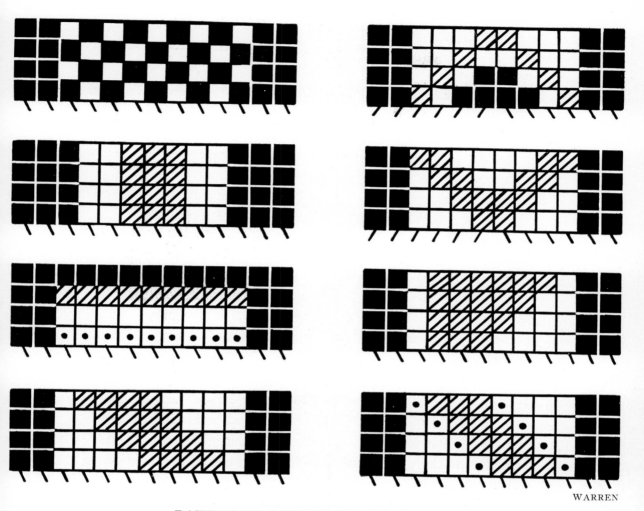

PATTERNS FOR CARD WEAVING

the woven material are more difficult to keep even when the cards
are turned in opposite directions.

It is wise to jot down on a piece of paper exactly what the
next turn will be when leaving one's work even for a short time. It

[99]

is difficult to correct an error, especially if wool warp is being used. Slipping rubber bands around the pack of cards whenever the weaving is put aside is a great help as well.

When the weft thread has come to an end a new piece may be added by placing the new length in the next shed. The short ends of the old weft may be cut off close to the fabric when the weaving has progressed an inch or so. The nature of the weaving will hold the ends in place without danger of raveling.

The bibliography will suggest references if one wishes to delve into the more complicated forms of card weaving.

Ingenuity will suggest many ways to finish the ends of the braid. A few suggestions will surely bring to mind others. The ends of the braid may be stitched several times by machine to prevent raveling and then the raw edges bound with cloth or thin leather (the tops of kid gloves or leathers of similar weight are usable). The loose ends of yarn may be knotted close to the braid and cut evenly to form fringe of the desired length; or a heavier fringe may be made by twisting two strands of yarn separately, then twisting them together. Other than these finishes are the braids made from three or four strands. Four-strand braid fringe is exceptionally attractive. It is a rare occasion when a commercial plastic or metal buckle forms a suitable addition to any of the hand-woven belts.

Grandmother Did This

Occasionally a design which uses greater freedom in line, motif, or repetition than that found in a pattern produced by card or finger weaving will be better suited to a particular dress. Sometimes too, the fabric from which the dress is made will be a more satisfactory background for a decorative belt than will another ma-

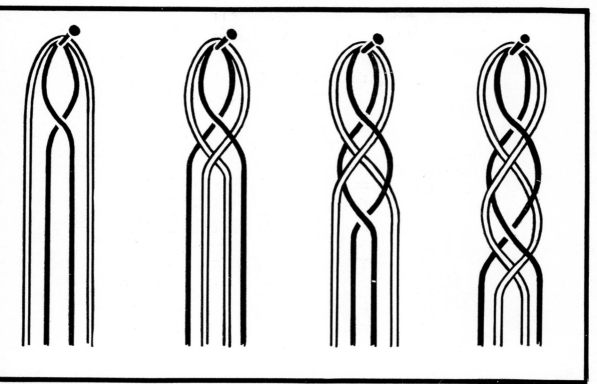

FOUR-STRAND BRAIDING

terial. Stitchery is one means for producing unlimited freedom of expression in the interpretation of a design and at the same time may be done on a piece of the dress fabric itself. It is not always, of course, necessary to do the stitchery on the dress material; other materials may be equally attractive as a basis for a well designed, decorative belt.

Needlework is something that the present day miss usually concedes to her grandmother. Do not for a minute imagine that this is a lost art buried under the mass production of our machine age. It takes to revival like a duck to water and it pays dividends for the time and effort it may take.

Two variations of technique not frequently used in making a belt will be considered in more detail here. It is to be understood, as we have mentioned before, that these are just suggestions presented with the hope that they may open the way to further experimentation on the part of the reader.

YARN ON FELT (OR WOOL)

After the fabric selection has been made, decide upon the length and width of the finished belt. Cut the belt to the desired shape, allowing sufficient material for seaming and fastening. Plan the design for the area to be decorated. This design may be a border following the length of the belt, or it may be a surface design consisting of small, repeated motifs. Draw the design on paper to actual size. To transfer the design to the fabric, pin the paper to the cloth and run small basting stitches along the lines of the design, taking care to go through the fabric at the same time. Then the paper may be torn away and the basting threads used as guide lines for the yarn embroidery. Another method may be followed.

EMBROIDERED BELT
by Barbara Warren

The paper design may be pierced along the lines of the design either by pricking with a pin or by using a seam marker. This perforated pattern should then be securely pinned to the fabric and powdered chalk pounced through the holes with a piece of cotton. If this method is used, it is essential to re-mark the transferred design on the fabric with a basting stitch, since the chalk guide lines will rub off during the process of embroidery. If one has confidence in his own ability, time may be saved by drawing directly on to the material with chalk.

In view of the fact that the design must be planned with an idea of some of the stitches that will be used in its execution, directions have been included for a few of the most usable and most quickly done stitches. With a small amount of practice, sufficient skill will be developed to produce a finished looking piece of work. While practicing these stitches, think of their possibilities in an actual design; they will suggest many original uses.

Often people beginning work of this sort have difficulty in selecting materials appropriate for use in combination. For convenience a table of suggestions has been prepared. (See page 106.)

NEEDLE POINT BELT

Outline stitch.

Chain stitch.

Chevron stitch.

Mexican stitch.

Cross stitch.

Lazy daisy stitch.

Satin stitch.

Blanket stitch.

Roumanian stitch.

French knot.

Pekinese stitch.

Loop stitch.

Feather stitch.

Couching.

Needle point.

Faggoting.

WARREN

On heavy or coarse textures:	Use one of these:
Wool suiting	Shetland floss
Felt	Tapestry or peasant yarns
Monk's cloth	Germantown or knitting worsted
Burlap, etc.	Cotton moss yarn
On medium textures:	Use:
Linen	Linen thread
Cotton	Linen or six-strand embroidery floss (dull floss is usually in best taste)
Wool crepe	Shetland floss or Shetland chiffon yarn
On fine textures:	Use:
Sheer wool	Shetland chiffon
Silks and velvets	Silk rope or floss
Sheer cotton	Six-strand embroidery floss

With the stitchery planned, the design transferred to the material, and the proper weight of yarn or embroidery floss selected, the actual embroidery may begin. Care must be taken to keep the stitches evenly and neatly placed and the tension of the thread correct so that the material will not be pulled out of shape. Do not plan a design which calls for carrying a long unsecured thread over the surface of the material, as it will be pushed out of position when used and may snag or catch on such things as furniture or buttons. A floating thread should be no longer than one-half inch.

The method of fastening the belt should be determined when the original idea is conceived. There are many methods which may be used, each one of them calling for certain allowances to be made when the fabric is first cut. One of the photographs will give a clear picture of one of the more simple means that may be chosen. It consists merely of a continuation of the lining fabric rolled back on itself to form a sufficiently large, decorative cylinder at either end of the belt. The lining was rolled around a fringed strip of the background material cut slightly wider than the width of the belt. Hooks and eyes were sewed to the under side of the cylinders to close the belt. This fringed extension was not necessary and might well be omitted in this type of closing.

Other methods for closing or fastening a belt are:

TYING: In this case the belt must be planned for additional length to be taken up by the knot.

LACES: In this method the belt is not planned to overlap. The ends may just meet or they may be separated slightly. Eyelets for laces may be punched and embroidered or they may be put in by a shoemaker. Plastic lacing hooks or rings may be obtained at the notion counters in most department stores. Cords may be made of strips of the basic fabric, the lining material, or of the yarn or floss used in the embroidery. If the laces are made of yarn or floss, a number of strands should be twisted or braided to make a firm cord.

BUTTONS: Any button of appropriate texture, size, and color would be suitable, but most attractive "buttons" can be made of wooden beads, cylinders made by rolling up strips of leather, or fabric, bits of dowel rod plus a small screw eye, and so on ad infinitum.

ZIPPER: When using this, be certain to get a zipper that opens at both ends.

BUCKLES: Generally speaking, an ordinary "store-bought" buckle does not look appropriate on a handmade belt. If the buckle is covered with yarn or with the fabric used in the belt, it seems to belong to it. However, one method which has proved successful uses several small buckles. These may be sewed to small strips of the fabric which in turn are sewed to the wider belt. Two or three may be used, depending upon the width of the belt.

The methods for closing belts which appear in the accompanying diagram have all been found to be satisfactory. Where leather is suggested as a likely material, the top of an old glove may be used. Sometimes it is possible to purchase leather scraps of assorted colors and weights at a leather supply house. Such scraps are usually sold by the pound and may be obtained at a reasonable cost.

Remember that ingenuity and inventiveness are as important items in the workbasket as the needles and yarns and flosses that are used for these crafts.

Appliquéd Belt

Numerous materials may be used for appliqué. Probably the most usable of the many which might suggest themselves is felt, since that fabric, when cut into shapes and applied to the foundation, has no raw edges to turn under and hem down. The entire design could be cut from colored pieces of felt and arranged pleasingly on the basic material with due consideration for the shape of the belt. The pieces which compose the design might be further elaborated with the addition of decorative embroidery. If this method is used, the design should be simple, with all of its parts well scaled to one another. Obviously, the success of the final product depends to a considerable extent on the care used in the selection and arrangement of the units within the design. If these various units are so detailed as to be difficult to cut from the felt and difficult to apply, the quality of the final effect is jeopardized. The omy of both time and energy. One advantage gained by the use of embroidery is that it permits a more flexible variation in scale because small stitches can be used in contrast to larger appliquéd units. Embroidery may also serve to tie isolated units of appliqué together into one well integrated design.

When selecting the colors to be used for either of these types of belts, the colors should be chosen with the design, the fabric, and the ensemble in mind. A simplified color scheme, as well as a simplified design, is usually the most satisfactory.

NEEDLE POINT BELTS

The advantages to be found in a belt made with needle point are numerous. In general, a belt made this way is definitely of a dressier type than most of those made with other methods. The design may be made up of fine units and intricate detail, and color may be used to produce an almost jewel-like effect. The technique results in a firm belt which may be a simple, straight, decorative band or may be shaped to repeat some curved or pointed line in the dress itself. Needle-point or cross-stitch canvas or a firm scrim makes an excellent foundation for the stitchery, which should be planned to cover the canvas completely. Sometimes a coarse but evenly woven material such as linen crash may be used advantageously.

APPLIQUÉ BELT

Petit point is not suggested for this purpose since it is too fine and would be too tedious a method for any but the most patient.

Yarns suitable to needle point should have a high twist in order that the design stand out clearly. Tapestry yarns are a very good choice and come in a beautiful range of colors. Peasant yarns are equally usable and frequently are found to be brighter in color than the soft neutralized tones of the former yarn.

Finishing the Belts

As embroidered belts do not look well on the back after the stitchery has been done, nor do they show to the best advantage if they are crushed out of their original shape, it is usually necessary to stiffen and line them.

Belt stiffening may be bought by the yard or crinoline may be used. In some cases the belt will not need much stiffening and a lining of grosgrain ribbon will give enough body to the embroidered fabric. Other lining materials are silks, taffeta, sateen, or the fabric on which the stitchery was done originally.

The stiffening should be cut to the desired width and length of the belt. Fold the edges of the embroidered fabric down over the stiffening and tack into place. The lining fabric should be cut about half an inch wider than the belt itself. The edges of the lining should be folded to the wrong side, then slip stitched to the belt securely so as to cover the material used for stiffening. This is a concealed lining or facing. However, the lining may form an important part of the design. By cutting the lining wider than the belt itself, sewing it to the belt with the right sides to the inside, and then turning right side out, the lining will extend over the edges of the belt to form a binding. This may be of a contrasting color,

WHITE EMBROIDERED JACKET
by Helen S. Petersen

Contemporary design uses strong, simplified motifs. The hand loomed fabric is a perfect foil for cross stitch.

value, or even fabric. This method was used in finishing the belt shown in the accompanying photograph.

Stitchery for Style

A well known fashion commentator has said that embroidery should never be used on a dress as it is apt to mark the dress as being "homemade." This seems too inclusive a statement, because it does not take into account many costumes which have been given added distinction by a smart note of decorative stitchery. It is true that often a dress has looked "homemade" as a result of *poorly designed* and *poorly executed* decoration. Sometimes it is the result of decoration which has been used to conceal basically poor structure in the dress itself. Occasionally it is the result of poorly selected yarns used in the stitchery or lack of consideration for the position of the decoration on the garment.

On the other hand, well planned stitchery may set the keynote of a very distinctive costume. A well chosen bit of such decoration will give individuality to an otherwise commonplace garment, and insures one against the possibility of seeing one's neighbor wearing a duplicate costume.

One need not make the basic dress. This may be encouraging to those who lack confidence in themselves as dressmakers. A first problem might be the injection of new life into an old dress. The present collar on the dress might be removed and replaced by a band of embroidery which could also be repeated at the cuffs: or if not there, on the belt. If the dress boasts pockets, those might receive the emphasis; or the sleeves, the yoke, or the blouse front; whichever seems to compliment the dress the most.

Should one buy a dress as the foundation for decorative needlework, be sure to select the garment with an eye for all the possibilities mentioned. Of course, all of the areas suggested should not be utilized for decoration on the same garment. Remember that restraint is a mark of individuality.

Some fabrics lend themselves to stitchery much more readily than others. Fabrics of coarse, but firm, texture are usually found more suitable and are more easily embroidered since they have more body. Among the summer fabrics that might be used are heavy linen, salyna, hopsacking, and crash; in the winter fabric group, flannel, wool crepe or rep, light weight, but firm, tweeds, broadcloth, velveteen, and others of similar quality are usable. If silk is used as a foundation for decorative needlework, very fine delicate stitches as well as suitable yarn or floss must be chosen in order to be in harmony with the texture of the fabric.

For the heavier materials Shetland floss of the regular or chiffon weight, or for a dressier garment angora, are most appropriate. A yarn having many twists to the inch is more difficult to use for embroidery, as each stitch seems to remain on the surface of the material rather than become a part of it. If the material is a wash fabric, the embroidery floss should also be selected for its washable qualities. Six-strand floss is usable with wash fabrics.

The stitches previously suggested in this section may be used singly or in combination to produce interesting decorative effects. Diagrams and directions for the working of more complicated stitches may be found in books devoted to the art of needlework.

Many articles in our wardrobes other than just belts and dresses can be used as a basis for attractive handiwork. Some lend themselves to a more formal and reserved type of design, others to a gay informality. Briefly they are:

SWEATERS

These may be decorated with an allover design of some small, evenly spaced unit, or the decoration may be confined to some structural point on the garment, such as the opening, the neck line, the pockets, or the sleeves. An informal note may be struck by the selection of the motif for the stitchery. Peasant designs may be the source of many fine inspirations.

NEEDLE POINT BUTTONS

NEEDLE POINT BELT

Twisted fringe was applied after the belt was completed.

FELT BOOTIES

A pretty departure from the usual baby bootie.

Chapter VII

Traveling Companions

VERY OFTEN A SIMPLE, BUT UNUSUAL ENSEMBLE OWES ITS IN-
dividuality to the decorative quality of the purse carried with
it. Many of us cannot afford a great variety of purses at the usual
department store prices, since genuine leather (and who wants imi-
tation leather?) is not inexpensive. To overcome this handicap, one
may devise any number of simple, easily made bags or purses that
will successfully point up the costume.

All sorts of fabrics, according to season, lend themselves to
this purpose; as, for example, felt, wool coating, velvet, heavy silks
and satins, velveteen, linen, and heavy cottons. Fabrics like these
may be used in such a way that the structural design of the purse
adequately augments the ensemble without the addition of decorative design. Sometimes this is preferable, especially when there is
already a great deal of pattern used elsewhere in the ensemble, as
in the case of a dress made of printed material. If the bag is to
be the outstanding decorative note, its surface can be enhanced
by embroidery, quilting, cording, or the combination of several
materials to give texture and color interest.

When considering either the purchase or the making of a
purse or bag, the type of costume with which it is to be carried
and the use to which it is to be put are of prime importance in both
the selection of the shape and the materials. Normally bags and

purses fall into four groups. The first and most used group would be made up of all those bags suitable for business, school, and street wear. These are usually sturdy, capacious, and simple. Most often, too, these purses are designed to go with the coat or suit, rather than any dress, that might be worn for those occasions.

Group two would include bags suitable for dressy afternoon or date wear. These may be designed to harmonize with a certain dress, and are frequently of a decided color rather than of the more neutral basic colors usually selected as the background for one's wardrobe. They may be more elaborate in shape and more decorative than the practical daytime purse.

The third group consists of the formal bags. These are small, since they are intended to hold only the indispensable lipstick and powder, keys, and, perhaps, a little "mad money." Their character may be practically conservative, or highly frivolous and decorative.

Group four contains the special purpose bags, utilitarian down to their core. Such would be beach bags, knitting bags, and kindred types.

In newspaper parlance the term "morgue" has a very useful definition. It is the name given to a collection of ideas and clippings garnered from here, there, and everywhere. Why not give this idea a place in one's own life? Build a personal file or notebook morgue. Seldom does one go into a shop, look at a magazine, or attend a social gathering without being struck by some new and clever ideas. Clip or sketch the idea before it slips from memory. It may not be used today, tomorrow, or perhaps ever; but sometime it may be fuel for a new addition to one's wardrobe. The use of a morgue does not imply slavish copying but rather a source of

A STENCILED BEACH BAG

by Mary Ellen Hustad

Stenciling is discussed under Fanciful Fabrics. This bag is made of white duck, lined with waterproof silk.

Photograph by Helen Ludwig.

inspiration. The shape of the bag one sees in a clipping of an exclusive model may suggest just what is needed to set off one's own ensemble. The design may be executed in entirely different materials from the original. In similar fashion, handles, closings, manipulation of material, and methods of decoration will bring new ideas to the observant individual.

Since this book concerns itself with decorative accessories, an embroidered bag from each of the first three groups will be illus-

KNITTING BAG

by Roberta Burbeck

The care with which a design is executed is responsible for much of the character of the finished product.

Photograph by Lloyd Matterson

trated here. Since the fourth group includes such a wide range of types, and since the construction and decoration of each of these types varies completely with the nature of the bag, they will not be discussed in this book. Instead, it will be left to one's ingenuity to fashion variations suitable to specific needs.

Strictly Business

Since it is of the utmost importance to have a large tailored bag and one which closes securely, a simple envelope style consisting of two large compartments closed with zippers has been selected.

THE STRUCTURAL DESIGN AND EXECUTION

First, the size must be decided upon. This must be thought of in relation to the individual's build and proportions (a very little lady with a very big bag looks as though she were going on a trip).

TAILORED BAG

The simple design embroidered in a very limited color scheme—two grays and bright red on black—gives distinction to this purse.

THOMAS

After the general size has been determined, the relationship of the length to the width is an important factor. Here one may follow the standards as exemplified by the Greek Oblong, 2:3, or a pleasing deviation from this ratio.

The interior of the purse should be planned in keeping with personal requirements. This would include the number of pockets, size of the change purse, and devices for securing cosmetics, cigarettes, and pencils. It is well to plan at the outset to fasten the change purse to the interior of the bag by a short length of hat elastic. This permits freedom of handling and at the same time insures safety when using the smaller purse.

The material for a daytime bag might be either felt or firmly woven wool coating of a color that fits into the wardrobe.

DIRECTIONS FOR CONSTRUCTION

Make a paper pattern that measures twice the depth but the same width as the size previously decided upon. Allow for half-inch seams on each of the two long sides of the pattern, and a full inch at each end. Cut two of these strips from the material. Linings may be cut at the same time, and to the same measurements with the exception of the top and bottom, where only a half inch need be allowed for hems. Two lining strips will be needed. Cut the pieces to make the desired pockets from the scraps of the lining fabric, which might be sateen, silk crepe, or rayon taffeta. Unless the outer fabric has a great deal of body or stiffness of its own, stiffening will be necessary. This may be buckram, crinoline, or muslin, depending upon the amount of additional stiffening required. If stiffening is used two strips should be cut without the seam and hem allowances. A piece of sheet wadding placed directly underneath the embroidered surface during the finishing of the bag plumps its sides with a professional touch.

Since the divisions of the purse are formed by stitching the material across from the center of one long edge to the center of the opposite edge and then folding on that line of stitching so that the short sides come together, it is necessary to place the pockets in the lining with this construction in mind. Remember that the open sides of pockets are at the top and not at the bottom. If one is not careful he may find his bag more individual than efficient!

If the outer surface is to be decorated with embroidery or by any other method, the piece which will be on the outside of the finished bag must be decorated before the purse can be sewed together. Detailed suggestions for embroidery and other methods of decoration will follow these directions for the construction of the purse.

Place the right sides of the two strips of the outer material

CONSTRUCTION OF THE TWO-SECTION ENVELOPE BAG

Cut and stitch outside fabric, right sides together, to within one inch of either end.

Cut, set in pockets, and stitch lining fabric.

Sew zipper closings to open ends of outer sections. Keep face of zipper toward inside and ends in line with the seams on outer section. Open zippers and turn section right side out, press. Push zippers into position to form headings; stitch.

Insert lining and stiffening, pull into position, and stitch through all fabrics through the center. Slip stitch lining to zipper tapes.

Fold on center line, slip stitch ends together.

WARREN

together and down the long sides only, stitch one-half inch from the edges to within one inch of the ends.

Sew the zippers to the open ends of the outer fabric. Keep the face of the zipper toward the inside and the ends of the zipper in line with the seams on the sides of the outer section; the edges of the zipper tape coinciding with the edges of the fabric. Open the zippers and turn the fabric inside out. Press the seams. Push the zippers down toward the center of the bag until the heading has been formed. Secure the headings with concealed stitches.

Put the two right sides of the lining sections together and stitch them one-half inch from the edge down the long sides. Do not turn inside out, but slip this section into the tube formed by the outer fabric. Slip the strips of stiffening between the lining and the outer fabric. If buckram is used for stiffening only one piece of it is necessary and it should be inserted between the decorated or outside fabric and the lining nearest to it. Use a piece of muslin for the stiffening between the inner layer of fabric and the lining. Pad the design with cotton wadding if desired. Baste or pin these layers of material together to prevent slipping. Be sure that all edges coincide; give especial attention to matching the design motifs at the sides of the purse. Find the point halfway between the open ends. Mark across from side to side with a chalk line or a basting. Stitch along this line either by hand or machine. If the stitching is done by hand, be sure to go through all thicknesses of the material. Fold the purse on this stitched line, pin in place, and slip-stitch the envelope sides together. If just the sides are sewed together, and not the zippered edges, there will be an extra pocket between the two sections. This may prove handy for a handkerchief or gloves. The decorative design may be of such a nature that the seam joining the two envelopes may be made a decorative feature by emphasizing it with appropriate stitchery and color, or by outlining it with cord.

To finish the lining process, open the zippers, pull the lining into place so that it fits without wrinkling. Fasten in place with pins or a basting. Fold under the raw edge of the lining to bring it within one-eighth of an inch from the metal or plastic edge of the zipper. This distance from the zipper will prevent the lining from catching when the zipper is opened or closed. Slip stitch or catch stitch into place.

For convenience, and also for a decorative touch, pulls may be added to the zipper ends. Any number of things will suggest themselves. The possibilities include tassels of yarn or of the fabric, wooden or composition beads, and commercial pulls purchasable at any notion counter. Small pulls, such as those listed, are especially effective if the zippers have been attached so as to open in opposite directions. This would give a balanced effect when both zippers are closed. Tassels or pulls of different colors help one to quickly identify the two pockets of the purse.

Bracelet pulls might be made of wooden curtain rings, plastic bracelets from the ten-cent store, or a large shaped fold of the material itself. If such a large pull is selected, one only should be used. A bracelet handle as described above is frequently more satisfactory if attached to the purse itself, rather than to the small zipper pull.

The Decorative Design and Its Application

Since the ultimate purpose of a daytime purse is that it be carried when one is wearing a suit or simple street costume, the design must also be considered from that point of view. Normally most ensembles planned for street wear are conservative in line and color; the decorative design on the bag should harmonize in idea. A simple geometric design lends itself best to such an interpretation. It offers a maximum in effect for a minimum of effort. The personality of the person for whom the bag is intended must be considered when planning the design. However, neither strikingly bizarre nor sentimentally feminine lines should be used for a daytime bag; they are more appropriate for sports or formal wear. Careful planning in this matter will produce a bag which can be carried over a long period of time; one which will not become tiresome or "dated."

A specific design will be formulated here. It must be remembered that this design will not be one suited to every type of individual. It is intended for a suggestion only, and as a point of departure for creative effort on the part of the reader. This plan follows the outline given in Chapter II for adapting a design.

1. COGNIZANCE OF THE SIZE AND SHAPE OF THE OBJECT TO BE DECORATED.

The original paper pattern used will be helpful in planning the decorative design for the already established size and shape of the bag. In order that it be accurate, fold in the seam allowance, and fold the paper, as one will the material, to form the center division. This will produce a simple rectangle of a given proportion.

2. REALIZATION OF THE ULTIMATE PURPOSE OF THE OBJECT.

The bag is to be a tailored, roomy, serviceable bag to be carried with tailored ensembles. For that reason the design should be planned so as to be conservative, fairly neutral in color, and simple in line. If planned in this way, it will fit more readily into the daytime wardrobe.

3. Consideration of the material involved in the process of the construction and the decoration of the object.

Black wool broadcloth has been selected for this purse. It is a sturdy, easily worked fabric which tailors well and is harmonious in texture with the average wardrobe. It is particularly adapted to the construction outlined above. However, some other fabrics would be equally suitable.

For the stitchery itself, wool yarn harmonizes best with the texture of the wool broadcloth. Three-ply Shetland floss or the somewhat more expensive tapestry and peasant yarns may be used. The last two mentioned are of better quality and produce a far richer effect. For the beginner, Shetland yarn is satisfactory and can be used very effectively. If one is fortunate enough to have yarn left over from some previous work, experiment with it on a scrap of the fabric or felt being used to determine its usableness. It may be every bit as good as the yarns mentioned.

4. The selection of source material suited to the idea, materials, and process.

From a portfolio of designs, reproductions of craftwork done by the natives of New Guinea, an interesting, conventionalized flower motif, treated very geometrically, has been used for the bag illustrated here. The unit in itself has a great deal of character and yet is simple enough to be appropriate. In the unit are lines which repeat and thus strengthen the rectilinear form of the bag. Though the motif is fundamentally geometric, its scale suggests an appropriate feminine quality. Likewise it is suitable to the background fabric and the stitchery to be used. Because of the nature of this design, very few colors are necessary to produce an effective product.

A knowledge of only a few essential stitches is needed to reproduce the design onto the fabric. The flower may be done in satin stitch, and the stem in two or three rows of outline stitch placed closely enough to appear as a solid unit. The straight-line

[127]

WARREN

NEW GUINEA—NATIVE DESIGN

[128]

leaves may be done in a single row of chain stitch. These three stitches not only produce a nice variation in texture but they also harmonize with the nature of the design. The directions for making these stitches appear earlier in this section.

5. ANALYSIS OF SOURCE MATERIAL TO DETERMINE THE MOTIF BEST SUITED TO THE PROBLEMS INVOLVED.

From the original New Guinea design the flower, stem, and leaf units have been selected.

6. ADJUSTMENT OF THE MOTIF TO THE AREAS TO BE EN-RICHED BY DESIGN.

The units have been arranged to produce a surface pattern composed of stripes. The scale of the original native design is in a great measure responsible for the character of the design. In order to preserve this quality, the same fine scale should be used in the adapted design. The size of the purse being constructed suggested the use of three rows or stripes of the flower unit separated by rows of the stem and leaf unit. From the photograph one can observe that the relative proportions of the two stripes of the design are subtle and pleasing, and not monotonous as they would have been had they been equal in width.

The background areas as seen in the original design have been omitted, and the leaves have been joined so as to produce a herringbone effect. By moving the petals close to one another, the design created by them produces an interesting rhythmic pattern. A simple, straight line of several rows of outline stitch marks off the top and bottom of the design.

7. FORMULATION OF THE IDEA ON PAPER.

It is well to think through the foregoing steps thoroughly before beginning to formulate the design on the paper pattern. This will save a great amount of time and energy and will insure a more satisfactory result. With the plan already in mind, the de-

WARREN

ADAPTED DESIGN

sign may be drawn to the exact proportions in which it is to appear on the finished product.

8. Careful checking of the design for adherence to the principles of design and good taste.

Refer to Chapter II. *Design.*

9. Completion of the drawing of the design.

Make any necessary changes in the design and adjust it for accuracy and clarity of drawing. Carelessness at this point is often responsible for inferior workmanship.

10. Planning the color combination and distribution.

For the purse shown in the photograph, black wool broadcloth was used for the foundation. It was planned to be used with a wardrobe built around black as a basic color. Two tones of gray, one quite dark, and the other light, were combined with a red of middle value. These were selected because they gave a good value range and the red gave a good color accent. Other colors might be used. Those chosen are conservative and harmonize readily with almost any other wardrobe color. They also seem suitable to the character of the design. Since red was the only true color used, it might have seemed spotty if placed at widely spaced intervals. For this reason it was used for the flowers which form an almost solid band of color. For the same reason the light gray was used for the leaves, which form an almost continuous line movement across the bag. The dark gray was reserved for the stem unit. This unit is spaced at the greatest interval, and would not have been appropriate in either of the other two colors. This second gray is really a transitional value between the light gray and the black of the broadcloth. It interrupts the strong rhythmic movement of the herringbone design without breaking it entirely, and in this way it forms a pleasant accent without being spotty.

11. APPLICATION TO THE OBJECT IN THE CHOSEN MEDIUM.

In order to insure the greatest amount of accuracy in transferring the design to the cloth, the original paper pattern should be pricked along the lines of the design, then fastened securely to the fabric to be used for the purse. Powdered chalk or whiting should be pounced through the tiny holes pricked in the design. Remove the paper pattern carefully and run a basting thread along the dotted lines. This will serve as a guide for the stitchery. If the object being made is large, it may be more satisfactory to transfer one line of the design at a time to the fabric. This will prevent the rubbing off of the chalk dots before the basting has been completed.

Embroider the design neatly and carefully in the chosen stitches. After this has been done, the basting threads should be removed, and the fabric pressed on the wrong side, using a damp cloth and a moderately hot iron. A sufficiently thick pad beneath the embroidered surface should be used to prevent any flattening of the stitches.

The procedure followed for the construction and decoration of this specific bag is an example of the method to be used for the construction and decoration of any other object, whether it be for the wardrobe or for the home.

Conversation Piece

We are usually our most feminine selves when we dress up for a tea, a bridge party, or a date. Perhaps one puts the best foot forward only to impress women friends, or perhaps one strives to cater to some gentleman's ego. For any such occasion a bag with a fragile feminine type of design seems appropriate. The design may be very fine in scale if one is a very little, delicate lady; or it may reflect a dignified feminine quality for the more conservative personality. The design should definitely not be in the naive, informal spirit of peasant handiwork. Motifs based on finely scaled geometric or graceful floral patterns seem to adapt themselves best to afternoon bags. The size of the bag and its general structural design should also suggest the more dressy occasion. Various constructions lend themselves to this classification.

The group offering the greatest number of variations is that which includes the pouch bag. This may be made on a frame; or it may be shaped and carried by bracelet handles, shaped loops, or braided cord. Any number of shapes might be used: circular, with a cord handle traveling around the sides and the bottom and left free at the top to form the handle; triangular, square, or rectilinear.

Small envelope bags may be made in a number of ways. Experimentation with paper will give stimulus to the imagination, and various shapes and ways of making bags of this nature can be evolved. More specifically a bag made of buckram and carefully lined may be incased in a removable, washable slip cover of heavy linen decorated simply with Italian hemstitching or embroidery. In this type of bag a muslin cover is usually placed over the outside of the buckram to act as a pad for the slip cover. Colored covers might be made so that the bag could be quickly changed to harmonize with various costumes.

Envelope bags may be fastened with buttons and loops, snap fasteners, decorative frogs, or a loop or slit through which the end of the envelope flap can be slipped.

Quaint drawstring bags are decidedly feminine and help immensely to create an air of fragility. These bags are made from a circular piece of fabric cut from one piece of material or made in sections (as an umbrella) of differently colored or textured pieces. The drawstring may be run through a heading on the bag or may be pulled through eyelets in the bag, or through loops, or rings sewed to the outside of the fabric. If any of the latter are used, there must be an even number of these to permit the cord to draw the bag shut correctly. Two cords should be run through the heading, eyelets, or loops. One of these cords is pulled to one side and one to the other to close the bag. The loops formed by the drawn cords will make handles for the little pouch.

The needle point bag which is illustrated in the chapter on design in this book is an excellent example of a conversation-making afternoon bag. The body of the long envelope shape is of black felt, and the design was worked in brilliant blue-green and black against a yellow-green background. A bag such as that pictured will go far toward creating an elegant costume from a simple ensemble.

Glamorous Gadgets

The formal bag gives one the opportunity to indulge in a bit of whimsy. As stated before, it should be small, and it may be frivolous. For that reason a little bag of unusual character will be described here. The idea for this odd little bag came from great-grandmother's sewing basket, where it served the practical purpose of harboring the elusive thimble. Someone away back in that time had utilized the shape of a beechnut for the purpose. If one makes this interesting little gadget he is certain to surprise his friends with an imaginative choice of accessories.

Owing to the construction of this bag, it should be just large enough to hold the minimum essentials for a very gala evening. The actual size will be determined by the amount of space needed for compact, keys, and a few coins.

FORMAL BAG

Just big enough for a few essentials.

THOMAS

The bag is made of three melon-shaped pieces of cardboard or buckram sewed together to form a little three-sided, nut-shaped box. One side is left partly open. To open, the two pointed ends are pressed toward each other to force open the unsewed side. When released, the sides spring back into place, safely closing in the contents.

This type of bag and the purpose for which it is intended suggest materials rich in nature, such as brocades, velvets, taffetas, metal cloth, and satin. If one is one's own dressmaker the bag might be made from scraps of the material used for an evening dress or wrap.

Directions for Construction

From a flexible strong cardboard cut three melon-shaped pieces which measure five inches at the longest point and two and three-quarters inches at the widest point. Draw the form with a smooth, regular curved line from point to point. If the cardboard

[135]

is thin, use it doubled, cutting six pieces of the described shape. Should buckram be substituted, six pieces will also be necessary. Paste or baste these thin pieces of cardboard or buckram together.

If the evening bag is to be covered with quilted material as is the bag shown in the photograph, the fabric must be quilted before it is cut to cover the cardboard pieces. For this process, the following materials are necessary: the outer fabric (satin was used in the photographed bag), sheet wadding, and light weight muslin. Two layers of wadding will be necessary if one desires the quilting to be quite puffy and soft. Stretching the quilted material over the cardboard forms smooths out the quilted effect considerably. Draw guide lines for the stitching on the muslin. In the photograph, the bag was quilted in a simple diamond pattern so that all the quilting could be done before the pieces were cut for the bag. However, if the quilting is to be done in a more elaborate design, the design must be planned to fit the curved, shaped surfaces of the cardboard. Baste the three materials together with the sheet wadding on the inside and the penciled guide lines showing on the muslin. It may be necessary to baste the fabrics together in only slightly separated lines to prevent the silk from slipping out of place during the stitching; sew by hand with tiny running stitches, or by machine, along the guide lines on the muslin, using a silk thread that matches or harmonizes with the satin outer fabric. Lay the three cardboard pieces on the quilted fabric, using care to place the forms in relation to the quilted design. With these shapes as patterns, cut the fabric, allowing for a three-quarter inch seam around each of the pieces of cardboard. Put a small running stitch one-quarter inch from the outer edge around each of the sections of fabric. Place the cardboard piece in position on the fabric and pull up the running stitch, drawing the edges of the fabric tightly over the cardboard. Fasten the thread to keep the material in position. Do this with each of the three pieces.

To line these sections, cut the fabric to be used one-quarter inch larger than the cardboard. One piece of lining will be needed for each section. Turn under the edges of the lining and slip stitch to the outer quilted fabric close to the edge and over the exposed surface of the cardboard.

Baste the three covered sections together to form the box-like bag. When these are basted accurately, overcast two seam edges very tightly and firmly down their entire length. Overcast the third side only one inch from each end, leaving the center portion open. Remove the basting threads. One will find that when one presses on the top and bottom of this little box, the unsewed length will spring open enough to permit a compact and other small articles to be slipped into it. If the tips of the sections are not sewed together, the cut ends of the gold cord used for decoration may be pushed through to the inside. This greatly facilitates the finishing details.

To further embellish the bag, a decorative braid may be sewed over the seamed edges. For the bag in the illustration a gold cord of a bit more than one-eighth inch in diameter was used. This was cut in lengths sufficiently long to permit twisting (or braiding) the three strands together from where they met at the top to form a loop long enough to slip over the wrist. Enough cord was also allowed to form three small loops to finish off the bottom of the bag with a stiff little tassel. Decorative cording should be sewed along the edges with an invisible slip stitch. When selecting a finishing cording or braiding, care should be exercised to choose a trimming that is harmonious with the other fabrics used to make the bag. Do not use a cotton cord on a satin bag.

[137]

SUGGESTIONS FOR DECORATION

Since the gold cord that was suggested has seasonal limitations, other materials may be used to enrich the box form. The side panels might be decorated with needle point, with silk embroidery, or with sequins according to the nature of the dress or wrap with which the bag is to be carried. Any embroidered decoration should be planned to fit well into the shaped panels and should be appropriate to the texture of the floss used for the stitchery. A silk floss suggests a finely scaled motif. If sequins are used, the entire surface might be covered or the sequins could be fastened to the fabric to produce a definite design.

Any bag that is designed for a very limited and special use may often reflect some particular liking of the individual for whom it is planned. It might be designed to add a touch of whimsy to some costume or to add a decorative note that is more strong than might be desirable in a bag that is to find more frequent use. An evening bag could well incorporate baroque motifs that might otherwise be considered elaborate or ornate. The fabrics that often appear in formal gowns—velvets, satins, and heavy silks—suggest materials and designs of a rich quality.

When an elaborate design is being planned for an evening bag, it is wise to keep the shape of the bag itself fairly simple and uncomplicated in order that the design which is to be applied will not find undue competition from the structure supporting it. Envelope bags with flap closings lend themselves well to all manner of decoration, whether it be bead or sequin trim, gold thread embroidery, or silver and gold leather appliqué. The front and back panels of the envelope form can be enriched with unit designs planned to fill the spaces entirely, or they might be edged with decorative border designs applied to frame the rectangular shapes.

The basic form can be made from scraps of fabric or from lengths of ribbon purchased at a department store. Since an evening bag is not expected to withstand hard wear, the materials used for the bag as well as for the trim can be of a more fragile nature than would be suitable for a bag for daytime use. Usually an evening bag is small, large enough only for the few essentials of lipstick, handkerchief, a bit of money, and a key or two. For this reason, the making of such a bag can be a project that is not too lengthy and yet one which will allow the craftsman to indulge a liking for rich material and design.

Chapter VIII

"Rich Man, Poor Man—"

OFTEN BUTTONS ARE THE ONLY DECORATIVE NOTE ON A DRESS or suit. And just as often it is very difficult to find the right buttons for a particular purpose; or on finding them, to discover that they are beyond the means of one's pocketbook.

The following ideas have been used successfully to give the proper decorative effect to a garment without too great a cost.

Leather Buttons

Small scraps of leather, obtained by the pound in lovely colors, from some leather findings store; suède banding, purchasable in trimming departments; or pieces of leather cut from discarded belts or the tops of gloves may be used to make attractive and different buttons.

If the leather is heavy enough, similar shapes of various sizes may be built up in pyramid fashion, glued together and punched for sewing to the fabric. These leather layers may be of one color or of various colors and may be held together with rubber cement or glue. The finished button should be firm enough to hold its shape under use.

Another method, and one suited to soft pliable leathers, is that of rolling the material into tight cylinders. The strips of leather

WOODEN BUTTONS

Designed by Barbara War-
ren, executed by Mark Doll

Some of these designs would
make attractive clips or pins
for sport clothes.

should be long enough to produce a cylinder well proportioned to the length that the button will be when finished. After the leather has been rolled tightly, it may be fastened by winding with a thin strip of leather of the same or a contrasting color. A small loop of this binding strip should be left at the back of the button to fasten it to the fabric. A similar button may be made from a long wedge-shaped piece of leather. The ridges formed by the narrowing width produce an interesting texture. The narrowest end may be extended to form a loop at the back of the button. A bit of glue will hold the layers of leather in place.

Wooden Buttons

These may be made in a variety of ways. The first thing that suggests itself is the wooden button mold and its attendant possibilities. The molds come in any number of sizes and may be enameled a solid color, waxed over the plain surface of the wood, or painted with some simple design with oil paint. A large brass

TO MAKE WOODEN BUTTONS

One needs these everyday supplies. Needle files are good standard equipment for craftsmen.

paper fastener may be put through the hole in the center of the mold and fastened through an eyelet in the dress. The metal top of the fastener may be enameled a color to harmonize with the dress or the button.

Careful workmanship is necessary to the success of a second type of button which may be made from such ordinary material as cigar box wood and doweling. This or any other thin wood may be sawed into simple shapes with a coping or jig saw. The top surface may be decorated with simple stripe or plaid designs made by cutting shallow grooves with the saw or a very fine file. Holes should be drilled through the button or a small screw eye inserted in the back of the button for sewing to the garment. Great emphasis must be placed upon the finishing of all edges of these buttons to insure a professional piece of work. The best method of finishing is to bevel all edges with a fine wood file, and to smooth every surface of the button with very fine sandpaper. Experimenting with both the saw and the file on a scrap piece of wood will lead one to discover endless possibilities resulting from the manipulation of the tools upon the material. Some of the effects which have been obtained and which may point the way to further developments in this technique are milled edges, as found in coins; deeply beveled edges further decorated with file cuts placed in step formation; cone shapes built up of two or more layers and held together in the sewing, or glued into place if the button is to be sewed to the garment through a screw eye.

After the wood has been thoroughly filed and sanded, various finishing methods may be followed. To preserve the natural color of the wood, apply two coats of white shellac. After it has thoroughly dried use a fine sandpaper or number 3/0 steel wool to remove the shine and any roughness. The final satin finish is obtained when a coat of floor wax is applied to the button. If the color of the wood seems undesirable, it may be altered by staining with regular wood stain, or by painting with water colors to produce colors other than browns. After the stain has dried the button should be finished in the same manner as described above.

Cork, a material which can be worked in much the same way as wood, except that it can be cut with scissors or a knife, may be purchased in sheet form at an auto supply house. Another form in which it can be used is the cylindrical bottle cork. The bottle cork variety may be cut into rounds of the desired thickness or cut lengthwise to form half log shapes. An interesting buckle may be made by placing a number of the half log shapes side by side upon a piece of fabric and sewing them securely into place. The stitches may be planned to form a decorative band of color across the top and bottom of the buckle.

Fabric Buttons

Aside from the usual fabric-covered buttons there are many other methods of handling fabric in the making of buttons. A simple cylindrical button may be made by cutting a piece of fabric the desired width, fringing the long edges just enough to produce a pleasing edge, and rolling it to the desired diameter. To secure the fabric in place, the cylinder may be bound at intervals with embroidery floss or yarn to produce an effective stripe down the length of the button. This may be done with a contrasting but harmonious color. Fastening these buttons into place is a simple matter; merely sewing them from the back is sufficient. If buttons of this type are used on a wash dress, small safety pins may prove more expedient than sewing.

Variations on this technique may be developed by rolling several colors of fabric together or one color around another. The effect of this is apparent only from the ends of the cylinder.

Should one wish to have the buttons covered commercially, the fabric may be decorated with needle point or other embroidery before it is sent to the tailor. Extreme care should be exercised in observing the proportions of the finished button when planning and executing the design on the fabric. It is also necessary to send the fabric to a reliable tailor to insure accuracy in the making of the buttons. The entire effect can be destroyed if the design is pulled out of shape or placed off center when the button is covered.

Felt is another fabric that lends itself to further manipulation for this purpose. It may be rolled and bound as suggested for the fabric buttons, or built up in layers as suggested for the leather buttons, embroidered, or appliquéd.

Metal Buttons

If one has access to a few more tools, i.e., a pair of metal shears, a drill, a ball peen hammer, metal files, pliers, a block of

METAL BUTTON EQUIPMENT

A few more tools are needed but all are easily obtained. The jeweler's saw frame and saw blades might prove the least easy to acquire.

wood, and a candle, simple metal buttons may be made very inexpensively. The two metals best suited to this purpose are pewter and copper, used singly or in combination. The simple forms suggested for the wooden buttons may be adapted to this medium as well, and they may be decorated with file cuts or by hammering with the ball peen hammer.

Buttons built up in layers need to be soldered together. This is a very simple matter if using layers of pewter, or light weight copper and pewter. Cut the layers of metal to the desired size and shape, then place upon a hard smooth surface and pound with a wooden mallet until absolutely flat. Unless this is done the soldering will not be successful. The two surfaces of the metal that are to be soldered together should be cleaned with an abrasive such as whiting, fine steel wool, or emery cloth, then coated with the ordinary soldering paste. Before putting the two layers together, a piece of lead foil cigar wrapper cut the size of the smaller piece of metal should be placed between them. Grasp this metal and soldering paste "sandwich" gently with a pair of pliers that have a smooth gripping surface. A spring clothes pin may be substituted for the pliers, though the wood becomes charred during the soldering process. Wave the metal forms slowly over a candle flame. Do not allow the flame to touch the metal as it melts pewter in an instant. It is even safer to place the metal upon an asbestos pad such as one uses when cooking, then hold pad and all over the candle. As the metal becomes warm, the paste flux will bubble from between the layers and the lead foil will melt just a second later. One can tell when this happens by watching for a gleam of molten metal at the edge of the smaller layer of pewter. When this occurs, withdraw the button quickly from the flame, place on a block of wood and press firmly with a second block of wood until the metal has cooled slightly. Speed and precision are needed to produce a good piece of soldering.

Since the lead foil method is scarcely strong enough for heavy copper, it is better to use a regular soft solder paste, which comes ready mixed with flux; or glycerine, or the regular paste flux, and wire solder (without the acid core). Follow the directions printed on the tube when using the paste form of solder. The wire solder method involves quite a different technique. Hammer the solder wire into a very thin strip. Cut off small slivers of the solder. Paint with the glycerine or coat with the soldering paste all metal surfaces that are to be soldered together and place them in position. With a pair of tweezers, carefully place the tiny pieces of solder as close to the joint as possible. Heat carefully over a candle. When the metal reaches the right temperature, the strips of solder will melt and flow between the layers of metal. Remove from the flame and allow to cool. Sometimes excess solder remains on the outer surface and must be filed away.

If filing would be difficult, the following method will leave a cleaner outer surface. Paint glycerine over each of the surfaces

METAL BUTTONS

Pewter alone or pewter combined with copper was used for these buttons.

THOMAS

to be soldered. Sprinkle finely cut solder wire over each painted surface. Hold each piece separately over the flame until the solder melts and spreads. Permit the metal to cool. If any of the solder particles fail to melt, file them down to an even surface. Repaint both pieces with glycerine, place them together, and hold over the flame until the solder has melted a second time. Remove and cool.

Place the button on a wooden block, and with a metal drill bore the necessary holes for sewing. A small loop made of copper wire may also be soldered on the back. Shape the loop like a written letter "e." The bits of wire extending at the sides furnish a base for soldering.

The quality of the finishing is the determining factor in the quality of the final product. All of the rough edges and surface solder must be removed with a file, emery paper, and finally, pumice. Number 3/0 steel wool is also useful for burnishing the metal surfaces. A satinlike finish is in far better taste than a high polish. It is well to note that metal buttons are quite heavy and should be planned for use upon a fabric with considerable body. This quality of weight also limits the size of the buttons. A necessary precaution when planning the design is the elimination of any sharp corners which might tend to catch in the fabric or injure the wearer.

Chapter IX

Mix or Match

For Frosty Fingers

THERE IS LITTLE DOUBT ABOUT THE FACT THAT A SNUG PAIR OF mittens is far better protection against wintry blasts than any pair of gloves ever will be. Most of us can remember that, as children, these were an accepted part of our winter's wardrobe. Perhaps the mittens were of a practical black Germantown yarn knit for us by a thoughtful grandmother, or perhaps they were of a less practical, but far more attractive, angora yarn. As we grew older, we discarded these childish things in the interests of sophistication and adopted gloves to protect our hands from frostbite. Of course there are many occasions to which gloves are a necessary requisite, but there are times when an attractive and gay pair of mittens will be useful additions to any wardrobe. On such occasions they may label one with an air of the ultimate in sophistication.

The cost of making a pair of these fanciful mittens is very slight—about fifty cents a pair—if they are made of coating that sells for three dollars per yard. One third of a yard of coating will make two or three pairs of mittens, depending upon the width desired for each mitten. There is no reason, either, why scraps of material left from previous sewing shouldn't be used, providing that the material is of the proper weight and quality.

Photograph by Lloyd Matterson

QUILTED MITTENS
by Dorothy Mereness

Another version of the mitten theme.

One will be fascinated by the speed with which the mittens can be made and by the effective designs that can be applied to them with a small amount of bright yarn and the use of simple stitchery. Mittens such as these are a welcome solution to the Christmas gift worries that beset those with large families or many friends. Since the steps for designing the embroidered decorations to be applied to the mittens were thoroughly discussed in the chapter on design, the following material will deal only with the construction of the mittens.

The materials needed are very few. One third of a yard of coating will make two or three pairs of mittens. If one plans to embroider any decorative units on the backs of the mittens, a plain fabric will be the best choice. However, undecorated mittens would be very attractive in a bright plaid fabric. The material should be heavy enough for warmth and wearability. Fleece coating is an excellent choice. If yarn embroidery is to be used, Shetland floss in one or more colors is suggested. Necessary tools include a needle with a large eye and a number eight crochet hook.

The width and length of the mittens will be decided by the width and length of the hand for which they are intended. Place the hand palm down on a piece of paper and draw around it with a pencil. Make the pattern slightly wider than the rough drawing. Straighten the outside lines on the drawing with a ruler. Keep the line which corresponds to the thumb side of the hand perfectly straight for this line is to be placed on the fold of the material. Flare the outer edge slightly at the cuff to permit ease of putting on when finished. Point or round the fingertip end of the pattern. Place the inside, or thumb side, edge of the pattern along the fold of the fabric, pin the pattern securely, and cut. Reverse the pattern, pin again to a piece of fabric, and cut another piece for the other hand.

To make the thumb hole, measure from the tip of the index finger to the upper part of the thumb joint—this length will determine the position of the top of the thumb hole. Then measure down across the thumb joint itself—this length will be the length of the hole. Cut the opening on the palm side of the mitten about one-fourth inch from the fold of the material. Round the hole slightly at the bottom and cut to a point at the top. It should be only about one-half inch wide across the widest part.

When making a pattern for the thumb section, draw around the outstretched thumb, allowing a bit of extra width for freedom of movement. Straighten the outer line with a ruler and true up the curve at the tip of the thumb. Join the upper and lower lines at the base of the thumb with a slight outward curve. Cut out pattern and adjust to fit thumb hole in mitten proper. Place the straight line on a fold of the fabric and cut the thumb section.

[151]

The diagrams which follow will serve as a brief review of the considerations to be met when planning a design for a pair of mittens.

Step 1. Size and Shape

Step 2. Purpose of the Object

THOMAS

THOMAS

Step 3. Materials

WARREN

Step 4. Inspiration for Design

WARREN

Step 5. Motifs Selected for Use in Design

[154]

Step 6. Motifs and Shape

Preliminary sketch of units

[155]

WARREN

Step 7. Trial Drawing

*Step 8. Careful checking of the design for adherence to the princi-
ples of design and good taste. In the trial drawing it can be seen*

[156]

that the design is somewhat lacking in rhythmical organization. The effect so far achieved is stiff as well as weak, especially in the stem and leaf area

Step 9. Corrected Design

Step 10. Design in Value

The mitten is put together with crocheting which should be done in a color that will complement that of the fabric itself. Crochet with Shetland floss once around the entire outer edge of the mitten fabric, working always on the right side of the material. Repeat this around the thumb opening and around the thumb section. If a design is to be embroidered onto the back of the mitten, it should be done at this point. Draw the design onto the fabric with tailor's chalk or outline it with basting threads. Embroider the decorative units with Shetland floss, using simple stitchery such as chain stitch, outline stitch, cross stitch, or satin stitch.

When the embroidery is complete, fold the mitten along the original folded edge and press it with a warm iron and damp cloth. If the embroidered side is placed face down on a piece of toweling or similar padding it will not be unattractively flattened out during ironing. Crochet the outer open sides together with the same or a contrasting color of yarn. In the same manner, crochet the folded thumb section along the top edge and then crochet into the thumb hole. Sometimes several rows of crocheting around the wrist opening will enhance the mitten because of the wide band of color or colors that this finishing touch produces. The stitches of all of the crocheting should be kept closely and evenly spaced in order that the final result will look professional.

To Top It Off

Some of the best ideas for tricky little caps and hoods may be garnered from drawings or photographs of peasant or period headgear. Probably the peasant costumes from rural European communities are most adaptable, for these need only slight alteration to fit becomingly into American winter sport wardrobes. However,

THE FINISHED HOOD
by Barbara Warren

The two vertical seams in the crown of the hood are made by faggoting together the two edges formed by cutting away the squares mentioned in the directions.

period costumes, such as those of the moyen âge, will tempt the imaginative person into planning amusingly different creations.

There will be no attempt to present a treatise on millinery in these pages, but rather a few concrete suggestions for caps or hoods that could be worn with skating or skiing costumes. Fetching little bonnets that are quickly and simply made will give

[159]

that final touch of the unusual that adds so much to a costume.

In planning a hood for an individual, it is best to build it, as much as possible, on the head of the person for whom it is intended. Whatever the source of inspiration for the general design may be, a few tucks here or an added fraction of an inch there will make the bonnet a pleasing frame for the face or not, as the case may be. The first plan or pattern may be done in muslin, and put together with pins. After a satisfactory effect has been achieved, the muslin may be used as a pattern for cutting the actual fabric.

Many kinds of fabrics may be used for these hoods. Felt, snow suiting, quilted challis, coating, corduroy, or velveteen are appropriate for wear with snow togs. These fabrics may be left plain or they may be decorated with quilting or yarn embroidery. If the bonnet is lined with a bright contrasting color, a turned back visor will show this bright color and will add a gay note to an otherwise plain hood.

It should be remembered that these hoods are designed not only for the decorative effect they produce, but also for a practical purpose. They are to be worn in the more severe winter weather and should be warm and comfortable; and they should stay put during expert or amateur participation in strenuous winter sport.

Directions for Making a Hood

The hood pictured is becoming to many people. It was originally made for an individual by the suggested method of planning mentioned before, i.e., that of designing it of muslin upon the head of the person by whom it is to be worn. It was based upon an idea suggested by a Dutch girl's hood. The woolen hood retains characteristic earmarks of its ancestry, such as the peaked top and winged side effect. To make it more suitable for winter sports use, it was designed to tie snugly under the chin. The peak was modified to a square line which was more becoming to the wearer and less extreme than a high pointed effect.

For warmth in a rigorous climate and for a texture that would be harmonious with the usual togs, wool fleece coating of the same kind as has been suggested for mittens was used for the hood. Incidentally, matching mittens were made to be worn with it. It was embroidered with Shetland floss in a very simple design.

To make this hood, cut a paper pattern to the following directions: Cut a rectangle eight by twelve inches. From the two corners of one of the narrow ends cut away a two-inch square of paper. The opposite end of the paper should be reduced from an eight-inch length to a four-inch length by a series of five evenly spaced darts which radiate from the lower edge. The longest and center dart is three and one-half inches in length, the shortest two and one-half inches. These darts form a decorative spoke arrangement at the nape of the neck. At the same time they bring in the lower edge of the hood back to make it fit the head snugly. At the upper edge the two edges formed by cutting away the square are brought together to create the squared-off peak. These edges are held together securely by faggoting. A seam allowance is unnecessary since the material does not fray easily and the stitchery is sufficient to protect the edges.

From the left-hand square corner of the lower back edge of the hood measure up along the side a distance of two inches. From the bottom of the center dart draw a slightly curved line up to the two-inch marks on the sides, thus rounding off the corners. Cut along this line. This curved edge should measure approximately five inches. Repeat this process from the center dart up the right-hand side of the hood.

Cut another rectangle from paper twenty inches long and six and one-half inches wide. Label one of the twenty-inch sides *front* and the opposite one *back*. Fold this rectangle in half, bringing the short ends together. Measure up three inches from the short ends and draw a line across from front to back. Along the short end measure in three inches from the back edge toward the front. From the last mark draw a straight line to the point where the first line drawn meets the front edge. This line should measure about five and one-half inches. Cut off the large triangle formed by these measurements.

On the folded end measure in five inches from the back edge. Along the front edge draw a slightly curved line from the lower corner to the five-inch mark. This curved line produces the winged effect on the hood.

Pin all of the darts into position and pin the back edge of the front section to the main part of the hood, beginning at center front down along either side. If the two lengths do not exactly coincide, they may be trimmed to match. Try on this paper model and make any necessary adjustments. The paper pattern may prove to be somewhat unyielding. Cutting the hood from muslin may prove more satisfactory for fitting purposes. The front section is to be turned back to form the winged effect.

Use this paper form as a pattern from which to cut the material for the hood. It is necessary to cut two front sections since one is to be used as facing.

Put the two front pieces together, and crochet around the edges with an evenly spaced single crochet stitch. Faggot the darts together and crochet around all edges of that piece. Pin the front and back pieces together and crochet together with another row of single crochet stitch, catching through the loops of the previous crocheting on both sections. Crochet a second row around all of the outside edges of the assembled hood. This may be done in a harmonizing color of yarn. Crocheted or braided cords finished with a yarn pompon or tassel fastened at the sides of the hood may be used to hold the cap snugly in place.

Decoration of the Hood

The method of fastening together the various sections of the hood is, in itself, quite decorative and should prove sufficient if a plain hood is desired. The costumes with which hoods are most frequently worn, such as ski suits, skating skirts, and jackets, may be made of a figured or plaid material which would make it necessary that the hood be plain.

The yarn used for crocheting the seams together and finishing the edges need not match the fabric of which the hood is constructed, but could just as well pick out and repeat one or more of the colors found in the costume. The most suitable area for the application of stitchery is found either on the area surrounding the face or on the crown of the cap.

In the hood used for the illustration, a very simple border following the upper edge of the cuff was used. It was made up of two rows of crosses, each cross formed by two horizontal parallel stitches over two vertical parallel stitches. A very small cross stitch of contrasting color was placed over the center of the large cross. A row of outline stitch was embroidered along the inside of the crocheted edge. This was whipped with a contrasting color to give a cablelike effect. For the embroidery the colors used were the same as for the crocheting except that one lighter value gave emphasis to the decorative stitchery. When the costume with which the hood is to be worn permits, a much more elaborate design may be applied to the front cuff. The hood itself finds its ancestry among peasant headgear, so it would seem most suitable to adapt one of the naïve, colorful designs found in peasant embroideries. These usually are of a type which cover the surface rather solidly. The nature of such designs calls for careful consideration of the colors to be chosen, because when used in so large an area, and so close to the face, they must be becoming to the wearer as well as harmonious with the complete ensemble. The more elaborate the decorative design, the greater the necessity to be guided by the shape of the section to be decorated.

The most suitable stitches for the more solid designs are the satin stitch, a chain stitch worked closely over an area, or an outline stitch done in the same way. Pompons for finishing the cord ends may match or contrast in color. The hood illustrated has one dark brown and one rust-colored pompon. To make these little balls of yarn is a simple matter. For the reader who is not already familiar with the process, directions follow:

Cut a rectangle of fairly strong cardboard the width of which is the same as the desired radius of the ball. Wind a goodly amount of yarn around the width of the cardboard rectangle. The more yarn used, the fuller the ball. After this has been done, slip a length of yarn, preferably doubled for strength, along one edge of the cardboard and under the yarn. Tie this short length of yarn as tightly as possible, drawing up all the wrapped yarns into a very small bundle. Cut the wrapped yarn at the opposite edge of the cardboard. This causes the cut ends of the yarn to spring out into a neat ball. Sew the ball onto the end of the braided cord used for keeping the hood upon one's head.

It is hoped that these detailed directions will serve only as an inspiration for other ingenious designs of one's own devising.

Chapter X

Leather Is Versatile

THOUGH MOST PEOPLE MAY NOT REALIZE IT, ARTICLES MADE of leather fill many of their daily needs. It is an interesting exercise to make a list of the leather objects with which one comes in contact most frequently. Probably the first item on such a list would be shoes; but wallets, small purses, handbags, belts, cases, books, and other items would make the list grow rapidly. Perhaps it is because leather takes just so important a position in our lives that it has always been one of the most popular of craft materials, yet there are reasons other than those of sheer usefulness which account for this as well. The "feel" of a beautiful piece of leather, the rich surface quality, the adaptability of the various leathers to simple tailoring or to supple draping, the fact that certain leathers are admirably suited to decoration by means of tooling or incising— all these factors contribute to the appreciation of this material as a rewarding medium for thoughtful craftsmen.

Because of its appeal, leather has been worked by all manner of people. Some have been true craftsmen and were guided by the canons of good taste and respect for the material which they were shaping beneath their hands. Unfortunately, many who have worked with leather have exploited the very qualities that have made leather a favorite among craft materials. It is the latter group who have almost ruined the acceptance of leather work as an artistic craft because of their unrestrained enthusiasm for the processes and effects of leather tooling.

Since tooling leather is extremely responsive to modeling, whether done sensitively or with tasteless abandon, there seem to have been more examples of poor work produced than of good, simply executed, and well planned work. Couple the ease of imprinting a mark upon the smooth surface of leather with an inability to plan a design suited to so beautiful a surface, and it does not seem surprising that the very mention of *leather tooling* is apt to send the thoughtful craftsman into a tirade against the misuse of the craft. Indeed, some have turned away from leather work as a craft for the very reason that so many poor objects have been made by insensitive people.

Fortunately, one need only to make a trip through a fine leather goods store or department to disprove the frequently expressed opinion that there is no leather work of any worth being done today. On such a trip, one will notice that the better objects stress the inherently beautiful characteristics of the leather itself. One will see that, where decoration has been used, it has been applied with restraint; and that, when tooling has been done, it has been carefully designed to enhance rather than to detract from the quality of the leather. Though it might seem necessary to exclude from a group of tastefully made leather objects the ornate saddles that are used in some parts of this country and Mexico, one must concede that expertly carved leather such as is used for these saddles does have its place, though it seldom appears among the accessories of the average home or wardrobe.

Since the variety of things which can be made with leather is great, it is very possible for the beginner to produce a fine piece of work providing he selects one of the less difficult articles as a

TOOLING CALF ENVELOPE PURSE

Front and back of bag: saddle stitched construction, incised decorative flap, tuck-in closing.

THOMAS

first problem. Leather work may range from an easily constructed little coin purse or belt to an exceedingly complicated handbag or similar object. One thing, however, is always true—leather work takes patience and time. Before beginning, one should accept the idea that he will try to make the finished piece as nearly perfect as one made by machine. Since the human error factor cannot be discounted, one must realize that machine perfection is an impossible goal; but as a goal, it eliminates any attitude that might accept carelessness on the ground that it is indicative of a precious homemade quality. An article made by hand will be of finer character than one of machine production only if all the principles of sound craftsmanship are faithfully followed.

Unless one is planning to make an article in quantity, jigs or forms similar to those used in machine production will not be of any particular advantage. Such mechanical aids do facilitate many operations and are largely responsible for the precision of workmanship in luxury leather goods; but quite without such special equipment, the handcraftsman can maintain a very high standard of workmanship. All the finished pieces reproduced in this book were constructed with equipment which can be obtained easily by the interested worker.

The Leather Itself

Information pertaining to the methods used for tanning raw hides into the various kinds of leathers available to the craftsman may be obtained from a library or any good encyclopedia. The processes are interesting, but a knowledge of them is not essential to one who is just beginning to use leather as a material for craftwork. However, it is necessary for the beginner to remember one important fact. *Only tooling leather can be tooled satisfactorily.* A tooling leather is one that has been prepared by a vegetable tanning process which causes leather to retain impressions made upon its surface with tools or stamps. A leather so tanned will also retain accidental impressions that might be made by one's fingernails, errors in tooling, or any similar pressure on its surface. Though quite strong, leather is truly the sensitive princess of craft materials and should never be handled without all the respect due such a princess.

Of the many kinds and qualities of leather, the best grade of *tooling calf* is usually found to be the most enjoyable with which to work. A good tooling hide has a beauty of its own, and lends itself to tailoring as satisfactorily as it does to modeling. Tooling calf comes in various grades, the heavier of which are the more easily tooled. In any hide, the heaviest and best section is that which runs down through the center. *Tooling cowhide* is somewhat less expensive than tooling calfskin and is suitable for sturdy belts or for any simple article where elaborate carving is to be done. Its weight limits its use to articles of simple construction, since it is not easily manipulated. However, the weight of cowhide does make it tool readily.

Tailoring leather, though it cannot be tooled, is stimulating to work with; and decoration may be added to articles made from it through the use of stitching, hardware, embroidery, or leather appliqué. The leathers used for tailoring are made from any of the animal hides normally tanned, and their surfaces may be either smooth or suèded. Like calfskin, tailoring leathers come in a variety of weights, an important factor in the selection of a leather for a particular craft product.

A *lining leather* will be necessary to the construction of some objects. Such a leather should be thin. Where strength is not re-

LEATHER DRAWSTRING BAG

by Marie Borchardt

This bag was lined with light weight buckram. After it was assembled and laced, a plywood base was glued to the inside bottom. Final lining was held in place by catching to the buckram and leather seams.

THOMAS

quired, skivers are ideal. Both suède and smooth leathers may be used for lining, but the purpose of the article being made should be borne in mind when selecting its lining since a suède lining is apt to soil more quickly than a smooth one.

It is best to purchase leather through a dealer or directly from a tannery salesroom. In either case, it is possible to see and to feel the skins that are available. The kind and quality of the leather has a great deal to do with the beauty of the object to be made; and seeing and feeling the various leathers available is a wise precaution, especially if one has the design of the object well in mind. A design using soft folds will demand a fairly thin and pliable leather, whereas a book cover or a portfolio will need the sturdy quality of a heavier leather. Since it is difficult to select leathers from printed descriptions, most handicraft supply houses will, for a small sum, send samples and price lists of the leathers they handle. If it is not possible to buy one's leather directly from a dealer, the small investment for these samples is well worth while. Listings of supply houses may be obtained through consulting a *current issue* of any magazine devoted to crafts or hobbies.

Handicraft dealers will frequently carry small kits made up with a leather blank and all the needed supplies for finishing a specific piece of leather work. The design for the particular piece of work will be included in the kit. Since these designs are almost always decidedly mediocre (though the materials in the kit may be top grade), it is usually best to devise your own. However, handicraft dealers will often sell pieces of leather cut to the approximate size one needs. This is one of the more expensive ways to purchase leather, but, if only a small amount is desired, it is sometimes more practical than buying a half or a whole hide.

If one expects to use more than just a small piece of leather, it is better to buy a whole or a half skin of the type needed. Skins are priced by the square foot, and leather so purchased is substantially lower in cost than that purchased in small pre-cut pieces. All hides should be examined carefully for blemishes. Animals have a habit of tangling with barbed wire fences or otherwise scratching themselves, and old scars often show on the leather. The price of a piece of leather varies with the number of flaws in the hide. As mentioned before, the center areas of the hides are best, but for the careful craftsman there is very little waste in a skin. The scraps may be used for buttons, straps, and linings. If the outer pieces are not too grained from rolling or handling, coin purses or similar small objects may be made from them. Graining is caused by rolling a smooth leather *finished side in*. Because of the ease with which leather is grained, *always roll leather with the finished side out* when it is to be carried or stored. Sometimes graining can be used to advantage since it is an excellent way to make odd scraps of leather match one another. Leather which has been grained has a good "feel" and is useful for certain objects if they are not too large.

Design and Construction

DESIGNING FOR LEATHER

Just as with any other craft problem, the designing of an article to be made from leather is the first step to be considered. Since leather articles are made for many different purposes, the use for which they are intended is of primary importance. This use will determine the nature of the structural design as well as the kind and quality of leather to be used. It might be wise to re-read the chapter on design before beginning to lay out the plans for a piece of leather work. One should remember that structural design is that part of the design represented by the object without benefit of embellishment. A leather-covered box may be decorated with tooling, but the shape and size of the box are elements of its structural design and must be planned carefully before any steps are taken in drawing the decorative unit to be applied to the basic form.

The importance of function cannot be overestimated. A handbag which is not easily opened and closed, or which is difficult to remove things from, is a nuisance and not a work of art however fine the craftsmanship that went into its construction. A book jacket that does not fit the book for which it was planned is a useless addition to one's library. Until the structural design is carefully and completely worked out, there is no need to plan the decorative design of an object.

To some, the beautiful qualities of leather are sufficiently satisfying without the addition of decoration. When tooled or other decorative elements are being omitted, the structural design becomes the entire design. The lines of construction, the silhouette, and the tasteful adherence to the functional aspects of the object often make further decoration unnecessary. However, these elements are equally important as the basis for all applied design and should never be lightly considered.

When decorative design is planned, it should compliment the well planned basic structure of the object. Because of the many forms which leather can take, it is impossible to give suggestions and admonitions that would cover them all. Certain general directions, however, should be helpful to the beginner.

Unless a design will increase the beauty of the structural design as well as the surface of the leather, it should not be used. Perhaps one could think of a leather object as similar to a piece of architecture. Often the structural shape of a building is not enhanced by decorative grillwork, changes in texture, or sculptured detail. Sometimes, however, such added ornamentation stresses and enriches the basic form. When this is true, the decoration is not only good but necessary. Decoration, whether used in architecture or on leather, should remain an integral part of the whole. Occasionally a lavish design may be used, but it should always be tasteful. An old leather-bound Spanish trunk is an elaborate piece of work, but the decorative way in which the material has been handled produces a richness of surface that in no manner impairs the structure to which it has been applied.

SPECTACLE CASE

*Suède leather, kid appliqué,
six-strand embroidery floss.*

THOMAS

After the structural plan for the object has been prepared, the decorative units may be planned. If tooling is to be used, the modeled design is usually best if it is held to simple forms which do not digress from the principles of good design as explained elsewhere in this book. Designs holding too closely to naturalistic forms are almost invariably poor, so sail boats and Scotty dogs, unless skillfully interpreted, are better left to the photographer.

Since the decorative design must relate to the structural design, planning the decoration for certain articles will require special care. The design on a handbag or purse which has flaps for closing, for instance, presents problems quite different from those met in designing a simple belt. An article with flap closings, such as a purse, should be so planned that any design placed on the flap will be a part of both the front *and* the back of the object. Portfolios present similar problems. The thickness of leather may cause design motifs to appear out of place when the flaps are folded down over the body of the purse or portfolio. This is particularly true of a continuous surface decoration which should never be planned except

[174]

LEATHER MOSAIC
HAT

Jig-saw technique used for colored suède which was stitched to a muslin backing. Seams were concealed by yarn embroidery.

THOMAS

on a paper pattern cut to the shape of the article. Such a pattern may be folded into position during the designing process in order that one may make sure that the rhythmic lines of the design will match in a pleasing manner. Areas within any decorative design should be related to the structure and so planned that they will not be broken by a fold or a stitched edge. Remember that design unity is highly dependent upon the arrangement of design elements to produce a satisfying effect whether the purse or portfolio is opened or closed. A marginal allowance should be made for edge stitching when it is going to be used.

When planning a design that is to be tooled, a black and white drawing should be made of the preliminary line design. Since tooled or modeled leather is somewhat like the bas-relief found on a coin (where no part is raised higher than the original surface), the design areas that are to be pressed into the leather should be darkened on the paper drawing. Tooling the surface of a piece of leather is essentially a problem in light and dark. The design can

[175]

only be seen accurately if it is worked out in black and white even though the final piece of tooled leather will be of one color.

When the structural design and the decorative design for a leather article are well planned, the craftsman is off to a good start. Time and care spent on these initial stages of the work will pay many dividends and will certainly not be wasted.

PLANNING THE CONSTRUCTION OF A LEATHER OBJECT

After the structural and decorative design of any leather project have been planned, paper patterns of all of the pieces necessary to the construction of the article must be made. Brown wrapping paper is a good material for these patterns. A ruler, scissors, pins, needle and thread, Scotch tape, triangle, and perhaps a compass and a French curve will be found useful for this step.

If the leather article is to be a case for something—such as blotter pad, book, or package of cigarettes—the particular object should be at hand so that accurate measurements may be taken. It is also wise to have at least a sample of the kind of leather that is going to be used, since its thickness is important in relation to the inside dimensions of any case. Unless the leather is considered in the planning, the ³⁄₃₂-inch thickness may mean that a case will be too small for the object it is to cover. Fractional differences are not too important in a purse, but a cigarette case that will not quite fit a package of cigarettes is rather useless. The thickness of leather is also a factor when one is planning a billfold or similar object which requires that two pieces of leather be folded together. *The outer piece must always be a little larger than the inner one.*

Using a straightedge, triangle, compass, or French curve as needed, make an accurate paper pattern of the article to be made of leather. Do not omit any section, but make all of the pockets, partitions, straps, buckles, and other parts. Allowance must be made on each section of the paper pattern for seams, folds, and overlapping parts. If corners are to be right angles and sides straight, use a triangle and straightedge to insure absolute accuracy. *Take time to be exact.*

After all pieces are cut, the paper pattern should be carefully assembled. A simple pattern may be pinned together; but for more complicated patterns, sewing will prove more secure. Scotch tape may be helpful in some instances.

Examine the assembled "dummy" from every angle. Check all its proportions. Determine whether it can be used easily. Does it look right? If it is a case, does it fit the object for which it is intended? Any errors should be carefully corrected; paper adjustments are far cheaper than leather mistakes.

When one is thoroughly satisfied with every aspect of the dummy, the pattern should be taken apart and pressed flat. Lay the paper pieces on the *right* side of the leather with as little waste as possible. The most important visible part of the planned article should be placed on the finest part of the leather. If one is expecting to tool the leather, a margin should be left around the pattern piece since it is not possible to tell whether the leather will shrink or stretch during the tooling. A quarter of an inch will be ample allowance for shrinkage.

Thought should be given to the pieces that will be on the outside of the article if it is to be folded. As previously mentioned, outer pieces will have to be slightly larger. A piece of leather planned to go around a book or a deck of cards, for instance, will have to be longer than the paper pattern. To determine just how much longer it must be, cut two small strips of leather of the weight being used. These should be equal in length. Place the strips together and fold in the center. The ends of the inner piece will extend beyond those of the outer piece. The amount of projection should be measured and added to the dimensions of the outer piece of the pattern. Attention to these small details will ward off later grief.

To determine the necessary allowance on a leather case, wrap some small solid object, such as a matchbox, with a strip of paper and carefully mark where the ends join. Repeat with a strip of leather. By comparing the marks on both the paper and the leather, the needed allowance may be gauged. A case must be large enough for easy use but never too large or it will lose shape quickly. Adjust the paper pattern to correspond to the weight of the leather.

After the foregoing steps have been carefully followed, the pattern pieces should be rearranged in the same relative positions on the *wrong* side of the leather. Draw around them for cutting. Tailor's chalk, a sharp crayon, or a ball point pen are good for this. Some leathers can be marked upon with a pencil, but usually such a mark is faint and not easily followed. When drawing a-round the pattern pieces, use some guide to insure clean, accurate lines.

To cut the leather, use a razor blade or a very sharp knife guided by a metal straightedge. A pair of extremely sharp shears or tin snips may also be used. Exercise caution when cutting a curved line; stay on the line and cut to produce a clean smooth edge. The kind and weight of the leather will determine which cutting method is best. Where there is any doubt, a small sample might be used to practice on.

Tooling Leather

After the design that is to be tooled has been carefully drawn, it should be traced on some fairly lightweight but strong paper. Typing paper may be used, but a good quality of tracing paper is somewhat more satisfactory. Indicate the outside edges of the piece of leather which is to be tooled, and be sure that the design is properly positioned within the area. The paper should be large enough to permit a margin of about one inch to extend around the lines of the shape. This will facilitate holding the design in place when it is being transferred to the leather. If the paper is too small for this margin, paste a number of tabs around its edge.

All the lines within the design should be clean cut and free from any unnecessary wavering or indecision. Plastic triangles and French curves are often helpful for sharpening the lines of a design. A French curve is an instrument which has a number of convex and concave curves of varying degrees. The hard edge of the French curve makes a good guide for redrawing any faltering line, and the various curves may be shifted about until one is found that coincides with the lines of the design. It may be necessary to shift the instrument a number of times for even a single flowing line of a design, but by doing this the recorded trembles of an unsure hand can be eliminated. The traced design must be precise; the tooling process itself will counteract any hint of mechanical coldness that may appear in the paper drawing.

Dampen the leather with a sponge or soft cloth *on the wrong side*, until dark spots begin to appear on the right side. When this begins to happen, turn the leather over and *dampen the entire surface* of the right side. Never dampen only a small area at a time,

[179]

for this will cause water spots which are extremely difficult to re-move. If for some reason the leather should become water stained, wet the entire piece with a cloth or sponge until it is thoroughly saturated. Allow to dry slowly. The best possible precaution is to work carefully to avoid any possibility of staining from the outset. Since the best grades of tooling leather are normally polished rather highly at the tannery, the right side tends to shed water and most of the dampening must be done from the back.

When the leather has been dampened according to the above directions, it should be placed upon some smooth hard sur-face—a drawing board is quite satisfactory for this. Place the trac-ing of the design over the leather using care to locate it in relation to the guide lines indicating the shape of the leather piece. The marginal edge of the tracing may be taped to the board, or thumb-tacks may be used to hold it in place. If tacks are used, take care not to puncture the leather or to press them too hard. If the head of the tack laps over the edge of the leather and is pressed into its surface, it will leave a mark. Keep metal tacks away from contact with the damp leather for some metals are apt to cause a dark stain which cannot be readily removed. Fasten the tracing paper very securely; as the paper absorbs moisture from the wet leather, it will begin to buckle.

If the design unit is a small one which can be traced quickly, it may be sufficient to fold the margins of the paper under the small leather piece to prevent its slipping.

A very hard pencil, HH or harder, may be used to transfer the lines from the tracing paper to the damp leather. The pencil should be sharpened well and then sanded to a blunt point. If a nut pick is used instead of a pencil, one must make sure that it is smooth and will not cut holes through the paper.

With the pencil or nut pick, go over all the lines of the design carefully and quickly while the leather is damp. Use a medium pressure and take care not to cut through the paper and scratch the surface of the leather. Follow the lines carefully, using a guide where necessary. Untraced lines will be easy to see, for the traced lines will be depressed slightly. Avoid all accidental pressure such as might come from the fingernails, buttons, or wrist watch. After the entire design has been outlined, remove the paper. The traced lines will be indented into the surface of the leather as guides for the tooling process.

TOOLS FOR MODELING, STAMPING, AND INCISING

Though one may purchase a wide assortment of tools for leather work, only a few tools are really essential. The quality of one's work is personal, and it is not entirely dependent upon the tool or tools which one may have access to. For the beginner, two nut picks will suffice. One should be rounded slightly at the tip to use for line work; the other pounded and filed into a spoon shape. Both should be smoothed with emery paper to remove any rough spots. Tools made this way must be tested on scraps of leather before using. Though nut pick tools have a tendency to darken leather, it is quite possible to produce creditable work with them.

Leather tools may be obtained through handicraft supply houses. When purchasing tools, one should select those of high grade steel with comfortable handles. The most important tool is the *regular modeler*. Usually this tool is made with a liner at the other end. The next most useful tool is a *deerfoot modeler*, which permits one to work very close to a form while tooling. Other useful tools are: a *diamond point modeler* which is good for corners, a *ball point embosser*, and an *edge creaser* which is used to tool

STAMPING TOOLS

Kitchen gadgets, commercial tools, carved dowel rods, linoleum blocks. Card case decorated with dowel rod stamps.

TOOLING AND ASSEMBLING EQUIPMENT

A variety of modeling tools, edge creaser, skiving knives, incising knife, pliers, slit punches, awls, French curve, triangle, button setting equipment, pin vise, wheel marker, spring punch.

a line a short distance in from the edge of the leather while beveling the edge at the same time.

It is sometimes effective to use a *stamping tool* to texture background areas after the preliminary modeling has been done. There are many metal stamps made for this purpose. They are made of short lengths of square or round brass rod one end of which has been cut to form some simple design of lines, dots, or geometric shapes. These stamps are held upright on the dampened leather and tapped with a mallet or hammer. Many textures and design arrangements are possible through combining the stamps in various ways. Unfortunately, there is some danger that such tools will be overused. Most of the Mexican and much of the western leather work brought home by beaming tourists is decorated with stamped designs which have been applied with neither discretion nor taste. It is always wise to test the stamps in various combinations upon a sample scrap of leather before using them on what is to be a finished piece.

Before investing in a commercial set of stamps, one might do well to give some thought to making one's own set. Very usable and attractive stamps can be made from large nails, hardwood sticks such as dowel rod, or from linoleum. To make a stamp from a nail, cut off the pointed end, smooth it flat with file and emery paper, and finally file lines across the flattened surface or nick its edges to make an interesting motif.

Designs may also be filed into the sandpapered end of dowel rods or hardwood sticks, or they may be cut into the wood with a knife. Since the ends of dowel rods and sticks are larger than those of heavy nails, the designs cut into them may be more elaborate. Simple leaf and flower forms may be used as well as the geometric shapes suggested above. After the design has been completely carved or filed into the stick, the end should be lightly resanded and dipped into spar varnish. Drain off all excess varnish and allow to harden completely. Thus protected, the wood fibers will not swell when the stamp is used on damp leather. The wooden stamps will not last as long as those of metal, but they will more than suffice for several pieces of work.

A linoleum block used for leather stamping should be very small, and it should be fastened to a piece of wood to facilitate handling. Usually such blocks are employed to depress the leather rather than to print it with dye. However, both wood and linoleum may be dipped into leather dye or textile paint and used to color and to depress the surface of the leather in the same operation. Linoleum stamps are cut in the same manner as a block for printing; directions for such cutting are given elsewhere in this book.

Many ordinary household items may be used for stamping tools. Among the things that have been found to be useful are thimbles, the leadless tip of a mechanical pencil, small bundles of brads tied together, garnish cutters, and darning needles. The imaginative craftsman will be able to find objects other than these for this purpose. Anything that leaves an attractive imprint upon the leather is a possible tool, though it is best always to test on a leather scrap.

To incise leather, one must have a razor-sharp cutting instrument of some kind. Though there are special knives made for this purpose, a single-edge razor blade or a stencil knife serves very well.

THE TOOLING PROCESS

There are four major methods of tooling leather—modeling, embossing or repoussé, incising, and stamping. The nature of the design planned for any leather object will vary according to the method used. Occasionally several of the methods may be combined to produce interesting results. Unless one has had experience with any one of these techniques, it is well to practice on a small article or scraps before applying oneself to a large piece of leather. There is nothing very difficult about any of the methods that will be discussed in this section, providing patience and care are used judiciously while one is working.

Whichever the technique that one uses, the preliminary steps are the same. If the leather has become dry during the tracing of the design, it must be redampened. When properly damp, the leather is placed right side up on a piece of glass, marble, or some other smooth hard surface which will provide a good tooling base. With a plastic straightedge and a line tool (sometimes called a veiner), go over all the straight lines in the design. Draw firmly enough to depress the line sufficiently for it to retain its character after the leather has dried. With equal care, deepen all the remaining lines in the design.

If a tiny bit of moisture appears at the tip of the liner, the leather is too wet and should be allowed to dry somewhat before it is worked. Wrinkling is apt to result if the tool is used on too wet a surface. After one has worked with leather for a little time, one will be able to gauge by the color and feel of the moistened surface the amount of moisture necessary for tooling.

When these preliminary steps have been successfully completed, the leather is ready for the actual tooling. The most commonly used techniques are as follows:

1. MODELING

Refer to the original black and white drawing of the design to ascertain which of the design areas are to appear higher than

BASIC LEATHER TOOLING TECHNIQUES

Simple border designs, such as would be very suitable for tooled belts, serve as excellent means for experimenting with the tools and methods used in elementary leather work. In the picture to the left, the design was produced with simple modeling and accented with polished brass paper fasteners and metal washers. The fasteners were inserted through the leather and secured at the back.

In the first of the examples on the opposite page, a similar technique was used but the metal washers were omitted. The second border on the right hand page illustrates an extremely effective use of modeling, stamping, and incising. The small circle units were stamped into the leather while it was damp, the running straight lines were incised, and the triangle forms modeled. The third example uses modeling and incising and adds another technique, that of background texturing. Texturing is a method which may be used with a number of variations and is one which produces interesting contrasts with the smooth surfaces of untextured areas. The last example on the page, a flowing leaf design, was done entirely with the basic modeling technique. Since incising lends itself most advantageously to straight line designs, curved units are usually best handled with simple modeling.

All the techniques shown on these two pages are described in detail elsewhere in this chapter.

TOOLED BELT

Simple modeling, buckle constructed over wire foundation, saddle stitched.

COIN PURSES

Simple modeling, with various lacing methods.

ENVELOPE BAG

Simple modeling, saddle stitched, one-piece gusset, tuck-in flap.

the rest. Locate these same areas on the moistened leather, and with the tip of the modeling tool directed *toward* the high area, move it back and forth *gently* until the background immediately joining the raised spot appears lower. It is best to hold the tool as one does a pen or pencil since that seems more natural and comfortable. The tooled area should slope away from the raised area for a distance of one-eighth to one-quarter inch depending upon the size of the background. Work carefully all around the high parts of the design in this manner *being sure to keep the modeler pointed toward the raised area all of the time.* Though the raised areas will appear to be higher than the background when this process is completed, they actually are not. This seems to be so, however, because of the tooled, sloping band outlining each part of the design. In tooling, the greatest pressure should be exerted at the previously traced and deepened line of the design. The amount of pressure should ease off toward the background areas in gentle transition. Accentuate any corners in the design with a little more pressure than that used for the rest of the tooling. The diamond-pointed modeler is an excellent tool for this.

With the modeler, gently bevel the sloping band of tooling so that there will not be a sharp ridge to mark the end of the tooling as it merges with the background. Numerous light strokes are better for this than a few made with excessive pressure. Though each craft has its characteristic tool marks, there is no need to add unnecessarily to their quantity. Overtooling will destroy much of the fine quality of the leather. The optical illusion created by lowering and beveling a small strip around the high areas will be sufficient to bring out the design in carefully tooled leather. The play of light and shade over the surface will be pleasing, and the leather will remain fresh in appearance.

It is best to work on this part of the tooling with the light—whether daylight or artificial light—coming from the front and at a rather low angle. Such a raking light heightens the effect of the tooling considerably and does much to offset eyestrain.

After the background areas have been carefully lowered and beveled, the raised areas should be detailed. Study the original design to determine the effect desired. Lines may be tooled into the raised areas with the liner or with the side edge of the modeler. One area may be made to appear to overlap another by merely treating the under section as another bit of background. As before, with the tool pointing toward the higher area, gently lower the area neighboring the part that is to be higher. The illusion is obtained quickly.

It may be necessary to redampen the leather now and then while the tooling is being done. Always remember to dampen the entire piece. After the tooling is completed, the leather should be set aside to dry.

2. Embossing or Repoussé

These terms are used to describe a tooling technique whereby parts of the design are raised above the original surface of the leather.

Following the same procedure as for simple modeling, tool the design into the right side of the leather. All detail as well as the main lines of the design should be carefully finished. When this is done, turn the leather over. Usually the main design lines will show on the back of the leather piece. If these lines are not apparent, place a sheet of carbon paper, right side up, under the leather and press over the lines from the right side. The carbon will transfer to the back of the leather along these lines, which are needed as guides to the embossing process.

RESTRAINED
EMBOSSING

Box: wallboard construction; cloth lined, leather covered with a light padding under the tooled cover. Rolled leather cover tab.

Belt Fob: tooled leather accented with metal. Bent copper wire attachment.

THOMAS

When only a small amount of embossing is to be done, the leather may be supported by the fingers of one hand while the other hand stretches the parts to be raised by manipulating the ball point

[191]

modeler beneath those areas. The slight pressure exerted by the supporting hand, coupled with the upward thrust of the tool, will stretch the leather easily. For large raised areas, the regular modeler is more efficient than the ball point tool.

When the embossing is more complicated, turn the already simply modeled leather upside down over a soft pad which may be made of layered felt, folded cloth, or modeling clay. With the ball point or regular modeling tool, work over all of the areas which are to be raised above the original surface of the leather. Do this gingerly, for leather cannot be shrunk back if it has been overstretched.

It is in the embossing process that much leather is ruined. If one's enthusiasm has a tendency to run away with one's judgment, the embossed forms may be so overdone that the design seems to be modeled almost in the round. When the modeling becomes more important than the leather, the effect is one of ostentation. Many designs which are otherwise quite fine have been cheapened with overstretching. A sensitive craftsman will practice restraint.

All embossed leather must be supported permanently from the back. This may be done with fine sawdust mixed with a small amount of glue or paste, cotton, kapok or similar fibrous material, or plastic wood. If fiber is being used and a firm backing is required, moisten the fiber slightly but not enough to cause any danger of water spotting the leather. Rest the tooled leather upside down on a soft pad and pack the filling material into the depressed areas until level with the back. One should exercise caution and see that the filling is kept smooth, for bumps carelessly left will soon be noticeable from the front after the article is in use. The filling should be held in place with a backing of thin paper, leather, or cloth. The nature of the backing is determined by the use to which the article is to be put. Box lids may be padded with sheet wadding so arranged that the highest areas of the design are supported by extra layers secured with paste. The springiness of such light padding often adds to the pleasure one feels when touching the leather cover.

3. INCISED LEATHER

The process of incising (or cutting) leather is one of the preliminary steps to the elaborate decorations on saddles made of heavy steer hide. It is a simple technique which is extremely effective with straight line designs that are not too ornamental or detailed. Incised designs may be combined with tooling or stamping though a design may be so planned that this is unnecessary.

Trace the design on to the leather according to the directions given previously. Define the lines after the tracing paper has been removed, and make certain that the leather is properly dampened. For the cutting of an incised design, use a regular incising knife, a razor blade, or a stencil knife. It is imperative that the blade, whichever is used, be thin and sharp. A straightedge should be used as a guide for the knife for all lines possible.

Holding the knife in such a way as to make a clean, perpendicular incision, cut along all the lines of the design to a depth of one-fourth—never more than one-half—the thickness of the leather. All cuts should be of the same depth, and they should be made with clean, sure strokes in order to avoid a burred edge. *Never cut through a previously made cut.* Since the tiny corners made by intersecting lines tend to become soft and frayed easily, allow a space of one-sixteenth inch between cuts. Damp leather cuts more easily than nearly dry leather, so the surface should be kept uniformly moist by sponging. The incising blade should be sharpened frequently on an oil stone to make the work more exact.

When the lines have all been cut, they may be opened by running the liner along the incision. The side of a small modeler may be used instead of the liner if the bottom of the "spoon" is held toward one side of the cut first and then toward the other. The cut lines should be opened carefully, for the edges of the leather have a tendency to wrinkle during this process.

The background areas of incised work are not usually beveled as are those in simple modeling. With either the regular or the deerfoot modeler, tool down the background areas so that one edge of the cut stands up straight and the other is compressed until it is not seen as a line. When this is done correctly, the effect is that of two layers of leather, one forming the design, the other the background.

Sometimes stamping or texturing is used in combination with incised work to further flatten the background and to add interest to the design. Though incised work is not difficult, precision is essential. As with the other techniques, preliminary practice is advisable.

4. Stamping and Texturing

In order to bring out certain portions of a design, it is often desirable to change the surface texture of background areas. One of the most simple ways to achieve this effect is to tap the leather with a blunt point of some kind. Small, closely placed depressions may be made with a small nail, an extremely hard pencil, the tip of the liner, or some other instrument. A mechanical pencil with lead removed will make tiny ring markings that are quite attractive. A darning needle may be used to prick the entire surface effectively.

When the area to be textured is large, there are many methods which may be used. The pattern made by pressing a thimble on the dampened leather surface will produce a texture quickly and interestingly. Closely spaced parallel lines may be drawn with the liner over such areas, or cross hatching may be tried. An active imagination is probably the best tool that one can have, for it will lead one to experiment with many kinds of equipment. Do all such experimenting on tag ends of leather.

For simple texturing, a helter-skelter free application of the tool being used will be found most satisfactory. Avoid creating unpleasant linear effects with a stamping tool, especially when working closely around some raised form within the design.

Decorative stamps are usually more bold in design than texturing tools. When working with such stamps, one should have some plan in mind, and the stamps should be set to form a definite pattern. The stamping instrument *must be held perpendicularly to the leather surface* and tapped squarely with hammer or mallet. Some practice is required before one can keep the pattern of the impressions even. Do not try to reset a stamp of definite design; the results are seldom satisfactory.

The smallest linoleum stamps are most easily handled if they are mounted on wooden blocks or sticks. Larger linoleum stamps may be used unmounted and may be pressed into the leather surface by stepping carefully on the back of the block. A mallet may be used to print the stamps, but it is difficult to obtain an even impression where a number of blows are required to print the entire stamp. With the larger stamps, it may be necessary to mark the back in order to insure its being placed in the correct position on the leather. As with other tooling methods, the leather must be damp for all texturing or stamping.

A Few General Suggestions

Although accidents are bound to happen—especially when one is learning a new craft—it is seldom that a project need be abandoned because of one. Remedies and precautions have already been mentioned, but a few further suggestions as well as a repetition of some of the warnings may help the beginner.

Always roll the leather with the right side out in order to avoid graining the fine surface. Once the leather has been grained, the marks are there to stay.

Since leather mars and scratches easily, use care to avoid accidental marking with rings, fingernails, or thoughtlessly handled equipment.

Always dampen the leather before any form of tooling is done. Sponge the wrong side first, then the right side. Dampen the entire piece of leather even when only a small portion is to be tooled. Should water stains develop, wet the leather thoroughly and place on an absorbent pad to dry slowly. The spots *may* disappear.

Never close damp leather up in a box or cupboard, for leather is particularly susceptible to molds.

Accidental marks made by slips of the tools are almost ineradicable. Stroking the marred surface gently from the top with the modeler and repeating from underneath may help somewhat to remove such marks. Sometimes the design can be altered a trifle to incorporate the mistake.

Work carefully and slowly. It is better to get the desired effect by tooling lightly several times than to exert too much pressure the first time. Only experience will teach one to gauge the correct amount of moisture and the amount of pressure needed to have the leather take definite form and to become satiny under one's tool. Always use restraint.

If the leather is cut all the way through because of some accident during incising, paste a thin piece of leather or cloth to the back to reinforce it. Tool this part of the cut line with extreme care.

When the knife has made a jagged, irregular cut, all one can do is to glue the rough pieces back into place and retool when the glue has dried. Such patching is not likely to be excessively noticeable when the work is finished.

If the leather wrinkles—because it has been too wet to tool well or because an edge has been undercut when incised—stroke the surface lightly in the opposite direction with the modeler.

Keep the hands clean. Be especially careful not to touch one's face and then the leather. The slightest trace of natural oil from one's skin will leave a stain on unglazed leather. Should this happen, use carbon tetrachloride or a similar grease solvent at once. Use it sparingly and do not rub the spot.

Since some metals darken leather, always use plastic straight-edges on damp leather. If one is using nut pick tools, use as little moisture as possible and do not over tool. These homemade tools affect only light-colored unglazed leather. Stains left by them may sometimes be removed by sponging the leather with a weak oxalic acid solution. One teaspoon of oxalic acid crystals to one cup of water is the proper mixture. Make it in a glass or porcelain bowl and avoid any contact with one's skin.

Metal Decoration for Leather Articles

Leather and metal are often combined to produce handsome results. The satiny gleam of some metals—copper, pewter, brass, or silver—mates beautifully with the rich texture of a fine piece of leather. Such combinations have long been favorites with craftsmen. When metal and leather are used together, usually one or the other material provides the decorative note. A well designed buckle of copper may be used to accent a plain leather belt, or the belt may be of tooled leather and fastened with a simple buckle of the metal. When leather and metal are combined, the total result should be tasteful and in accordance with all the principles of design and craftsmanship—each should compliment the other.

Among the readily available metal decorations that may be used attractively on a leather surface are nailheads such as are used on fabric. Nailheads are fairly inexpensive, and a setting tool may be purchased for a small sum. On very thin leather, these nailheads may be applied according to the directions supplied by the manufacturer. However, if the leather is heavy, it may be necessary to make small holes for the prongs beforehand. To do this, press the nailhead into the leather to mark the position in which it is to be set. Punch the holes with an awl, a coarse needle set into a pin vise, or with a sewing machine (turn the wheel by hand). Insert the prongs of the nailhead through these holes, and set the nailhead with the instrument provided for this purpose.

Copper or brass rivets may be effectively combined with leather. Industry uses a great variety of rivets not all of which are suitable for leather decoration. Large, split-shank rivets are too heavy for such use, but tiny rivets are satisfactory. These may be so applied as to produce border designs, all over designs, or accents to tooled or cut designs.

Roundheaded paper fasteners may be obtained in a number of finishes and sizes. These may be inserted into the leather in the same manner as in paper. They may be used alone or in combination with small flat washers to produce a larger metal unit. Leather decorated with paper fasteners should be lined in order to cover the metal shanks which are bent against the wrong side of the leather.

Occasionally, metal buttons are suitable for adding a decorative note to an object. The methods for fastening such buttons will be determined by the shape of the button itself. Bits of attractive metal jewelry, copper, brass, or silver wire, old coins—all of these may be used; but never without consideration as to the appropriate results to be obtained. Imagination must always find its foundation on good taste.

Coloring or Dyeing Leather

Style trends change frequently, and various methods of coloring leather are apt to follow the year's fads and fancies. It has been some time since the polychrome effects were considered in good taste. Though formerly done, fortunately coloring a design to heighten its realism is now out of favor. There never was a time, for that matter, when work of that kind rightly belonged in the field of good applied design. There are occasions, however, when it seems desirable to color small areas of leather. This should be done only when the design is enhanced with the addition of color. It should never be done to create an illusion of realism.

When small areas of a tooled or an incised design are to be colored, the work is done with a soft brush or a cotton swab dipped into a leather dye or photographic tinting water color. The surface of the leather must always be entirely free from dirt and grease before the coloring is applied. The leather may be cleaned by sponging lightly with denatured alcohol or carbon tetrachloride. In order that the pigment will penetrate the leather evenly, the piece to be dyed should be dampened as for tooling.

[199]

Present day taste usually prefers natural or solid color leathers. If a colored leather is desired, it is best to purchase it ready-dyed. Tanneries do a better job of dyeing leather than one can do at home, though it is by no means impossible to dye small pieces of leather satisfactorily. It is best to provide one's self with a good leather dye. Where that is impossible, use a dye manufactured for coloring wool. Whichever dye one uses, prepare it carefully in accordance with the directions given on the container. Be sure to strain the concentrated solution through several layers of fine cloth before using. For dyeing the leather, it will be necessary to have a container large enough to immerse the entire piece of leather at one time. Fill the container with dye of the proper strength to a depth sufficient to cover the leather adequately. Before attempting to dye the leather which one is intending to use, test the solution on a scrap of the same leather. Remember that color almost always becomes lighter as it dries. The dye bath must be *cool*. Soak the leather thoroughly in clear water, then place in the dye bath. Keep it completely submerged while in the solution. To prevent any precipitation from settling on the leather, keep the liquid moving a bit either by stirring or by moving the container with a gentle rocking motion. When the color is as deep as one wishes, remove the leather and rinse quickly in clear water. Drain it, and place upon a pad of newspaper to dry. It is important to remember that leather may shrink during the drying process. Allowance for possible shrinkage should be made when cutting the piece to be dyed.

Only unglazed, light-colored, vegetable-tanned leather can be dyed in the manner described above. However, much of the calf used for tooling is of this type. Since leather dye has the same affinity for one's hands as it does for leather, one will be wise to wear rubber gloves while doing any dyeing.

Craft supply houses carry a number of coloring agents which may be used on leather. Among these are quick-drying enamels which remain flexible and do not peel or crack, lacquers and waterproof inks, and alcohol and water soluble dyes. The manufacturers of these products supply directions for their use which must be followed explicitly. The only general directions possible to give are: be sure that the leather is absolutely clean and free of grease, work carefully, and let one's best judgment be his constant guide.

An *antique finish* is one which changes the tone of the leather and deepens the effect of the design by highlighting the raised units. Leather so treated is toned by applying a mixture of oil paint thinned with turpentine to the glossy, dry surface. The paint mixture is rubbed from the high spots almost immediately, but is allowed to remain in the depressed areas to accent the tooling. Usually blue and brown oil paints are mixed together for this purpose, but one should experiment with various colors to determine which is best on the leather one is toning. A subtle variation in color is better than too great a contrast.

Preparing the Leather for Construction

PROTECTING THE SURFACE

Ordinarily, assembling the separate pieces of leather into the completed object requires that the leather be handled considerably. If the leather has been glazed or polished at the tannery, it already has enough surface to protect it. As an added precaution, however, it is well to polish the surface with a cream wax, Venetian shoe cream, or Fullustre. The latter is a product prepared for use on linoleum floors, but it has been proved a good protective coating for leather.

Smooth but unpolished leather may become soiled during the tooling process. Should this happen, general griminess can be removed with saddle soap. The feel of leather cleaned with saddle soap, which requires very little water, is always improved. Follow such cleaning with a light waxing.

Unfortunately, suède leather cannot be protected in any manner. One must exercise extreme care while handling such leather, particularly as the velvety surface becomes soiled much more easily than a smooth one.

TRIMMING AND SKIVING

If shrinkage allowance was made when the leather pieces were originally cut, all edges must be trimmed to the exact measurements of the pattern. The cleanest edge is obtained by cutting with a razor blade along a metal straightedge held in the proper position. Be sure that *all* pieces needed in the construction of the object are trimmed to the correct size.

The construction of most articles requires that two or more pieces of leather be fastened together in some manner. If the leather is thick, the result may be clumsy in appearance as well as difficult to manage during the sewing or lacing processes. Leather may be made thinner by *skiving*.

Skiving knives may be obtained in two principal forms. One has a broad blade almost two inches wide and sharpened at the broad end. One can make a satisfactory knife of this type by grinding the end of a putty knife to a sharp cutting edge. The corners of such a knife should be rounded slightly to help prevent accidental gouging of the leather during the skiving. These broad-bladed skiving knives are especially good for skiving large areas. They are used for thinning down leather by cutting small shavings from the flat surface. *Cutting strokes should always be directed away from the body.*

The form of the other type of skiving knife is similar to that of a paring knife sharpened along one side. Edges of leather are thinned or beveled very well with a knife of this kind.

Before attempting to skive leather, dampen it slightly as for tooling. Use a piece of heavy glass, marble, smooth hard wood, or some like surface under the leather. Except where the work otherwise demands, the skiving is done on the wrong side of the leather; so usually the leather is placed upside down on the working surface. If finger clearance is needed, place the skiving base on a box or a pile of magazines to raise it above the table. A newspaper under everything will permit one to let the chips fly where they may.

Place one hand on the leather *between* one's body and the area to be skived. Hold the leather in place firmly. With the knife held in any way that comfortably permits the blade to be almost parallel with the leather, cut away small thin chips from the section to be thinned. If one is inexperienced, it is wise to start cutting gingerly rather than to risk cutting too deeply. The skived portion should taper gradually from the thin edge to the main body of the leather.

It takes some practice to produce an even thickness with skiving. A careful sandpapering of the skived surface will help the beginner finish the task more accurately.

The thickness of the leather, the use to which the object is to be put, and the particular part that the skived piece is to play in the finished construction will all dictate the amount of leather that is to be cut away. Sometimes it is necessary to remove all but the smooth top surface of the leather. At other times it may be necessary to remove only enough to facilitate folding. Generally, however, the leather should be skived thin enough so that two layers will be as thick as one piece originally.

Skiving suède can best be described as a worrying process. Suèdes pull and stretch in all directions during skiving. It is helpful to fasten the leather securely with thumbtacks or a heavy weight at the edge farthest from the worker. Holding the near edge firmly, one may skive between the two secured edges.

Remember that one is working with an extremely sharp blade when skiving. Use every precaution to avoid accident. Work carefully and slowly, and never use the knife between the body and the free hand.

Construction Processes

CHECKING AND PLANNING

Before attempting to assemble any parts of the article being made, one should spread the pieces flat on a table in the approximate positions they will take in the finished piece. All corners should be tested for accuracy of angles, and all edges measured for straightness and length. An eighth of an inch in error may detract much from the final appearance of the object.

Next one should study the layout to determine just which seam could be stitched first to the greatest advantage. One may think that a handle on a handbag is a finishing touch, but it might make construction far more simple if the handle is fastened to the gussets as a first step. *Each piece of work presents its individual problems.* It is sometimes advantageous to reassemble the original paper pattern and to note the steps while doing so. In problems involving complicated construction, such notations can be immensely helpful.

The following construction processes are not necessarily presented in the order that one might need them. It would be well for the beginner to familiarize himself with all the processes by reading through this material. Later, he may refer specifically to certain sections when the need arises. It is useful to know just what the various construction methods are when planning any project, for this gives a wider range in which to think creatively.

Gluing and Pasting

Although one may purchase adhesives especially prepared for leather work, it is not necessary to do so. Three ordinary and easily obtainable adhesives were used for all the examples of leather work shown in this chapter. One of these may be made at home and is a paste which is highly recommended by the leather goods trade. It is particularly good to use since it has a high adhesive quality and remains flexible after drying. For these reasons, *rye paste* is extremely useful when one wishes to hold thin lining leathers in place.

Since rye paste is quickly absorbed into leather, it is best to coat the leather surface immediately a second time before putting the layers together. The paste spreads easily and may be put on the leather with a small varnish brush. One may make this adhesive according to the following directions:

Rye Flour Paste

2 tablespoons rye flour	1 cup water
¼ teaspoon alum	a few drops oil of cloves

Mix the flour, alum, and a little of the water to a smooth cream. Add the remainder of the water and cook over low heat. Stir constantly until the mixture is cooked to the consistency of a thin white sauce and is translucent in appearance. Long, slow cooking will increase the "stickiness." When sufficiently cooked, remove from the stove and add the oil of cloves. Rye paste can be kept for as long as a year if put in a closed jar and kept in a refrigerator. Occasionally the paste may separate, but it can be restored by stirring.

Higgins Vegetable Glue, a commercial preparation, is a good all-purpose adhesive. It is less watery than rye paste and may be used satisfactorily to fasten cloth and paper to leather when this is necessary. Since this is a rather heavy adhesive, it is best applied with a flat brush that has short, fairly stiff bristles. Should the paste be too thick to spread smoothly, it may be thinned with water.

Where strength rather than flexibility is the important factor, a good glue should be used. *Le Page's Glue* has been proved excellent for such purposes as fastening two layers of leather together securely for the punching of holes or slits for lacing. Glue dries quickly and must be used carefully. If it is applied too thickly, it may penetrate the leather and cause stains which are impossible to remove. Should cold weather cause glue to thicken, it may be necessary to place the container of glue in a pan of hot water. Glue warmed in this fashion will spread more easily. If it seems desirable, the glue may be thinned with a little vinegar.

LACING AND STITCHING

Preparing the cut edges. All leather edges that are to be laced must be straight and entirely free from any frayed appearance. If dark leather is lighter where it has been cut, the edges may be touched up with dye or waterproof ink after they have been trimmed correctly. This must be done before any shellacking or waxing, or the coloring will not penetrate. Where it is impossible to complete the final trimming neatly and accurately with a razor blade, fine sandpaper may be used to smooth the edges. Should the leather be too soft to sand, a bit of shellac should be applied to the raw edges to stiffen them for this process. When a number of layers of leather are to be laced together, it is extremely important that the edges be well finished.

After it is as even and as straight as possible, the edge should be tooled with the modeler to a slight bevel. An edge creaser, a tool made for this purpose, may be used instead of the modeler. It is a tool which may be used to draw a line in from the edge of the leather while beveling it at the same time. Though this tooling, whether done with edge creaser or modeler, may be sufficient it is sometimes advisable to give the edge of the leather a hard smooth finish. Paste may be rubbed into the leather until the edge is smooth, or wax may be used. On very heavy leather, luggage manufacturers use varnish. Suède leathers must be left soft since most finishes stain them badly.

Lacing and stitching are the two most widely used methods of holding layers of leather together. Each of these methods has many variations. For lacing, the edge of the leather must be prepared by punching holes of the correct size or by cutting slits through which the thong may be laced.

The most satisfactory work will be done if the layers of leather to be laced are held in position with a small amount of glue. After the edges have been glued together, the *top layer* should be marked lightly to indicate where each hole or slit is to be placed. These marks should be evenly spaced and parallel to the outer edge. The guide lines for round holes should be at least ⅛″ from the edge of the leather, or the leather may be so weakened that it will tear during the lacing process. It is advisable to observe the same distance from the edge when slits rather than holes are being used.

LACING AND STITCHING

From the top: over and over lacing, two tone over and over lacing, cross stitch or crisscross, button hole or loop lacing, Florentine lacing, back stitch (front and back view), saddle stitch, two thread one needle stitch, machine stitching.

When holes are to be punched through the leather, one should allow ⅛″ between holes. Measurements for the dots to indicate where the holes are to be punched must be gauged by the size of the hole to be used. All corners should be rounded slightly, and there must always be a hole punched in each corner. It may be necessary to adjust the marks for punching according to the distance between corners. To make the holes, a *leather punch* will be needed. The handiest type is a four or six tube spring punch with which holes of various sizes may be made.

Always have all layers of leather held together securely with glue before punching any holes or cutting any slits. This is very important.

Although it is somewhat simpler to lace a seam that has been prepared with a series of punched round holes, a more attractive and finished appearance results when slits are used instead. It is possible to purchase *thonging chisels* or slitting punches with one, three, or four prongs. Such tools are expedient, of course, but a nail or a small screw driver can be fashioned into a workable chisel without much difficulty. When a nail is used, the end must be pounded flat, filed to a width of ⅛″, and sharpened on an oil stone. A screw driver does not need to be flattened. Usually one can be obtained in the width desired and need only be sharpened. The cutting edge of the chisel should correspond in width to the thong which one is using for the lacing.

As for punching, mark a light guide line ⅛″ in from the edge of the leather. Do this on the right side. With a single prong chisel, cut a slit diagonally across all corners to be laced. These corners should be slightly rounded, and the slits should be placed ⅛″ from the edge of the curve. The position of the rest of the slits will have to be planned in relation to these corner cuts.

Normally, the space between slits should be the same as the width of each slit. It is sometimes necessary to increase or decrease the distance between slits a trifle in order to come out right.

Since it takes quite a bit of force to cut through several layers of leather, it is wise to place a board or a thick magazine beneath the leather to protect the table surface. Hold the chisel firmly in a vertical position and strike it with a hammer or a mallet. Unless the chisel is held correctly, the slit in the bottom layer of leather will be undercut and not in line with that in the top layer. Each cut must be positioned exactly. Staggered cuts will give a very careless appearance to the laced edge. One will find it helpful to sit on a low chair while using the chisel; it simplifies the work by making it possible to keep the tool absolutely vertical while the cutting is being done. It will be necessary to open each slit with a nut pick or awl before each stitch is taken when the lacing is in process.

Goat skin lacing, which may be purchased ready cut from most craft supply houses, is the most satisfactory thong to use. Though there is a plastic thong on the market, its appearance is unattractive and use of it will tend to cheapen the article being made. Leather thong comes in various widths—those most frequently used are ³⁄₃₂″ or ⅛″. Since too long a thong is difficult to handle, one should never attempt to use a length greater than three feet. Longer lengths of thong than this are apt to get frayed and dull-looking from being pulled through the holes or slits so many times. Where a long length is needed, shorter pieces may be *spliced* together as the work progresses.

To splice leather thong, cut off the top layer of the thong being used so that it tapers back about ½″. Do the reverse on the new length of thong, cutting off the bottom layer from one end. Glue the two ends together. When the glue has dried, lacing may be continued. Some care must be used until the splice has been worked up.

It is possible to buy thonging needles, but they are often more nuisance than help. To sharpen the end of the thong so that it may be inserted easily into the holes or slits, cut it at a diagonal. Dip the pointed end into shellac or fingernail lacquer and allow it to harden before using. If the tip of the thong becomes frayed during lacing, recut it on the slant and dip the new end into the hardening agent.

Over and Over Lacing. A thong which is $\frac{3}{32}''$ or $\frac{1}{8}''$ wide is best to use for this simple stitch. A length three times that of the distance to be laced will be necessary. It is best to begin the lacing where two thicknesses of leather are being fastened together. With a nut pick or awl, open a small part of the seam near the first hole to be used. *Do not start at a corner.* Insert the tip of the thong through the hole in the piece of leather forming the back of the article being laced. Pull the thong through until only a half inch or so of the thong remains. Tuck this small end out of sight between the two layers of leather and fasten it in place with a touch of glue. Bring the long end of the thong up over the edge of the seam and insert its tip through the next hole bringing it out at the back of the leather. Always work from the front of the article, pulling the thong out at the back. Pull the thong neatly to form an overcasting stitch. Keep the smooth polished side of the thong uppermost to avoid having to straighten it out after the loop has been pulled taut. Continue this simple over and over stitch around the article being laced. After every dozen or so stitches, stop and tighten those last taken by inserting a nut pick or awl under the loops and pulling up the slack. The stitches should be too tight to push from side to

Over and Over Lacing

Cross Stitch, or Crisscross Lacing

Two Color Over and Over Lacing

Buttonhole or Loop Lacing

Splicing Thong

Saddle Stitching

Back Stitch

Two Thread One Needle Stitch

side, but not so tight that they pucker the edge of the leather. Put two stitches in each corner hole.

When the lacing has been completed, there will remain the hole in the top layer of leather at the place where the work was begun. Insert the thong through this hole, cut it off to one-half inch, and tuck this end down between the leather layers as was the first end. New thong may be added in this manner anywhere along a double thickness of leather. However, on a single edge, or at any place where such ends might appear bulky, the thong must be spliced.

After all lacing has been done, place the work on a hard surface and flatten the edges by tapping them lightly with a hammer or wooden mallet.

Cross Stitch or Crisscross. This is a variation of the over and over stitch. Punch the holes or slits in the regular manner, but be sure that there are an *even number*. To do the cross stitch, one should lace as for the simple over and over stitch but using only every other hole. When the article is laced around in this manner, it should be laced in the *opposite* direction through the holes that were skipped the first time. At the corners, put two stitches into the hole with the thong that would normally use that hole, and only one stitch with the other thong. There are *three* stitches at each corner with this type of lacing. Begin and end the lacing in the same way as described for the over and over stitch.

Two Color Over and Over Lacing. For this type of lacing, the holes may be punched a bit closer together than for the previously described methods. This should not be done, however, if there is any danger that the edge might tear. With one color of thong, do the over and over stitch using every other hole. When this is completed, use another color of thong and lace through the holes skipped before. Work in the *same* direction as with the first lacing.

The Buttonhole or Loop Lacing. This stitch produces a more decorative edging than those described above, but it is not as simple to execute as the others. The guide lines for the buttonhole stitch should be placed ³⁄₁₆″ from the edge of the leather. Holes or slits may be used and a narrow ³⁄₃₂″ thong is best. The thong will have to be about six times the length of the distance to be laced.

Hold the edge to be laced toward the body. Insert the thong from the top and pull through at the back leaving a short end extending from the first hole. As with the other lacing methods, the lacing should be started in an inconspicuous place and at a double thickness of the leather. Bring the thong up from the back, and insert into the next hole to the right, pulling it until only a small loop remains at the edge of the leather. Put the end of the thong through this loop *from the top toward the bottom*. Tighten the loop through which the thong was just passed by grasping the thong close to the leather at the back. When the loop is snug against the edge, pull the thong the rest of the way through. When almost tight, pull the thong toward the *left* and then toward the *right*. These last two motions seem to produce a neater and firmer stitch. Bring the end of the thong up from the back again and insert into the next hole, pulling until a new loop is formed. Repeat the procedure above, and continue repeating until the article is completely laced. Remember to keep the smooth side of the lace on top and to pull up all stitches equally as they are made. Buttonhole lacing produces an attractive edge only when it is done carefully.

To fasten this type of thonging, work around the article until the starting point is reached. Remove the short end from the first hole and lace through the hole with the end of the thong just being used. Cut off this end one-half inch from the last stitch and skive it from the wrong side until very thin. Touch the skived surface with a little glue and slip this end under the first stitch made, through the lacing hole, and bring it out to the back of the leather. Fasten the first end of the thong in the same manner. After the ends are dry, they may be cut. When using the buttonhole stitch, one will find that three stitches at each corner are more satisfactory than two. As before mentioned, the corners should be rounded a bit before the stitching is begun.

Florentine Lacing. This is a lacing method which is particularly appropriate on large portfolios or bags. It is nothing more than the simple over and over stitch, but is done with strips of thin, pliable leather about ⅜" wide. Lacing for this method may be purchased ready to use, or one may cut it from a suitable piece of leather at home. Kidskin is the most satisfactory for this purpose.

Since the lacing leather is so wide, round holes are better than slits when Florentine lacing is to be done. The distance between holes should be the same as the width of the lacing so that each stitch will just touch the one next to it without overlapping. The distance of the holes from the edge of the leather should be the same as that between holes. It is important that the lacing fan out nicely as it comes through each hole. In order to cover the edge at the corner adequately, three stitches should be made. Because of the width of the lacing, somewhat more length will be needed than for the ordinary over and over stitch. The amount will vary with the width being used.

Stitching. Usually the leather work that appears most professional is constructed with stitching rather than thong lacing. Though stitching takes longer, it is well worth the added effort. If the leather is not too heavy, stitching may be done on a sewing machine, but most often it is hand work.

[215]

Tailor's buttonhole twist, shoe twist, or linen are the most satisfactory threads to use, but occasionally one may have to resort to substitutes. Select a smooth, strong thread of several ply. Some crochet cottons are excellent for stitching purposes. If necessary, the color of the thread may be changed by dyeing. When the thread is dyed, one must be sure to dye more than enough for the article to be sewed. Tie the thread to be dyed *very* loosely in a hank, wet thoroughly, and dye to the desired depth of color. Remember that any color will tend to lighten as it dries. After dyeing, the surface of the thread may be improved by rubbing with beeswax.

The guide line for stitching may be placed closer to the edge than for lacing. On thin leather, $\frac{1}{16}$" from the edge and 8 to 10 stitches to the inch will be found suitable. For heavier leathers, a $\frac{1}{8}$" margin with as few as 5 or 6 stitches to the inch is appropriate. The thread used should be proportionate in weight to these measurements.

The marking for the stitches may be done in several ways. Whichever method is used, the edges of the leather should be prepared properly according to the directions given earlier in this section. A light guide line should be marked in the correct place. A spacing wheel may be used to indicate the stitches. These wheels are available in several sizes. For most leathers that are light enough for hand tailoring, a seamstress' seam marker has the correct number of teeth per inch. When a spacing wheel is used, it is helpful to employ a straightedge or cardboard template to keep the wheel on the guide line. The wheel should be placed into position carefully so that one prong coincides with a definite spot such as an angle formed by the guide lines, then run forward along the line with enough pressure to mark the stitches clearly.

One may also mark for each stitch along the guide line with

the aid of a ruler and some convenient pointed tool. A pair of dividers may be used for this method.

After the marks for the stitches have been made, one must punch the holes for the thread. To do this, one may use an awl, a coarse needle inserted into a pin vise, or a sewing machine. When a sewing machine is used, the thread should be removed and a heavy needle placed in the machine. Turn the wheel of the machine by hand and guide the leather so that the needle punctures the holes in the right places along the line. Put a piece of paper between the leather and the machine to prevent the feed bar from scratching the under surface of the article. It is possible to pierce quite heavy layers of leather with a sewing machine needle if the work is done slowly and carefully.

The stitch regulator may be set on a sewing machine which may then be used to mark and punch the holes in a single operation. However, the thickness of the material has a decided effect upon the stitch regulator of the machine. It is very important to remember that, though the regulator is set for stitches of a fixed length, the stitches will be shorter where the material is heavy and longer where it is thinner. Two layers of leather will have stitches of a different size than one layer unless adjustments are made on the machine.

It may be possible to sew the leather on the machine, though this depends upon the weight of the machine and the thickness of the leather. Sometimes the needle must be lowered a bit in order that the stitches may be formed completely. If the wheel is turned by hand rather than by motor, the stitching will be more regular since any slight variation in the thickness of the leather affects the action of the feed bar when the machine runs at normal speed.

Saddle Stitching. One of the most satisfactory methods of

hand stitching is saddle stitching. Two needles are used alternately to produce this effective stitch. Thread two needles, and start both threads from between the layers of leather with one thread emerging from one side of the seam and the other from the same hole but on the other side of the seam. Do this at any convenient point along the line to be stitched. Tie the short ends of the two threads together allowing enough length to permit rethreading into a needle when the stitching has been completed. Saddle stitching employs a running stitch, each needle going through the entire thickness of the seam—through the same holes—but from opposite sides. After each stitch has been made, the threads should be given a tug to tighten the stitch. Though it is as ungraceful as 'cello playing, if one holds the leather between the knees while stitching, better work can be done. The sewing should appear exactly the same on both sides. After the stitching has been completed, untie the short ends left at the beginning, re-thread into the needles, and run them down between the layers of leather to the inside of the article. Fasten the ends with a bit of glue if necessary.

An effect similar to that of saddle stitching may be obtained by using but one needle and thread in a single running stitch around all seams. When this is finished, the work is reversed and the stitches filled in on a second time around. It is not possible to keep these stitches as tight and as even as with true saddle stitching, but it is a useful method where strength is not a prime factor.

Back stitch. Though the back stitch does not appear the same on both sides of the leather, either side has a decorative effect. From the top, the back stitch resembles saddle stitching whereas the reverse side appears as a stem or outline stitch.

As for all hand stitching on leather, the holes should be marked and punched before the sewing begins. Start the thread

QUILTED SUÈDE BOX BAG

with adjustable shoulder strap.
Hand stitched construction over
a heavy cardboard box. Slanting shoulders are reinforced
with heavy buckram. A dowel
rod, split and suède covered,
forms the rigid top. Snap fastener closing.

THOMAS

from between the seams, bringing it through one of the holes on
the top surface. Take one stitch all the way through the leather at
the hole to the *right* of the starting point. For the next stitch, bring
the needle up from the back through the hole to the *left* of the starting point. The third stitch will be down through the first hole used,
and the fourth will be to the left of the hole to the left of the
starting point. Proceed in this manner until the entire seam is sewed.
Tuck the ends of the thread out of sight between the layers of
leather. If one wishes to have the decorative cablelike stitch on the
top surface of the leather, the sewing must be done from the reverse side of the work; or work from left to right, skipping one hole

[219]

to the right, coming up through it for the next stitch exactly as one might embroider stem stitch.

Two Thread, One Needle Stitch. This is a fine, decorative stitch which may be done easily and quickly. It is especially suitable where rows of heavy stitching are used for decoration only.

A heavy thread, which need not be particularly strong, is used on the top surface of the leather. The under thread should be lighter in weight but as strong as possible. It is not necessary to take the heavy thread from the spool. Secure the free end of the top thread at the starting point by putting it through the hole in the top layer of leather and gluing it beween layers. Hold the long length or the spool to one side and out of the way, but keep it on top of the leather. Thread the lighter, stronger thread into a needle. Fasten the end of the thread between the leather layers at the same point at which the heavy thread was fastened. Bring the needle up through the hole to the top surface. With the left hand, hold the heavy thread either just above or just below the line of holes punched in the leather. Whether the thread is held above or below does not matter, but one must be consistent throughout the stitching process. Bring the needle over the heavy thread and insert it back through the same hole. Pull on the working thread gently until the top thread has been pulled down half way through the thickness of the leather. Repeat in the next hole to the left. Two thread sewing is quick and effective and permits many decorative variations.

HELPFUL SUGGESTIONS FOR HAND STITCHING

Always use a needle that is coarse enough to open the hole for the thread used. When too light a needle is used, the thread will bulk up at the eye of the needle and sewing will be extremely arduous. Added to this is the danger that the thread will fray and break before the sewing is completed.

A pin vise set with a needle as coarse, or slightly more coarse, than the needle being used for the sewing will be found useful for enlarging holes at difficult points in the leather. Pliers may be used to help pull the needle through the leather if one finds this hard to do with the fingers.

Kinks and fuzziness can be prevented if the thread is waxed by pulling over beeswax.

When stitching a single thickness of leather, one should try to have the thread long enough to more than finish the length of stitching. This is necessary, because the only way that one can secure short ends on such a piece of work is to wrap them over and under previous stitches on the wrong side of leather.

For saddle stitching, use threads of unequal length in order to avoid having to fasten both ends at the same place. It is simplest to let the thread ends dangle until all of the stitching is finished, then to re-thread each end into a needle and insert it into a seam.

Sometimes it is most expedient to start sewing in the middle of a seam. This is especially true when gussets are being sewn into position. When doing this, start with a thread twice as long as is convenient to use. Tie it in place loosely, with half of the thread left dangling to be used up in stitching from the other side of the starting point. This procedure will do away with having to fasten more than the minimum of thread ends.

In the construction of more complex articles, it is often difficult to sew the last seam since the almost completed article permits little freedom of movement. Gussets often present such a problem. It is sometimes helpful to sew the last gusset into place in a piecemeal manner. Start at the center bottom and sew up about

one inch on one side, then an inch on the other side. Work this way—from one side to the other—until the sewing is finished.

When assembling a billfold or other article made up of two pieces of unequal length, glue the ends together so that the edges coincide. Stitch from *near* one corner to where the leather will fold when the article is in use. Continue the stitching on the outside layer only for about one-half inch, then sew through both layers again.

Buckles, Fasteners, and Buttons

Because metal and leather may be combined harmoniously, commercial buttons and buckles may often be used on hand-worked articles. These should be selected with thoughtful regard to the design, the character of the metal, and the scale of the object. Wooden buttons and buckles are equally suitable in texture for use with leather. The illustrations in this chapter show examples of buckles made entirely or partly of leather. When it is not possible to find a pleasing manufactured buckle for belt or purse closing, one must be made. The examples shown in the photographs should give the interested craftsman ideas for similar fastenings.

Some purses and cases may be closed successfully by tucking flaps under straps or into pockets which have been planned as part of the structural design.

Snap fasteners furnish still another form of closure. Craft dealers supply the necessary parts and the setting tools. A setting outfit includes a pair of anvils and a machine hammer. The snap buttons are made up of four pieces: cap, cap rivet, spring, and spring rivet. The anvils fit the opening in the base of the rivets which are inserted from the under surface of the leather. The machine ham-

LEATHER BUTTONS AND DECORATIVE UNITS

Top row shows reverse of buttons to demonstrate fastening methods; rolled buttons have bent wire backbones; cylindrical buttons have dowel rod centers.

SUÈDE LEATHER BELTS

Top belt closed with button and button hole. Lower belt fastened with salvaged buckle which was re-covered. Decorative units are applied with paper fasteners.

THOMAS

mer has one end to fit over the spring, the other or concave surface to cover the cap or button top.

To attach a snap button, punch a hole large enough to accommodate the cap rivet where the button is to be. This will usually be on the flap of the object. Fold the flap down into position, and mark the place where the spring, or bottom, is to be placed. Punch a hole at this point large enough to insert the spring rivet. These holes should be the exact size needed or a bit smaller. They can be stretched with a bodkin or similar object, but too large a hole allows the fastener to slip out of place. Insert the cap rivet on top of the large anvil. Place the button cap on the eyelet. Place the large, concave end of the hammer on the button cap. With a good square blow, strike the top of the machine hammer with a mallet until the rivet has spread and secured the button. One good blow is usually enough. Too much force is apt to mar the button surface.

The spring portion of the fastener is set in the same way. Use the small anvil under the spring rivet which has been inserted through the leather from the wrong side. Place the spring on top of it, then the small end of the hammer on top of the spring. Strike with a mallet as before.

For concealed fasteners of the snap type, those available in notion departments for heavy material may be used. It is necessary, when using these, to punch holes in the leather with an awl or coarse needle for each of the cap prongs since too much resistance will be offered unless this is done.

The familiar zipper makes a good, secure closing for leather articles. These closings may often be sewed into the leather with a sewing machine. However, when the leather is heavy, or where the position of the zipper makes a machine out of the question, the zipper must be sewed into the article by hand.

MEXICAN INDIAN LEATHER WORK

Lunch bag, money belt, harness belt. These are interesting examples of decoration by means of lacing, stamping, eyelets, and buckles.

Reinforcement Materials

Tooling leather is usually heavy enough to hold its shape very well. This is particularly true if the article is lined as it ordinarily would be. Box type bags or articles made of lightweight leather will probably need more body than the leather provides. Soft suèdes almost always need some reinforcing material.

Much can be learned about construction if one rips open a discarded purse which was made commercially. Perhaps not all the materials found in the manufactured article are readily available, but if one considers the purpose and characteristics of the reinforcements used, satisfactory substitutes can be found.

For foundations of varying degrees of rigidity, the following materials are good: *fiber-board* is available in red, brown, or black and has a smooth surface. It is made in a number of gauges from number 14, the heavy, to number 20, the lightest, and those in between have their particular uses depending upon the need of the craftsman. Fiber-board is tough without being brittle.

Millboard is somewhat brittle, a mottled gray color, and most useful in the thinnest gauge. *Strawboard* is yellow, soft, lightweight, and easy to cut and work. *Wood pulpboards* are white, soft, and brittle. The light weights are very suitable for interior reinforcements. These various boards are often found in the home in the form of tablet backs, cartons, laundered-shirt inserts, and suit boxes.

Occasionally paper is heavy enough to be used in reinforcement. Unglazed paper is easier to work with and is less apt to "rattle" when the article is in use. *Kraft paper* is especially good because of its strength. It is a brown wrapping paper. *Blotting paper* has absolutely no "rattle" and is thick enough to add to the quality of feel of thin leather. It should be pasted to cloth to keep it from breaking. *Felt paper* is constantly used by manufacturers. It is very soft, flexible, and of dark gray color. Only occasionally does some of this material find its way into the home. Sometimes mail order houses ship fragile objects wrapped in a soft fiber sheeting of this type. If one must, one may substitute sheet wadding for this material.

Among the fabrics used are all grades of buckram, crinoline, linen, drill, and muslin. For padding qualities as well as reinforcement, one might use a flannelette or the heavier swansdown which is napped on but one side. Fabric is used where punching or stitching might weaken the leather, or where the leather needs added weight and is to be used in soft folds. Paper padding, in such an instance, cannot be used. For heavy padding, cotton or wool batts are suitable.

Lining Materials

The purpose of the object as well as the material used in its construction will dictate the type of lining material to be used. The

[228]

best wearing materials are leathers. Among those suitable for linings are kidskins, sheepskins, and suède. Skiver, the thinnest available lining, is too thin to add any strength or to withstand much strain. However, it adds to the appearance of an article to a degree equal to that of other leather. Whether or not it should be used will best be decided by the nature of the object.

Many fabrics are suitable for lining. Among these are silk, rayon, velvet, and cottons. Many notion departments carry made-up linings, complete with pockets and often with zippers. One can use such linings if the correct size is purchased before the article is made.

Assembling

Except in severely tailored purses and boxes, the lining, padding, and reinforcements are seldom fastened solidly to the outer leather. It is usually best to tack the padding to a paper or cloth reinforcement with a bit of glue. Turn the edges of the lining over the paper shell to cover the padding and to help secure it. Use glue along the edges to hold the padding, lining, and reinforcement in place.

If leather that is being used for a pouch bag seems too soft to hold its shape well, it is wise to use a firm cloth reinforcement. The leather and the cloth should be cut at the same time and to the same size. Sew the fabric and leather together using "in seams" for this purpose. Turn right side out and line with an attractive lining that corresponds to the shape and size of the bag. Whenever possible, stitch along the top edge of the lining and leather to fasten the two together. This is best done by hand. If this is not possible, glue may be used. Paste is not strong enough to fasten a lining into position and should never be used. Rubber cement may be substituted for glue.

Where the leather is not excessively heavy, a thin leather piping, corded perhaps, is attractive and will add to the body of a bag. Piping, which is of lightweight leather, is added between the seams of the article. It may be stitched from the inside or the outside whichever method is practical. If the piping leather is very thin and is being stitched *over* the edge seam, the edges of the piping should be folded under. Piping used this way resembles a binding.

It might be useful and informative to study the construction of a commercially tailored bag which was fairly firm to the touch. From the inside out, these are the layers of material which made up the purse that was taken apart:

1. The silk lining, complete with small pockets for mirror, comb, coin purse, and other feminine accouterments. The top edges of the pockets were piped with leather. Zippers were used on some pockets.

2. A layer of cheesecloth pasted to a piece of heavy paper. The cheesecloth was used to keep the paper from splitting. The flaps had added cardboard stiffeners.

3. Sheet wadding, cut slightly smaller than the rest of the material.

4. The outside case of leather.

Very often, fastening gussets into place becomes a difficult sewing problem. It may help to dampen and fold the gusset into its final shape before attempting to sew it into place. Begin the sewing at the center bottom of the gusset at all times. Work alternately from side to side. Before attempting to sew a gusset to the outside leather, the edges of both should be skived. When properly thinned down, the edges can be glued together for punching, for lacing, or sewing. If bits of glue are not sufficient to hold the gusset into place, it may be tied into position with soft thread such as darning cotton. These tacking threads may be removed as the sewing progresses.

The corners of rectangular gussets should always be rounded somewhat. If a gusset is lined with some reinforcing material, cut a piece from that material wherever the gusset must fold.

Bulldog clips and flat wire paper clips are useful for holding glued edges in place while they dry. One should always protect the leather with pieces of firm paper between it and the clips. If the gusset and the main body of the purse cannot be marked and punched for stitching at the same time, one must be very sure that the number of holes and the distance between them correspond on each piece. Allow some extra length for any gusset that goes around a corner.

And always, always keep the hands clean while working.

Final Surface Care

All smooth leathers will benefit from a final cleansing with saddle soap. Use very little water when doing this cleaning. Polish the leather afterwards with a soft cloth or with the palm of one's hand. If a harder surface is desired, use any of the waxes or creams mentioned previously in this chapter. When using a paste wax, put a small quantity of it *inside* several layers of soft cloth to apply it. Use the wax sparingly. It will produce a surface on the leather that will feel fine to the touch. Excess wax which may be left in depressed areas on the leather surface turns white and is difficult to remove. Wax carefully.

Suède may be resurfaced with a medium fine sandpaper. This must be done carefully. A fresh appearance may also be given a

FABRIC AND SUÈDE LEATHER COMBINATIONS

Pouch Bag: rigid cardboard and buckram base covered with suède and topped with plaid wool reinforced with canvas. Handles of suède-covered cable cord secured by a pewter ring slide. Envelope Bag: wool body decorated with suède leather appliqué. Additional color units added with wool embroidery. The design was adapted from Mayan stone carving.

suède leather by rubbing its surface with a scrap of the same leather.

Any fine piece of leather which has been carefully worked into a beautiful and useful article should be worthy of good care. The surface, if properly groomed, will resist dirt and soiling for longer periods. It will remain lustrous and pliable. The appearance and the "feel" of a well kept piece of good leather amply repay one for the small amount of effort that must be expended to protect its surface.

Chapter XI

Paint and Wood

To some people home is where they hang their hats. A few moments of thought given to this state of affairs will uncover several easily changed contributing factors. Usually, when a home, or better a house, no longer acts as a central living unit, it is not because the physical setup is lacking. Palatable meals may still be set on the dining room table every day, inner spring mattresses may still lure one to rest at night, but the house often has an unattractive personality. It may be drab, colorless, and unimaginative. It is well to determine whether or not the rooms are arranged interestingly, or if the appointments in the house are things which have become contemptible through prolonged familiarity.

Current magazines offer many suggestions for redecorating a single room or an entire house. Modern commercial advertising constantly puts new ideas and plans before the public, most of whom spend at least part of their day in a home, whether it be a mansion, a bungalow, or a rented room. Sometimes the plans or suggestions as outlined in the articles involve costly refurnishing or remodeling. If one can afford to do so, this is unquestionably one of the most satisfying ways of injecting new life into the commonplace.

Perhaps a better understanding of the problem of making a house take on the personality of a home might be brought about by comparing the house to the wardrobe. Small things, cleverly and tastefully selected in the way of accessories may brighten a dull wardrobe or mark it as individual. In just the same way can small accessories, well selected and used in a home, add to its atmosphere. One might call these little things the grace notes of a harmonious home. We do not mean to suggest that one clutter up his home with knickknacks of heterogeneous selection, but we do wish to impress him with the fact that a few well chosen accessories will go a long way toward brightening a room.

Many small accessories may be made at home after the housework is done. And many such accessories will not only add sparkle to the house but may be used for very acceptable Christmas or birthday gifts. Some of the articles suggested later in this section are things for which one cannot even find duplicates in our larger stores. Most of them can be made at a very low cost and with a minimum of effort and will repay the individual who creates them.

After reading through the directions which follow, it may seem to the reader that we have selected a rather unrelated group of craft problems. This is true to a certain extent, but careful planning will coördinate articles made into a harmoniously related group. There are among these articles things which may be used not only decoratively but also in the utilitarian sense.

In planning anything which is to find a useful place in the house, it is first necessary to consider the relation of the article to the things with which it is to be combined. This involves consideration of all of the material on design and its principles as presented in the first section of the book. Not only should the principles apply to the object itself but also to the object as seen in relation with all of the other things it may be used with, i.e., the room decorative scheme, the furnishings, the textures, and the other accessories of the room. It should also reflect the personalities of the persons using the room, since it is to be a measuring stick of their tastes.

Plates and Bowls

One of the very easiest items to make and one which is very attractive and useful may serve as a welcome first lesson. We give this suggestion at the beginning of this section since it concerns an article which is very quickly completed. It is a plain wooden salad bowl, painted on the outside with some bright color—blue, or red, for instance. How may it be used? Fill it with fruit and use it for a centerpiece on an informal table. Use it for salad or popcorn. A large salad bowl may be accompanied by half a dozen individual bowls to add gay spots of color to an otherwise ordinary table. The large bowl might be painted blue, and the smaller bowls various other bright harmonizing colors. Remember, the bowls are by nature informal, so your colors may be informal as well.

Bowls for this purpose may be purchased at the five-and-ten-cent store. If the outer surfaces have been waxed—they usually are—the wax must be removed completely with sandpaper before the paint is applied or the paint remains tacky indefinitely. Oil paint or enamel may be used to put the color on the bowl. The paint may be put on with an inch-wide paint brush and should be so applied as to keep the surface free from brush strokes. If one chooses to use enamel, there will be directions for its use on the can in which it comes. Two coats should be sufficient to cover the the surface well. After the first coat is thoroughly dry, sand it lightly with number 4/o sandpaper or number 3/o steel wool before applying the second coat of paint. When the final layer of paint is dry, wax

PAINTED BOWLS
by Kate Anderson

Decorative when empty; delightful for serving dry food.

both the inside and the outside of the bowl with either a paste or liquid wax. This will protect the painted surface.

If one wishes, and if one has faith in his ability, one might paint a simple border design in contrasting colors around the upper edge of the bowl. This should be done with a small water color or oil paint brush after the surface of the bowl has been painted, but before the bowl has been waxed. Such a design may be very simple, a scalloped edge with a dot between each scallop, for instance. It will add a note of distinction to the bowl if carefully drawn and painted.

Sometimes a design placed on the inside of the wooden bowl is more effective than a border design. This is particularly true if the bowl is a shallow one where the outer edges curve under so as to obscure any outer decoration. However, if a design is to be placed in the center, the bowl must be used either as a purely decorative object or as a container for dry foods—nuts, fruits, popcorn, etc.—since one must be able to clean it by wiping with a damp cloth

RUSSIAN BOWLS AND BOX

Native designs from the far flung reaches of the earth are worthy of being added to one's collection.

THOMAS

only. When planning a design for the center of the bowl, several things must be considered. The design is to be applied to a curved surface so the measurements should be planned for the curve rather than just from side to side. And since the design is to conform to a circular form, it is essential that it be well related to the structure. Probably a design based on a circle would be most successful for this problem. After the design has been planned on paper, its various units may be cut out to be used as patterns. This makes transferring the design to the bowl much simpler, in as much as it is difficult to adjust the complete paper design to the inner curve. The separate pattern units may be placed in position in the bowl and then outlined with a pencil. Of course before this is done, it is necessary to remove any wax surface that may have been on the bowl when purchased.

In summing up the types of designs suited to the decoration of a bowl one finds that there are: a border on either the outside or the inside of a bowl, the inner circular motif, and, if desired, an

MEXICAN PLATE

*Another good design to adapt
to one's own needs.*

THOMAS

allover design applied to either the outside or the inside of the bowl.

For finishing the inside of the bowl follow the directions as given above for the outside, namely, shellacking and waxing.

Another possibility for useful decorative objects may be found in wooden plates which make serviceable serving trays. These plates may be stood on edge to form a background in a grouping of several related objects. A decorative arrangement such as this will create an interesting note in a dining room or kitchen, according to the type of design used on the plate. The wood itself suggests an informal setting and should be combined with like objects and be used in a room of the same spirit.

These wooden plates cannot be as easily purchased ready-made as the bowls. For this reason, it may be necessary that they

WOODEN PLATE
by Ardis Swanson

The repetition, with variations, of the small scallop motif unifies the design.

Photograph by Helen Ludwig.

be made by someone having access to a lathe. Any town which has a carpenter will also have a lathe—sometimes a high school boy who can use school equipment may be found to turn out one or several plates.

Since it may be impossible to purchase these plates, it is necessary to furnish a pattern to the carpenter. The most usable designs follow two main types. The first is modeled after a standard dinner plate but may be made to almost any dimension. It has a rim proportioned to the size of the whole plate. If one takes the measurements of a dinner plate of pleasing design and increases or decreases the relative measurements of the flat inner portion and the rim according to the same ratio, it may serve as a standard for the wooden plate. The second design and one particularly useful for serving is without a rim. It is a flat plate with the outer edge

WOODEN PLATE

by Barbara Warren

A stylized figure such as this is far more effective than one weakened by sentimentality.

Photograph by Helen Ludwig.

turned up slightly to give depth to the plate. It is somewhat easier to plan a design for this type of plate since one need not consider the rim as a limiting factor. The design may be planned in much the same way as was the design for the inner surface of the wooden bowl.

When planning the design for the plate first mentioned, it is essential that the rim and the center be thought of as related to one another. A border design following the rim with the center left plain is one successful method. Another reverses this process and puts a design in the center with the rim left plain or painted a solid color. A third treatment involves the decoration of both the center and the border. If this is done, it should be remembered that either the center or the border should receive the most emphasis and that the other should complement the dominant part of the design.

WOODEN PLATE
by Marian Ogard

Simplicity is the keynote of this distinctive design.

Photograph by Helen Ludwig.

The beauty of the wood should play a prominent part in the finished product and it is not usually advisable to cover completely the center surface of these plates with paint. Frequently the grain contributes a great deal to the character of the design, and certainly the inherent color of the wood is often so beautiful as to warrant preservation. A simple design which makes use of these qualities is in the best taste and will give the most satisfactory results. Occasionally imperfections in the wood such as knots or too dark areas occur. Sometimes they may be incorporated into the design, but often such flaws make it necessary to cover the wood completely with paint.

After the design has been painted on, these plates are finished in the same way as the wooden bowls, with shellac and wax. However, since they come from the carpenter without any protective

SECTIONAL CANDLE HOLDER

The richly gay decoration and the extremely simple forms unite to produce an exceptionally attractive centerpiece of an informal character. The sectional plan permits a variety of arrangements.

finish having been applied, it is necessary that they be thoroughly smoothed with sandpaper and given a single coat of white shellac before the design is put on. This acts as a filler to close the pores of the wood. It also protects the raw wood from becoming soiled with handling. When the shellac has thoroughly dried, sand it lightly and just enough to remove the shine. Oil paint or enamel is suggested for the painting. If oil paint is used, one should thin it with turpentine only enough to facilitate handling. If it is thinned too much, it is apt to run along the grain of the wood and thus obscure the design.

Tea Tiles

Another wooden craft article for which materials are more easily obtained is a tile for use under hot dishes, or as a decorative note in itself. It is a small square of wood set up on fat round little legs made of wooden kindergarten beads. A simple but effective design may be applied to the colored surface, then finished with a spar varnish, which is heatproof as well as waterproof. One of the nicest features of this tile is the low cost of the materials necessary for its making, and if more than one tile is made, each one costs proportionately less, since some of the needed materials can be used over and over again. The supplies that one will need are:

One piece of *unwarped* pine, bass, or similar wood. A good size for most uses is three-quarters inch thick by six and one-half inches square. This can be obtained at the local lumber yard, cut to size for about ten cents. The cost is usually lower on quantity orders. Four round wooden kindergarten beads (purchased at five-and-ten-cent store or a store handling school supplies, usually listed in phone directories under the heading of book and stationery stores).

Sandpaper, medium and very fine, four flat-headed nails (shingle nails) long enough to fasten the beads to the tile. Water color paints of the ordinary school box variety, and a small jar of white tempera paint are used. White poster paint is a good substitute for the tempera. Oil paints may be used instead of the water colors. If oil paints are preferred, then the technique given for painting wooden bowls should be followed. Use a watercolor brush big enough to hold paint well, but be sure it points up for the small areas and lines. Spar varnish is used as a finish. Ordinary var-

TEA TILE

by Dorinda Johnson

An entertaining design of great simplicity.

Photograph by Helen Ludwig.

nish is not practical for this purpose. The varnish is most easily applied with a brush about one inch wide.

To make the tile, the wooden block should be sandpapered to a smooth finish, rounding all edges and corners slightly. The desirable character of the wood itself is lost if the corners are rounded too much. A certain severity of line is preferable to a soft, curved edge. When sanding the flat surfaces of the wood, be careful to work with, rather than against, the grain.

If desired, the wood may next be colored. This coloring process is done by mixing clear water color paint and water to the desired value and intensity. Be sure to mix an ample amount so as not to run short of paint while working. Paint all surfaces of the block as quickly as possible with a fairly large brush. If the color

[245]

does not appear dark enough, apply a second or even a third coat after the first coat is almost dry. Another method of coloring the wood is by the use of leather or batik dyes. A dye bath of the desired color and in a quantity sufficient to permit completely submerging the wood is necessary. In order to prevent warping the wooden block, the dye must be strong enough to dye the wood to the right value and intensity instantly. The strength of the dye may be easily tested with small scraps of the same wood as that being used for the tile. After the tile has been dipped into the dye bath, it should be stood up on end to drain and dry. Do not force the drying process by placing in a warm place, for that often causes the wood to warp and crack.

When the paint or dye has dried into the wood, trace the design, planned carefully, onto the top surface. If an error is made at this point, the entire surface may have to be resanded, since the traced lines cannot be erased.

Prepare the colors one desires to use for painting the design by mixing transparent water color with some of the white tempera or poster paint. The tempera will give body to the paint and will prevent its running out of the boundaries of the design and along the grain of the wood. It also gives the paint an opaque quality which enables one to apply one color directly on top of another with satisfactory results. Varnish will change the appearance of the colors slightly. In order to prevent disappointment, it is wise to varnish over trial patches of color. These need not be painted on wood; the trial colors mixed and tried on paper will serve the purpose well. Varnish has a yellow cast, even when the most transparent kind is used, so that either the hue or intensity of the colors is changed in almost every case.

Paint the design. If the design calls for black in some of its areas, use the plain black water color without the addition of white. Use water sparingly. The paint should be just liquid enough to cover the surface of the wood easily without becoming caked. It may be necessary to apply more than one coat of paint to some parts of the design.

After the design has been painted onto the tile surface and around the edges if desired, the tile is ready to have the legs attached. Nail one round wooden bead onto each of the corners of the underside of the tile. Measuring one-half inch in from each corner on the diagonal has proved satisfactory. Sometimes the wooden beads come in a variety of shapes. The cylindrical and square beads can also be used for legs if the design is in character with that form.

The final step in the process is that of varnishing the tile to preserve the design and to make it heat resistant. Apply the spar varnish in two or three successive thin coats, allowing the varnish to dry between applications.

The design itself should be carefully considered. If it is kept very simple and conventionalized, or geometric, it will be more attractive and in far better taste than if a realistic basket of flowers or a Scotty dog is used for the decorative motif. Many Swedish designs are particularly appropriate for this practical, decorative article.

Painted Boxes

Boxes, too, may be decorated. Many common commodities come packed in wooden boxes that lend themselves to this treatment. To mention just a few: cigar boxes that have mitered corners; cheese boxes, the round as well as the square; dried fruit boxes, stationery, chalk, and many others. Besides these packing boxes, it

RECLAIMED CIGAR BOX

A spirited design, five wooden beads (four were used for legs), and a little time.

is possible to purchase very attractive wooden boxes for only a few cents at ten-cent stores and book and stationery stores.

The uses for these decorative boxes are unlimited. The small ones are fine for cigarettes, pins, costume jewelry, sewing supplies, and a dozen other things. The larger boxes, the round cheese box for instance, afford convenient storage space for hats, knitting or sewing, or toys. Give a box to any member of the household and he will find a use for it. Either the oil paint or water color processes may be used to finish the boxes. The surfaces should be prepared carefully, of course, before any process is employed. Boxes have so many possibilities for decorative treatment that every box designed offers at least two more ideas for other boxes. There is the top cover, perhaps the most obvious choice for decoration. Except that it may be rectilinear rather than round, it lends itself to exactly the same variety of treatments suggested for plates. The sides of the box might be the center of attention, or the outside of the box may be painted a beautiful, rich color that harmonizes well with the sur-

WOODEN BOX FROM POLAND

Just border designs were used. Similar ones might be adapted to wall hangings, draperies, or place mats.

THOMAS

roundings, and then an interesting design placed inside the top cover, to be enjoyed every time the box is opened.

After one has experimented on simple objects as have been mentioned, it is hardly safe to look at the panels of a cupboard door or breakfast nook windows without being stimulated to action. Utmost care must be taken when undertaking the enrichment of anything so permanent as furniture or architectural details of a room. Every part of the room must be considered in relation to the planned design. Are the draperies of such nature that another design can be added without competing with them? Is the furniture simple enough? Is the spirit of the room itself of informal nature? Other suggestions are beside the point, since anyone who has become interested in this craft will find many opportunities to make use of it. Great is the satisfaction to any one who has become proficient in this process when comparing it with the results obtained by the frequent misuse of commercial transfers or decalcomanias of poor design.

MEXICAN BOX

Boxes such as this are a valuable aid when learning space division and shape harmony.

THOMAS

The beautiful texture of wood has a great appeal to many people, and if one belongs to this group he may hesitate to superimpose any design motif upon the natural grain of the wood. Such a person might investigate the possibilities of several products manufactured by General Finishes, Inc., 111 South Second St., Minneapolis 1, Minnesota.

Chapter XII

Fanciful Fabrics

IT IS INTERESTING TO ENUMERATE THE VARIOUS USES OF TEXTILES in the room in which one ordinarily spends the evening. The upholstery upon the chairs, the rug, the draperies, and the glass curtains, wall hangings, table scarves, pillows—to mention the most obvious. These will demonstrate to one how important fabrics are in the home, and the close relationship they bear to the other furnishings of the room. Because of this widespread use of textiles in the average home, a wider scope for the application of design presents itself. The use of fabrics is one of the most important items in the decoration of one's home, owing to the fact that they are used in such large areas, and play such an important role in determining the complete color scheme and the spirit or personality of any room.

Not all the fabrics in a room lend themselves to home crafts. For instance, it would hardly be practicable to attempt to design a large piece of upholstery or room-size rugs. On the other hand, hooked rugs of a small scatter size, or a needle-point chair seat or footstool cover, or a wall hanging, among other things, are very feasible. The article which is least familiar to the average person and which one seldom finds used in homes, is the wall hanging. This may be used not only as a substitute for the ordinary framed picture, but as a decoration is often far more suited to the other

BLOCK-PRINTED DRAPERIES

(*Courtesy of the Milwaukee WPA Handicraft Project.*)

The well proportioned stripes furnish a splendid complement for the bold motif.

BLOCK-PRINTED SCREEN

(*Courtesy of the Milwaukee WPA Handicraft Project.*)

Stenciled material would be equally satisfactory for this purpose.

BLOCK-PRINTED MATERIAL

(Courtesy of the Milwaukee WPA Handicraft Project.)

Only two small blocks are necessary for this feminine pattern—a single flower and a length of stem bearing eight leaves.

textures used in the room. Wall hangings frequently complement the spirit of the room more adequately than does a picture, since the wall hanging is usually designed for a particular area in a given room. There are a number of techniques adaptable to wall hangings which range from the very simple to the intricate.

Old Art into New

Block printing is one of the more simple techniques and has innumerable uses. It can be used expediently for making greeting cards, book plates, table covers, and draperies as well as attractive wall hangings. Block-printed material, either paper or cloth and designed to suit one's fancy, can be used for making book covers, pages of books, wrapping paper, covering for boxes, and for unusual bags or purses. The possibilities are limited only by one's ingenuity.

As a rule materials for block printing are not too difficult to assemble. The linoleum may be obtained in two forms: mounted blocks, or battleship linoleum which is used for floor coverings. The blocks are carried by art supply shops; the battleship linoleum in floor-covering departments of most furnishing stores. It is often possible to buy remnants or scrap pieces.

There are tools especially manufactured for this craft consisting of V- or U-shaped gouges; or razor blades and pen knives may be used. The best printing medium is regular printer's ink, though oil paint may be used. For cleaning up and protecting the work table, one needs plenty of old newspaper, rags, and turpentine. Kerosene is effective for cleaning off the printing blocks, rollers, and glass if turpentine is not handy. Never use the kerosene as a thinner for the ink or paint. A piece of glass or a smooth stone slab is necessary for rolling out the ink or paint. A rubber or composition roller, called a brayer, is used to apply the ink to the cut linoleum block. A photographer's squeegee roller works well on small blocks. This is a small rubber-covered roller which can be purchased for about twenty-five cents, though for long usage, gelatine rollers of a six-inch length are preferable. The latter must be hung up when not in use as they have a tendency to flatten, especially in warm weather.

If cloth is used to print upon, it should not be of too coarse a texture, because ink will remain only on the upper threads, destroying the effect of the design. Percale, pongee, linen, or fabrics having similar textures are suitable.

Careful, even painstaking, attention should be given to the

BLOCK-PRINTED MATERIAL
(*Courtesy of the Milwaukee WPA Handicraft Project.*)

Strong rhythmic movement and value contrast are responsible for the spirit this design displays.

preparation of the block for printing. If the linoleum has a hard, waxy surface, sandpaper this off carefully with fine sandpaper. If desired, the sanded surface may be painted with white poster paint or flat white oil paint to facilitate tracing the design. Commercially mounted blocks frequently come with a white surface.

Trace the design very accurately upon the block. Graphite paper underneath the design is an expedient method; or the back of the design may be blackened with a soft pencil. *Precaution:* If the design depends upon a certain direction of line, either to the right or to the left, it will have to be traced in reverse upon the block. This applies to lettering especially. It is provoking, to say the least, to find words on greeting cards turned backwards.

Using a simple motif over and over in simple repeat patterns gives attractive results. If this is desired, measure the parts of the

CUTTING A LINOLEUM BLOCK

(Courtesy of the Milwaukee WPA Handicraft Project.)

An area is outlined with a V-shaped groove before being gouged out.

motif that serve as connecting units very carefully in order that they may match when used in this manner.

Slow, exact cutting of the block pays dividends later. Before making a single nick in the surface of the linoleum learn the principle that all parts to be printed are left the original height of the linoleum, unprinted areas are dug out or cut away.

In general there are three main techniques used in cutting:

1. OUTLINING the entire design with a V-shaped gouge or a razor blade. When using the razor blade cut around the design, holding the blade at an angle slanting away from the part of the design to be printed. This is to prevent undercutting. Then cut a line all around the design, holding the razor blade slanting toward the printing surface of the design. This cuts a V-shaped groove all around the design. A block cut in this manner is called a white-line block; when printed, the design appears in lines only.

[256]

A COMPLETELY CUT
BLOCK

*(Courtesy of the Milwaukee
WPA Handicraft Project.)*

*Each unit is broader at its
base than at its printing surface.*

2. ROUTING. Proceed as for outlining; then, with a U-shaped gouge or pen knife, dig out all areas not to be printed.

3. DETAILING. This is a combination of methods 1 and 2. By using the tools in various ways to show the direction of the stroke of the cuts and varying the width of the cuts, very interesting results may be obtained. Analysis of blocks cut by others, close observation of prints made from blocks, and actual experimentation will develop skill in cutting blocks this more elaborate way.

There are a few pitfalls one may avoid if the following rules are kept firmly in mind:

1. Wide spaces are cut deep. This prevents paper or cloth from picking up excess ink that may have gotten on the background areas.

[257]

2. Narrow spaces are cut shallow.

3. Deep vertical cuts are bad, undercuts are worse. Fragments of the linoleum break off, leaving ragged printing edges.

4. Square off the outside edges of the block with a vertical cut, not slanting either in or out. The block is more easily keyed into its proper position for printing if this rule is observed.

About the time enough cutting has been done on the block to let one recognize the design there is a great urge to rush the task in order that a print can be made. It is wiser to take the time to test results frequently while cutting in order that one may forestall accidents. There are two popular methods: Put the block, cut surface up, under a piece of paper. Hold the paper securely, then rub the lead of a soft pencil back and forth over the block; the cut surfaces will appear white or very light gray in contrast to the raised parts. Or if brown or gray linoleum is used, the cut parts may be filled with starch or talcum powder, then the raised parts wiped off clean. A white-surfaced block may be blackened with ink if this method is to be used.

It is wise to have both the original design and the one traced on the block worked out in dark and light to be used as a cutting guide. Darken all parts to be left the original height of the linoleum.

The actual process of printing with a linoleum block is simple. All the attention given to careful preparation of the materials used will be well repaid later. The cloth or paper must be free of folds or wrinkles. Prepare the cloth or paper for printing by indicating guide lines with pencil dots (not lines) pointed off where the corners of the block are to be placed. Spread the material out

ALL READY FOR PRINTING

(Courtesy of the Milwaukee WPA Handicraft Project.)

More than one brayer is a convenience for multicolor work. Neatness and order are a necessity for all crafts.

Washable printing ink in an infinite range of shades may be obtained through the Artco Printing Ink Corporation, 1715 West Canal Street, Milwaukee 3, Wisconsin. No setting process is required, but it is recommended that the material be laundered before the ink is applied.

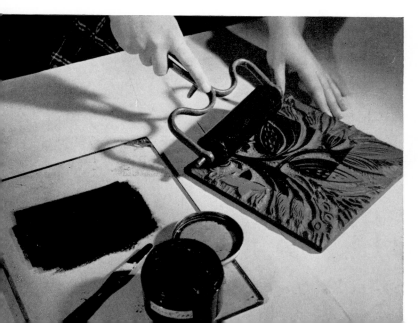

INKING THE BLOCK

(Courtesy of the Milwaukee WPA Handicraft Project.)

A squeegee roller would prove a good substitute for the professional brayer.

(*Courtesy of the Milwaukee
WPA Handicraft Project.*)

*Pounding the block with a
mallet is one of the best ways
of applying pressure.*

over an even pad of newspapers; then tack it down to a flat surface if necessary.

Printer's ink or oil paint may be used, the ink preferred. If it is necessary to thin the ink, use a reducer produced by the ink manufacturer; for the oil paint, use linseed oil or turpentine, but this should be done very cautiously. Oil also slows down the drying process. Either the ink or the oil paint should be of a tacky consistency.

Place a little of the ink (or oil paint) on the center of the piece of glass. Roll the brayer over it until the ink is nicely distributed upon the roller and the surface of the ink is velvety rather than shiny. Roll the brayer back and forth over the cut surface of the linoleum until the block is covered completely with a thin coat of the ink.

With the inked side down, place the block in position on the cloth (or paper) as indicated by the pencil dots. There are several ways of producing the pressure necessary to make a perfect im-

THE PRINTED RESULT

(Courtesy of the Milwaukee WPA Handicraft Project.)

Finger smudges or marks made by a block that slipped would mar the work beyond repair.

pression of the design upon the material to be printed. The size and nature of the problem at hand will dictate the best method. Some favorite procedures are listed.

1. Pound the block with a wooden mallet over its entire surface to transfer the ink to the cloth, or

2. If the block is small, pressing everywhere with one's thumbs is often sufficient, or

3. Have the material and pad on the floor, step on the block a number of times, facing in different directions in order to distribute the pressure evenly. The preceding methods are especially suited to printing allover patterns on large pieces of material.

4. Book plates and greeting cards may be printed by putting the padding, the paper to be printed, and an unmounted piece of linoleum on a very thin board, then on top of all of this a piece of tin, or heavy cardboard. Put all this through an old clothes wringer.

PRINTING WITH AN IRREGULAR BLOCK

(*Courtesy of the Milwaukee WPA Handicraft Project.*)

Both convenience and economy are often served by cutting the block the shape of the motif.

5. Ink the block as usual and place upon the paper. Press into place firmly. Turn the block cut side up so that the paper is uppermost. Rub over the entire surface gently with the bowl of a tablespoon. Be very careful the block does not slip at any time. Remove the block, re-ink, and print as before.

Always clean the glass, roller, and blocks thoroughly with turpentine or kerosene when through printing at any time, even though the entire process is not finished.

Block printing need not be confined to printing with one color. A separate block is needed for each color used. Until one has practiced this craft enough to gain considerable confidence, limiting oneself to a few colors or values is a wise decision. The more complicated procedure for multicolor block printing follows. Take time to think through each step before going ahead. It is worth the extra effort.

HAND PRINTED MATERIAL

(Courtesy of the Milwaukee WPA Handicraft Project.)

It is not the subject matter but the manner in which it is used that determines the success of a design.

1. Cut a master block first. The entire design outlined with a V-gouge is used for this.
2. Ink the block very thoroughly.
3. Make a print on hard-surfaced paper.
4. Place a second linoleum block, cut to match the master block, carefully upon this fresh print. Register the corner accurately. Press gently to make the paper adhere to the new block. Turn the block, paper adhering to it, upside down and rub the paper with a tablespoon to transfer the design to the linoleum.
5. Allow this block with the printed design upon it to dry before attempting to do any cutting. The ink will smudge if not dry and will cause inaccuracies.
6. Indicate upon this block all the areas to be printed in any one of the colors needed in the original design.

7. Cut the color block carefully, following the guide lines of the master block, or the cutting may be done with a fractional allowance for overlapping.

8. Prepare a new block from a fresh print of the master block for each color desired. After all have been printed, cut away all the areas of the master block not to be printed in the darkest color. Each color block should have raised areas for a single color only. Cut all other parts away.

9. In printing, start with the lightest color first, the darkest last. This last should be the master block. On the reverse side of each block, mark corresponding corners plainly to avoid turning the block accidentally and hence printing upside down.

Borders on wall hangings present their own problems. Suggestions for designing corners were made previously. A few hints for avoiding difficulties during printing follow:

A special corner block may be cut. This facilitates printing but adds to the cost of the finished product. When planning for a special corner block, care must be taken to measure the border blocks accurately to insure a perfect fit around the center unit. The border may be printed either before or after the center of the hanging has been printed.

The center area should be measured off with a row of pencil dots against which the border blocks are placed. Mark the base on the back of the block in order to avoid reversing it when laying it on the cloth. Every fraction of an inch of the border must be accounted for before printing a single unit of the border. It is probably safest to follow this procedure. Have a piece of material large enough to allow for very ample margins. Using the border blocks

BORDER DESIGN WITH SEPARATE CORNER BLOCKS

PLANNING AND PRINTING A MITERED BORDER

[265]

as units of measure, plan the placing of the blocks as accurately as
possible. Use faint pencil dots to indicate the position of each during the printing. After all has been carefully planned, start printing
in the middle of the top border. Work out from this unit to both
the right and the left until the desired amount of border has been
printed. Next, print the two top corners and continue with first
one side, then the other; finally the bottom corners and the bottom
border. The center of the wall hanging may now be printed, adjusting the inner margins for pleasing proportions. This seemingly backward procedure prevents gaps or unfortunate overlapping, because
the linoleum block simply won't stretch or shrink if the last space
to be printed and the size of the block are not the same.

When printing borders without special corner blocks, the
corners are mitered. Before printing, indicate with light pencil marks
the center square or rectangle; draw in the diagonals. Extend these
lines an equal distance beyond the corners, the distance depending
upon the width necessary to accommodate the border. Connect the

BLOCK-PRINTED MATERIAL

(Courtesy of the Milwaukee WPA Handicraft Project.)

Two blocks identical in size were printed alternately.

ends of these lines with a faint dotted pencil line. Measure the sides of the central square or rectangle thus formed and point off the exact center of each side. Lay the border block with one corner at this mark and print. Follow this procedure, printing until the corner is reached.

Fold a piece of paper of a size large enough to serve as a mask and lay the folded edge along the line extending from the center unit, pinning or tacking down the paper so that the corner about to be printed is neatly bisected, the paper protecting the part of the corner to be formed by the border not yet printed. Print the uncovered area in the same manner as before, right over the masking paper, the result being, after removal of the block and the paper, one-half of a mitered corner. Repeat this process in the other direction from the center mark. The printing is continued in this manner on the remaining three sides of the center motif. The resulting border will have an unbroken movement around the corners of the hanging.

BLOCK-PRINTED
MATERIAL

(Courtesy of the Milwaukee
WPA Handicraft Project.)

*This design requires that the
two blocks be perfectly keyed.*

THOMAS

MEXICAN PRINTED
FABRIC

*The handling of the bird motif
is an excellent example of an
informal and spontaneous effect
in design.*

Stenciling

Stenciling is equally as effective for wall hangings as block printing. It offers some advantages not found in a block-printed textile, since it permits the use of a wider range of colors and the covering of larger areas with color. Another distinct advantage is that of enabling the craftsman to see just what his results are going to be during the process itself. It is usually found that the materials required for the making of a stenciled wall hanging are less expensive than those used for block printing.

There are numerous other projects for which stenciling may be used. It may be wise for the beginner to experiment with this new technique on some small item before attempting so large an article as a wall hanging. In general, stenciling may be used as a means of applying surface decoration wherever block printing would be suitable; and in addition upon wooden and metal objects such as furniture, boxes, woodwork, and plastered walls. The materials are quite easy to assemble. The sten-

Photograph by Helen Ludwig.

STENCILED DRAPERY
by Helen Ward

Inexpensive Osnaburg was used for these draperies.

cils themselves are best when cut from a flexible, hard-finished cardboard. It is possible to buy stencil board, but the results obtained when using Manila tag board or very heavy wrapping paper are satisfactory. The cutting is done with a razor blade, small pointed scissors, or a special stencil knife.

The designs for stenciling may be very elaborate, using many colors, or as simple as a polka dot stenciled in only one color. Somewhere along the gamut of possibilities is a degree of complication suitable to anyone. When designing the unit to be used keep in mind that each color calls for a separate stencil, with each "hole" in this particular stencil surrounded completely by at least a small pathway of the stencil board. To some this pathway between all units of a stenciled design is the distinguishing characteristic, for it is the type of stenciling used by many interior painters for years. Not many of these old stenciled borders would pass as good designs, for they are weak and spotty in appearance. A carefully executed stenciled design need not have a single trace of the background material separating the various colors used unless it is desired for part of the design itself. However, this pathway serves as a protective mask during the stenciling process, so it does appear on the separate tag board stencils.

Tubes of oil paint, turpentine, a piece of glass or an old plate, and a palette knife or other device for mixing the paint, along with thumbtacks and clean rags, are about all one needs besides the tag board or heavy paper. As is true with block printing, the material upon which the design is to be stenciled should not be too coarse or flimsy in nature. Osnaburg, sugar or flour sacking, linen, crash, sailcloth, and dull-surfaced oilcloth are all suitable. The purpose of the finished product will have to govern one's choice.

EQUIPMENT FOR STENCILING

One or more sharp cutting instruments, a stencil brush, stencil board, oil paint, and a piece of glass to mix it on are the tools of stencil craft.

As mentioned before, a stencil will be needed for each color. Trace all the sections of the design which are to be in one color onto one piece of the stencil board. Allow at least one inch of margin around the outside of the entire group of spots to be cut out. This provides a thumb-hold quite necessary when doing the actual stenciling. Follow the same procedure for each color, taking care to trace each unit accurately or the finished piece will not key.

With a razor blade or scissors cut away the outlined sections. It is advisable not to use more than four colors, at least on one's first project. If one uses four colors there will be four stencils.

If the stencils have been cut from square or rectangular cardboards of a uniform size, the following method may be used for keying: Make a frame from a large piece of cardboard by cutting in the center of it a hole the size of the small cards upon which the design has been cut. Hinge the stencil sections with gummed tape to the sides of the hole in the frame unit. This will look very

[271]

much like a doorway with four doors, each one hinged to a different side of the opening so that any one of them may be used separately. It will be necessary to determine which edge of the small card should be hinged to the frame in order that the stencil may take its proper position when turned down over the opening in the frame. Test the accuracy of the position by turning down any two at a time and holding the frame up to a strong light. The cut out areas should just meet or overlap evenly just the smallest fraction of an inch. If gaps or large overlaps appear, shift the small cards at the hinged side, or trim the cut edges judiciously until a satisfactory matching is effected. This is termed "keying." When in use, these flaps are turned down one at a time over the portion of material to be stenciled, starting with the one through which the lightest color is to be stenciled. When done carefully, and if too much paint has not been used, the various colors will not smudge. Clean, clear-cut edges are characteristic of a good stenciled design.

A second method of keying and one which sometimes is more easily used, especially for allover patterns, is as follows: Trace the entire unit on as many cards as there are colors in the design, but cut each card so that it accommodates only one color as before. Now on the second stencil, or the one to be used for the next to the lightest color, cut peepholes that fit accurately over two, better three, parts of the areas stenciled through the holes in the first card. It is not necessary or even advisable to cut out the entire areas. They may be just small holes that register a sharp corner or a distinguishing curve in the design. Let these holes be well separated and far enough away from the areas to be stenciled through this card to prevent the bristles of the stencil brush accidentally carrying an unwanted color onto the material exposed by them. If the design permits, the same peepholes may be cut into the remaining cards.

KEYING A FOUR-SECTION STENCIL

[273]

STENCILED WALL HANGING

by Ruth Justine

The vigor of this design be lies the fact that only three stencils were used.

If not, cut them elsewhere; it is care that counts here. Test the keying of the stencils by holding any two of the cards up to a strong light to see if the outlines of the design on one card coincide with the peepholes and cut out areas on the other one. A stenciled area is always a bit smaller than the hole through which the paint has been applied. This may be compensated for by a slight overlapping of areas when keying the design. Be sure to correct all errors even though one or more of the cards has to be cut over more accurately.

When the stencils are keyed satisfactorily, mix a sufficient quantity of oil paint of the desired color to permit stenciling all the areas of that particular color. Do not thin the paint with turpentine without testing the consistency first on a piece of the fabric to be used. If thinning appears to be necessary, do so with great care. Paint which is too thin will run under the stencil edges and cause a blurred design. Spread a thin layer of the mixed color upon

STENCILED WALL HANGING

by Jean Montgomery

A small design such as this lends itself to block printing as well.

Photograph by Helen Ludwig.

the surface of a piece of glass or a plate. Keep the remainder of the pigment in a compact mass covered with waxed paper to prevent it from drying before it is needed.

The material should be firmly tacked to a smooth surface. Place the keyed stencil in the desired position upon the material. Fasten the stencil down with thumbtacks and, if using the hinged type, fold the first stencil over into position. Apply the paint gingerly. First tap the flat surface of the stencil brush into a thin layer of the prepared paint, using care not to get too much paint on the bristle ends. Hold the brush perpendicular to the material and tap the bristles briskly with short, swift strokes over the exposed area of material until the desired color has been obtained. Shading may be accomplished by varying the amount of pigment used within an area. Interesting surface textures may be obtained by experimenting with various brush strokes and through the application of more than one color within a single area. Keep the underside of the stencil free of paint. Always clean the brush thoroughly in turpentine and wipe it well on a rag before using it for another color.

The time required for the paint to dry depends upon the amount of paint applied and the weight of the fabric used. In most cases the paint should dry out overnight, but this is not always true. Try to prevent the paint from forming a thick coating on the surface of the material. When stenciling a piece of fabric, the fibers of the material should absorb the paint. This is accomplished by tapping the brush more frequently over any area rather than using more paint to obtain darker values. The texture of the fabric is an integral part of the design and should not be obscured by too much paint.

The color may be set by covering the material with a cloth dampened in a fairly strong solution of vinegar and water and pressing it with a hot iron. Usually fabrics treated in this way can be washed if care is taken. This is not always so, however, because the quality of paint varies. It is well to test a small piece of stenciled fabric for color fastness.

Experience will develop ways and means suitable to each individual and to the task at hand, but a few variations of procedure may be of assistance. Scotch tape or masking tape will hold stencils firmly in place when thumbtacks are impractical. Just the steady pressure of one's fingers is sufficient to keep small, simple stencils in place.

A large wall hanging or a decoration to be stenciled directly on a wall may be attacked quite differently if the design calls for good sized motifs that are not repeated over and over. If this is the case, draw the design very lightly directly upon the surface to be decorated. Any small units that are used for allover or border pattern within any of the large areas may be omitted from the drawing and taken care of by the usual procedure, but all the large areas do not necessarily require a true stencil. Instead cut a variety

WALL HANGING

(*Courtesy of the Milwaukee WPA Handicraft Project.*)

The main lines of a design of this type might be drawn directly upon the fabric. The characteristic clean-cut line of stenciling could be obtained by using a variety of curved and straight line shields; only the clover leaf requires a regulation stencil.

of curved and straight-edged pieces from sheets of tag board. Have the pieces wide enough to permit one to handle them easily. Twelve inches or more is a good length. Firmly hold or tack the piece of tag board which happens to be cut with the right curve along the corresponding line drawn upon the design. Stencil the area thus protected; then shift that curved mask along to another part of the line or substitute a piece that fits better. Not many pieces will be required. Start out with a few straight strips, a large and smaller circle, a piece shaped like an S, a shallow concave piece, and a shallow convex piece. A roll of waxed paper or a bread wrapper or two that may be snipped for small pieces now and then is a handy addition to one's equipment.

Sometimes one wishes to stencil a spot within a spot, and there is no way of holding the parts of the stencil together without destroying the unity of the design. A piece of stencil board cut to the right shape and size, and held in place with pins or thumb-tacks, solves that problem. It may be used to protect the material while color is being applied, or to protect the color while another color is being stenciled in an adjacent area. These protective pieces used independently of the stencil proper are called positive stencils. The cards into which holes are cut are called negative stencils.

A very satisfactory textile color is distributed by the American Crayon Company of Sandusky, Ohio. It is easy to use, and when the very simple directions for setting the colors are followed accurately, the colors are resistant to fading and are washproof.

Oil paints are not satisfactory for stenciling upon paper. After a few hours an unsightly ring of oil begins to appear around the colored areas. Poster, tempera, and water color paints are far better for this purpose. The procedure is the same. Never use too much paint.

For quick effects colored chalk may be used on fairly rough paper. The chalk is powdered and pounced through the stencil. Decorations made with this medium are not practical unless kept under glass as a framed picture or set by blowing a fixative upon them. A dilute mixture of denatured alcohol and shellac, sold for fixing charcoal drawings, may be applied with an atomizer. Just as good, and easier to prepare, is a mixture of one tablespoon of mucilage in one-half cup of water. Have the design thumbtacked to a flat horizontal surface and blow this fixative over it so that the mist falls down upon it. Do not disturb until quite dry.

PLACE MAT AND NAPKIN SET
WITH MATCHING TEA TILE

All the articles pictured above were stenciled with textile colors. The border design on the simple place mat repeats the movement in the tendrils of the plant form on the napkins.

Chapter XIII

Decorative Needlework

WALL HANGINGS HAVE BEEN DISCUSSED AT LENGTH UNDER
other techniques; but for the woman who enjoys plying an
embroidery needle, decorative stitchery lends itself admirably to the
making of decorations for walls, and of course, to many other objects that might add an individual note to one's home. To anyone
the least bit sensitive, the so-called art needlework shops or departments are really chambers of horror. It is amazing to find that so
many sweetly sentimental boys and girls, "cute" little puppy dogs
(or kittens, to say nothing of squirrels and ducks) can be maligned
to such an extent. If one looks carefully, one might find a fine adaptation of a Swedish tapestry, or directions for simple decorative
edges on linens for various purposes; but there is an overwhelming
display of "real" roses, daisies, and forget-me-nots, stamped hither
and yon upon otherwise beautiful material. The same may be said
about most of the stamped articles offered for sale in needlework
sections of magazines, or of the transfers so profusely filling pattern
books.

The designs found on stamped goods, or offered to the public on transfer patterns, are generally poor in that they lack suitability to the use to which they are put. Many are realistic to the
extreme; others add to this mistaken conception of design a great
deal of sentimentality. The actual organization of many of these

DETAIL FROM MEXI-CAN AYATE

A rich collection of source material is a good antidote for that helpless feeling.

designs is very loose, lacking almost entirely the desired quality of unity. When the design is stamped upon the material, all too frequently the same design is used for aprons, bedspreads, dish towels, and rompers for the baby without regard for the structural design of the object to be decorated.

Designs should be suitable to their use. We have rather universally accepted the humor of walking over a bed of cabbage roses every time we cross the floor to the other side of the room, and few people would buy scatter rugs nowadays that have a lifelike portrait of Rover taking his nap. Unfortunately, we have not let this understanding of the harmony of idea to be expressed in a design carry over to all household objects. Little kittens are often scorched on the handles of hot skillets, luscious purple grapes twine themselves up over the shoulders of dresses, and glasses are often wiped and polished upon images of themselves. This statement deals with a number of ill-conceived ideas concerning design. The little kitten should have been conventionalized to the point that it had become

[281]

an interesting motif, based upon the animal form, but not a realistic representation of the animal. The grapes, besides being too realistic, do not strengthen the structural design of the dress. They, too, would have to be conventionalized to give character to the garment. The pictures of utensils upon towels is too obvious a label, the texture of the linen ordinarily dictates the use. A simple border in suitable colors would be ever so much more attractive hanging over a towel rack.

While dealing with the matter of suitability of design, it might be well to mention the use of monograms. That form of decoration has been misused to such an extent that monograms have fallen into disrepute. A monogram should always be considered a design, not merely a label. If it is good, it will serve both purposes. When making a monogram, the source of inspiration is one's initials. These should be treated no differently than a flower or an animal used for this purpose. It should be simple, of beautiful proportions, consistent in size and shape with the object to be so decorated, and finally, placed upon that object in such a way that the structural design is given added strength. If these suggestions were followed, there would be few script or old English letters trailing off a pillowcase on the diagonal, or on blouse fronts telling the passerby that one's name is Jane.

It is hoped that the preceding paragraphs do not discourage anyone. It is merely hoped that they will create the desire to find truly excellent source material. A few suggestions for sources are: English crewel embroidery, Scandinavian tapestries, peasant embroideries on wearing apparel, Mexican decorative stitchery, and Oriental needlework. It is not necessary that one find actual examples of stitchery for inspiration. If one knows a few simple stitches,

MEXICAN EMBROIDERY

This type of handicraft furnishes abundant source material for today's needlework.

THOMAS

and has an active imagination, a painted box, a bit of beautiful leather tooling, or perhaps some simple wood carving is all the idea one needs. Just by way of caution: some designs are not suitable to development in stitchery, but are better expressed in some other medium, for instance, stencil, or perhaps batik.

MOTIF IN CHAIN STITCH

*(Courtesy of the Milwaukee WPA Handicraft
Project.)*

Pretty as Pictures

After one has tentatively considered a suitable design for a
wall hanging in a specific room, one's attention should be turned
to a fabric that answers one's needs. It should be harmonious in
texture to the other textiles used in the room. It should be consistent with the idea of the design, and above all, have a texture of
its own that permits the stitches applied to it to become almost an
integral part of the fabric, rather than remaining conspicuously upon
the surface. There are a number of fabrics that fulfill these specifi-
cations, for instance, the finer monk's cloth, linen and linen crash,
and Osnaburg, which can be dyed a desirable color or used in the
natural state. Other drapery fabrics, woolen materials, and cotton
crashes add many possibilities. For a very social home, some silks
and satins are suitable.

[284]

For the stitchery, yarns are very good. The most suitable are the Shetland flosses, Germantown, and tapestry and peasant yarns. Among the cottons are six-strand embroidery flosses and moss yarn. For wall hangings there are really no suitable linen threads; the soft textures are too fine, and those heavy enough to give character to the design are apt to be stiff and wiry.

The character of the design itself will suggest stitches most suitable for its portrayal. Some of the most adaptable stitches are: the chain in all its variation, the cross stitch, outline, darning, and satin stitches.

Assuming that a design has been planned that satisfies the requirements, it is necessary to transfer it to the material. Some designs, especially those worked in cross stitch or darning stitch, are easily executed by merely counting the threads of the fabric. This is not too difficult, since a fairly coarse material is ordinarily used for wall hangings of this type. For other designs, the motifs may be traced upon thin paper, then basted to the fabric. The stitches to be employed are then carefully worked over the paper. After the embroidery has been completed the paper is torn away from the stitches. If this method is used, be careful to place the long lines of the motifs with the thread of the fabric. It is possible, of course, to trace the design upon the fabric, but very often the pencil or carbon marks discolor the embroidery floss or smudge the plain background areas.

The actual stitchery should be executed with the utmost care. Long floats of thread should be avoided because they easily catch and snag. The stitches should be firm enough to have character, but not pulled so tightly that the fabric becomes warped.

To finish the hanging, it should first be pressed carefully, face down on a well padded board. A damp cloth helps to steam

THOMAS

EMBROIDERED DRAPERY

by Helen S. Petersen

A simple, bold design carried out with roving couched into position and accented with balls cut from ball fringe.

the fabric back into shape and renew its original finish. After that fold back the raw edges enough to form the margins necessary to set off the embroidered design. If the turned back edges are wider than one-half inch, the excess material is best cut away. A lining should then be slip stitched to the top and sides. If the bottom edges of both the lining and hanging materials are hemmed, but not stitched together, the wall hanging will lie more flatly against the wall. The principle there is the same one often applied when lining a coat or jacket; for a space directly in the back, the lining is not fastened to the hem. The hanging may also be lined by cutting a piece of suitable material the same size as the embroidered fabric, the two placed face to face, then stitched on the machine around the sides and top. The bottoms should be hemmed separately when this method is used also. Suitable lining materials would be sateen or percale, depending upon the choice of the material of the hanging itself.

The lining may also be considered as part of the design. In this case it is cut large enough to permit suitable margins to be brought over the hanging to form a colored border. The corners should be neatly mitered. If this is done, the lining material should be carefully selected for texture and color.

To hang a wall decoration of this type, whether embroidered, stenciled, or produced by

JUVENILE WALL HANGING

(*Courtesy of the Milwaukee WPA Handicraft Project.*)

This hanging shows an engaging freedom.

some other medium, rings or tabs should be provided at the top through which a rod may be placed. For the rings, wire or bone are suitable. The wire rings are best sewn to the back, concealed from view. The texture of the bone rings is harmonious with many of the fabrics suggested for use as wall hangings and therefore may well be fastened to the very top edge of the hanging if desired. In

CROSS STITCHED
WALL HANGING

by June Sigsworth

*Local farming was used
as the inspiration for the
design.*

[288]

case the natural color of the rings is not harmonious, they may be dyed by soaking in a cup of dye solution. There are also on the market rings made of plastic material in a number of pleasing colors. If rings are not available, tabs of material may be made and applied to the back, or again to the top edge.

Rods may be either of wood or metal and should be appropriate in color. Usually the less conspicuous the better, since an over-elaborate rod will detract from the character of the hanging.

The rod should be suspended from the picture molding by means of two wires or cords that hang vertically and parallel to each other. A single wire or cord forming a triangle above the hanging (or a picture for that matter) leads the observer's eye away from the hanging to the picture hook up in the vicinity of the ceiling. This is hardly complimentary to the hanging itself.

More Stitches and Time

While a wall hanging offers a fine opportunity for the use of needlework, many homes do not have the right wall space for such decoration. This does not mean that embroidery for household accessories need be relegated to the guest towels hanging in the bathroom. Among the articles which might be enhanced with stitchery are many that will take their place in the living or dining room to add to the character and individuality of that room.

Pillow tops may be decorated with simple conventionalized or geometric designs. These may be based on border designs or well scaled allover designs of simple units. If one chooses to make a pillow top, there are several points to be remembered. The embroidery should be simple in character, should harmonize in line and spirit with the furniture in the room, and should be done with

WOVEN MAT AND NAPKIN

The motifs employed for the design of this Swedish place mat and napkin are adaptable to embroidery.

THOMAS

stitches which will withstand the often rough handling that a well used pillow receives. Many stitches lend themselves to this purpose; namely, cross stitch, chain stitch, outline stitch, needle point, and a closely worked satin stitch. Long floats of yarn, which are apt to catch and pull, should be avoided. The texture of the fabric and the yarn are also important considerations and should be selected with thought for the rest of the room. The pillow may be planned to repeat the color of the upholstery fabric used on the furniture, or it may repeat some accented color found in the decorative accessories in the room. It is wise, however, to avoid colors so bright that they tend to focus the attention on the pillow itself.

Frequently one wishes to protect the top surface of an end table or some other piece of furniture in the room. Or perhaps in the dining room, a few attractive changes in place mats would be appreciated. Table scarfs and place mats may be made quickly and inexpensively and may be very attractive if done with simple and effective designs. Well planned proportions and well selected colors

EMBROIDERED MAT
AND NAPKIN

by Helen S. Petersen

The embroidered motifs are well placed and in scale with the linen upon which they are used.

THOMAS

used in a border design of simple stripes or units will provide adequate and distinctive decoration. For table scarfs, the fabric may be as informal as heavy monk's cloth or of finer textures such as linen. On the heavier textures, yarn may be used, and on the finer textures, a floss of appropriate weight, such as six-strand embroidery floss. Place mats should be planned to be of the correct size for the china, silver, and glass as well as for the particular meal of the day for which they are intended. A good luncheon size is eleven by eighteen inches. They may be made of the finest linen, delicately embroidered or hemmed with single hemstitch, ladder stitch, antique hemstitch, or Italian hemstitch for more formal occasions when fine china and glass are used; or of heavy linen, cotton crash, or like textures for more informal occasions. Color selection is important since the mats should harmonize with the dishes to be used with them, as well as with the general color scheme of the room. For the more informal occasions, bright colors may be used. Very attractive informal mats may be made quickly by stitching rows

ONION SACKING
TABLE MAT

Coarse nets, jute cloth, or various sack materials are all quickly decorated with cotton rug filler.

THOMAS

of bright but harmonious colors of rickrack trimming in a striped border on either end of the mat. Plain, solid-colored napkins repeating one of the colors in the braid would be attractive with them.

Mats and scarfs need not necessarily be trimmed with borders. Small motifs made up of geometric forms in two or three colors may be arranged over the surface of the fabric in an allover design. Remember always that a simple, unified design well related to the structural lines of the fabric itself will be in far better taste than elaborate or realistic motifs of the sort seen all too frequently.

Guest towels and finger towels may be thought of in much the same way as place mats and table scarfs since they are of about the same proportions. The fabric may differ in as much as it should be selected for its absorbent qualities. Simple border designs, allover designs, or a single well planned unit placed so as to be attractively displayed while the towel is hanging on its rack are wise

DETAIL FROM NEEDLE POINT CHAIR SEAT

by Helen S. Petersen

Variety in texture has been attained by changing the direction of the stitch in alternate stripes.

THOMAS

selections. Monograms may be used, but should be considered in the light of the paragraph dealing with them at the beginning of this section.

Needle point has been mentioned as a possibility for pillow tops. This particular technique has many other uses in the home as well. Chair seats or footstool covers done in needle point may be beautiful in texture and design. Most department stores sell partially completed needle-point canvases, but these are usually of inferior design, consisting of realistic wreaths of roses or the like. One may plan designs from well selected source material belonging to the period represented by the furniture in the room, or from related periods. Here, too, simple geometric or conventionalized motifs will be the most successful. It is not essential that the design be executed in a wide range of colors. A few well chosen colors will probably be more pleasing than a great variety.

HOOKED RUG

(*Courtesy of the Milwaukee WPA Handicraft Project.*)

The strong movement of the design is counteracted by closely related color values.

HOOKED RUG

(*Courtesy of the Milwaukee WPA Handicraft Project.*)

A simple repeat is one of the most adaptable of designs for a rug.

HOOKED RUG

by Barbara Warren

Solid or broken stripes are a welcome relief from the floral patterns so frequently employed for hooked rugs.

Always Under Foot

Any library reference shelf will provide well detailed books on the art of making hooked rugs. For this reason, we are omitting a lengthy discussion of them here. However, we do feel that a brief mention of the possibilities of this technique and of the materials which may be used for it will encourage some to do further research along this line.

A HOOKED RUG

(*Courtesy of the Milwaukee WPA Handicraft Project.*)

A welcome departure from the usual hooked rug design. This rug would be most appropriately used in a distinctly modern setting.

HOOKING A RUG

(*Courtesy of the Milwaukee WPA Handicraft Project.*)

The appliance shown in the photograph is one of the best for the craft. It may be purchased in the needlework departments of most large stores.

DETAIL FROM AN OLD QUILT

Heirlooms such as this furnish good source material.

THOMAS

APPLIQUÉ PLACE MAT

PATCHWORK PILLOW TOP

Abstract designs lend themselves admirably to modern patchwork. This pillow top combines appliqué and regular patchwork techniques.

THOMAS

Scrap materials which might otherwise be discarded may be saved and cut into lengths for such rugs. Woolen fabrics from old garments may be dyed to the colors desired or may be used in their original color if it is suited to the design. Silk stockings and underwear may also be dyed beautiful, subtle colors and worked into rugs. Yarns may be used, but as it is usually necessary to purchase these, the original cost of the rug is a great deal more than if waste materials are used.

Striking abstract designs for modern rooms are well adapted to this old technique. One will find that most of the designs shown in references dealing with hooked rugs are of the realistic flower garden sort. Research, however, will uncover reproductions of lovely old colonial designs which may be used as they are or may be modified to fit into many interiors.

[298]

APPLIQUÉ COMBINED WITH QUILTING

(Courtesy of the Milwaukee WPA Handicraft Project.)

This technique is adaptable to wall hangings and table covers as well as to coverlets.

Needles for hooking rugs may be purchased in the needle-work departments of the larger stores. Burlap or monk's cloth is usually used for backing for these long wearing rugs.

Priority on Patches

It would be fun to list all the ideas for the uses of patchwork and appliqué one might conceive while turning the pages of any one of the fine books available on old patchwork quilts. Perhaps one has to be in an analytical mood, but once he has begun thinking about the possibilities of this technique, he is likely to wail because time passes too quickly! Just the borders found on beautiful old quilts could be used as the decorative design for tablecloths, place mats, draperies, smocks, beach coats, or robes. The units making up the body of the design lend themselves to mats, pillows, chair seats, holders, and unusual bags or purses. Or one might make a miniature version of a complete quilt, quilting and all, and use it as a most distinctive table cover. After all these ideas are taken care of, adaptations based on the designs would permit one to continue on and on.

Once the craftsman is familiar with the technique, he may wish to employ contemporary designs. The illustrations in this section will provide some good suggestions, and the drawings in the chapter on design might have been made to order. There are a few technicalities to keep in mind. If the finished product is to be laundered, be sure that all the material used has been shrunk before any of the pieces have been cut. It is also necessary to keep the correct position of the warp and weft threads throughout the work. This care prevents unsightly puckers later. All edges must be carefully prepared. In true patchwork each edge becomes part of a seam and is thus protected, but frayed edges might appear on appliqué unless the edge of each applied piece were turned under evenly before stitching into place. Firmly woven materials may be sewed to the foundation material with a diagonal overcast stitch; these small

APPLIQUÉ WALL HANGING

(Courtesy of the Milwaukee WPA Handicraft Project.)

The introduction of embroidery unifies the entire design. The freedom of the design is the noteworthy element of this work.

THOMAS

EGYPTIAN APPLIQUÉ

The large simple forms and fine distribution of values provide a good object lesson.

THOMAS

APPLIQUÉ DRAPERY

(Milwaukee WPA Handicraft Project.)

THOMAS

APPLIQUÉ DRAPERY

(Milwaukee WPA Handicraft Project.)

stitches can later be covered with decorative stitches. Simple couching as well as couching combined with other stitches such as the buttonhole stitch are the types most often used. Chain stitch is likewise effective.

A very effective wall decoration can be made from an appliquéd panel mounted in a picture frame. When the work is to be protected by glass in a manner such as this, less attention need be paid to the edges. Textures which would be most unhappy partners if sewed together for a place mat that would be laundered can be combined in appliquéd pictures to give interest and variety. Embroidery is a nice addition to give accent to some of the areas.

Our great-grandmothers produced some very beautiful appliqué and patchwork, but there is another source well worth investigating. The Egyptians make many interesting pictures of cloth in appliqué technique. The colors are bright and the design is highly stylized. The most effective of these panels are almost room high, but small squares about the size of a pillow top have much of the same spirit.

The Seminole Indians of Florida have developed a distinctive use for patchwork. Intricately designed geometric arrangements of brightly colored percales are machine-stitched into bands of fabric which are sewed together to produce gay yardage. From this uniquely designed material, which has an individuality all its own, full gathered skirts and fanciful blouses are made. The fabric thus produced is brilliant beyond description. However, the same method might be used with a more subtle assortment of colors than is used by the Indians.

In this patchwork technique, borders vary in width from one inch to three inches. Each border is slightly different in design, but the repeated use of the geometric motif and the frequent repetition of colors from one band to the next produce a harmony that is quite delightful. Material of this nature is suitable for a number of purposes other than wearing apparel alone. Draperies, pillow covers, or even bed spreads would be effective if coördinated colors were selected.

The Indians often sew the bands of patchwork together with rickrack covering the seams. There is no reason why bias binding in an appropriate color might not be equally effective. One of the advantages of a technique such as that described here is that it makes admirable use of small scraps of fabric that are not large enough for other purposes. Anyone who does much of her own sewing will be well aware of the many bits of material which seem to accumulate so quickly and for which there seems to be no use whatsoever. Time, a little ingenuity, and some imagination may, with the method outlined above, empty the scrap bag and add to the home or the wardrobe.

Chapter XIV

Practical Portfolios

THERE IS A CERTAIN FASCINATION TO THE CONSTRUCTION OF portfolios that might well be strong enough to make this craft one's major hobby. Drawing ability is not a prerequisite, for one may choose material distinctive in design and color in the shops with which to make the book covers or similar projects. At the same time this craft provides a splendid way of using stenciled or block-printed fabric or paper.

Only slight variations of procedure need be considered in order to successfully carry through any number of projects based on the fundamental principles of construction. Everyone's problem is quite apt to be specialized. The following directions for a telephone book cover are typical and should prove helpful as a starting point from which departures may be made.

DECIDE UPON THE MATERIAL TO BE USED FOR THE COVER

Heavy cardboard used for book binding comes in fifty-pound bundles. The weight or thickness of cardboard is designated by a number. This number actually represents the number of sheets in the bundle, so that the smaller the number, the thicker or heavier the cardboard. Number 30 therefore would be thicker than number 40, etc. Number 30 is recommended for portfolios in general. Smaller notebooks could be made of lighter weight material, usu-

ADJUSTABLE PORT-FOLIO

(*Courtesy of the Milwaukee WPA Handicraft Project.*)

The wide strips of binder's linen used to fasten the flaps to the cover make this portfolio adjustable to either a few or many plates.

ally large ones of heavier material. Keep the covers in scale with the size of the book.

If one is using cardboard that happens to be on hand, examine some of the books one has. Most covers are almost an eighth of an inch in thickness. It is quite possible to employ suit boxes, tablet backs, or the cardboards the laundry uses to fold men's shirts around; paste as many layers together as required to make cardboard of the desired thickness. Be sure to place under a heavy weight, and allow several days for drying. Warped covers are most unpleasant. Discarded posters or display material from the local stores are very useful. Just remember to paste the brightly colored sides together when fabricating the cover board; the bright inks might discolor the material used to cover the book.

Cut and trim all edges with a razor blade. Use a metal-edged ruler and be sure the corners are square. When binder's board is purchased for a particular project the dealer will cut it for one, but he charges so much per cut. It's rather costly unless large quantities

LEATHER AND CLOTH BOUND BOOK

An adaptation of leather tooling techniques to simple book binding.

THOMAS

are being used; then one's own time may be worth a great deal more than the ten cents or so it costs each time the knife falls.

Some sort of cloth is needed for the back binding. Paper is not strong enough to withstand any wear on this part of the book. There is upon the market regular bookbinder's linen, which comes in a variety of colors and textures. The price of the linen varies, depending upon the quality desired. Dress linen, crash, hand toweling, drapery and slip-cover material, as well as sailcloth, cotton suitings, percale, ginghams, and denims are all suitable and are sometimes more attractive for particular problems than are the commercial bookbinder's linens. The book linen has been impregnated with a substance which makes it very durable. For most uses in the home, material from one's piece bag will be quite suitable.

Fabric or paper may be used for covering the front and back covers. If fabric is selected it should be of a firm weave—any in the foregoing list would be suitable. The design (if a patterned material is used) and color should be carefully selected to harmonize with the surroundings. This may be the place to add pattern interest if plain colors predominate, or to come smashing through with a color note that makes the color scheme of the room distinctive.

If paper is used it should be fairly tough. Kraft paper is ideal, but is not always suitable in color. Construction paper—the heavier

*The soft toned chintz is far
more pleasant on the desk
than the taxicab advertisement it conceals.*

THOMAS

of the usual colored papers—is good if not too old. Old paper cracks
at the corners because it has become brittle with age. Commercial
cover papers give one a wide selection and are not very costly. Wallpapers open up still another possibility, and after one once learns
to visualize the finished product before any work has been done
on it at all, ideas for the uses of materials, alone or in combination,
will be so numerous that the average person just couldn't get all
the books visualized made. One does have to sleep, even though
a beautifully bound leather portfolio for the desk is ever upon one's
mind.

The portfolio will need a lining. Choose any of the afore-
mentioned materials, but remember the little matter of suitability.
It's fun to introduce drama in the lining of a book. If the book
cover from necessity had to be plain, here is an opportunity for
striking pattern, or for some color to be brought to full intensity.
It has something of the same effect one experiences when a brilliant bird is seen for just an instant as it flies across the field of
vision.

[308]

PORTFOLIOS AND SCRAPBOOKS

(*Milwaukee WPA Handicraft Project*)

Types vary with the use of each folio.

THOMAS

The choice of an adhesive is important. Use Higgins Vegetable Glue, really of a semi-opaque pastelike consistency, or any other library paste that is permanent. Some adhesives fail to hold after several months. Pastes have different effects upon colors also. Avoid one that stains the fabric or cloth easily. Rubber cement deteriorates and a strain may make the cemented parts give way after a short time. Glue is useful to have on hand and is used in one step. It is too difficult to use for ordinary pasting. Mucilage is messy too, and does not hold well enough.

The recipe given in the Boy Scouts' Handbook for bookbinding paste is satisfactory; or if the paste is to be used immediately just flour and water boiled together until transparent and of rather pastelike consistency will do. Rye flour is superior to wheat flour for this purpose.

A few more materials will be needed. A thin coat of white shellac or clear lacquer may be put on the finished cover. This helps to keep it clean and to harden the surface. A little wax or Venetian shoe cream is all that one needs on leather. Too high a polish is out of keeping with the idea of a book. In many cases it is not necessary to coat the surface of the book at all. The use to which the book is to be put will decide this.

Use cord, carpet warp, leather thong, or wire to fasten the book into the cover. A telephone book is revised several times a year, so it is best to have a means of readily replacing the body of the book.

Measure the Book for Which the Cover Is to Be Made

Be accurate. When measuring the thickness of the book do not compress the pages, but measure it as it normally closes. Skimping on this measurement might cause the covers to spring open at the front of the book.

Prepare All the Materials Necessary for the Construction of the Cover

The foundation cardboards should measure ½" wider and ½" longer than the telephone book. Cut two pieces. Notice that ¼" has been allowed for extensions of the cardboard cover over the edges of the original paper cover of the directory. For a smaller book this extension is about ⅛" on each edge. In a straight box binding, such as this portfolio, ¼" is also allowed at the back edge. In a regulation book of the nature of a textbook or novel the back of the book proper extends slightly beyond the cover boards.

Of thinner cardboard cut two pieces. The length of one piece of cardboard should match the length of the cover boards, the width should be ¼" wider than the thickness of the book to compensate for the thickness of the cover boards and the thickness of the cloth (or paper) used to cover the cardboards, as well as for the thickness of the lining papers. The smaller piece should be ½" shorter to permit the cords or thong to function without extending beyond the top and bottom of the book. It should be ½" narrower to prevent crowding the cover boards when the book is closed.

A strip of the cloth or bookbinder's linen is needed for the back binding. The width of the piece of bookbinder's linen or cloth used for the back binding is optional. As it is placed across the back and over the back edge of the cover boards a pleasing relationship of areas should be sought. If striped or patterned material is used the design will also govern the width. A stripe or motif should be cut to the best advantage of the design. Bookbinder's linen or leather is sometimes so heavy that a lapped seam would be too thick. In that case the edges of the binding material and the cover cloth or paper are just brought together neatly rather than overlapped. If overlapping is desired a ⅛" or ¼" lap is adequate. This amount then must be allowed on both sides of the binding material. The length of the cloth or binder's linen should be 2" greater than the length of the cover boards.

Cloth, paper, and leather are all suitable for covering the cardboard. Two pieces are needed. The width of this material is somewhat governed by one's decision when determining the width of the back binding. One should allow for the following: If the seam is an overlapped one or if the material, such as the chintz used for the telephone book cover, might ravel easily, and is thinner than the binding material, allow ¼". Add enough to take care of the part of the cardboard not covered by the back binding (this measurement varies with the project). For turning over the edges, add another inch of material. The length should be 2" greater than the length of the cover boards.

Paper is most frequently used for lining the covers of a book. Cut two pieces. The lining papers are cut just enough smaller to permit about ⅛″ of the edge of the material used to cover the outside of the book to show inside. A larger area of the cloth or bookbinder's linen will show on the inside at the center of the book.

Cut a third piece of paper two inches longer and two inches wider than the smaller of the two strips of thin cardboard to be used for the back.

To increase the strength of the back binding, cloth is used to line the inside of the back of the book. A strip is cut long enough to extend one inch beyond the front and back hinges, but should be the same length as the lining paper.

CONSTRUCTING THE COVER

Provide plenty of old newspapers and clean rags before the actual construction is begun.

Paste the two cover boards and the back board to the strip of bookbinder's linen or cloth. A one-inch shellac or varnish brush is a great convenience for quick pasting.

Be sure the strip of cloth or bookbinder's linen is cut on the thread or has followed the pattern of a stripe or other design. Press out any wrinkles present. Put a coating of paste on one side of the larger back board. Place it in the exact center of the reverse side of the bookbinder's linen or cloth. The ends extending at the top and bottom should each be about one inch long, the side pieces equal, the size depending upon the project at hand.

Lay the two cover boards in position, one on either side of the back board. Leave a space that equals the thickness of the cardboard one is using between each of the covers and the back board; this is necessary to allow the book to close. Sometimes the cloth

Pasting Back and Side Sections to Backing and Cover Fabrics.

Two Methods for Mitering Corners of Cover Fabric.

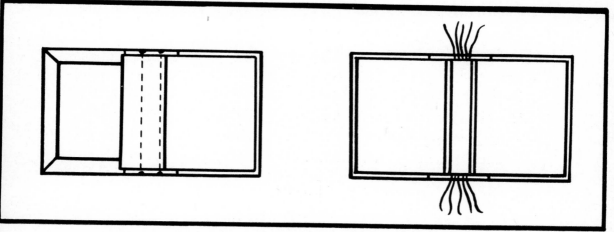

Pasting Lining Sections and Corded Section into Portfolio.

TELEPHONE BOOK COVER

shrinks when the paste moistens it, so this space may have to be increased. Place a mark on the cover boards to indicate where the back binding extends. Put a coating of paste just over this narrow strip of the cardboard and put the cover board back into position at once. Do this to both cover boards, working as rapidly as possible. Rub out any wrinkles or air bubbles with a soft clean cloth. Before the paste has a chance to dry, place the phone book in its correct position between these covers to make certain that enough leeway has been allowed to permit the covers to close and to remain so when the book is at rest upon a table. There should be enough slack present at this stage to allow for the cover papers and lining still to be used in the next steps. If too tight a fit, adjust quickly before the paste has set.

Paste the extending ends of the binding to the inside of the book. Pull down very tightly over the edges of the cardboard. Press the material firmly into the cracks between the pieces of cardboard. If the material is thick it is better to cut gussets over these cracks, extending up to within ⅛" of the edge of the book.

Cover the large pieces of cardboard with the decorative cloth (or paper).

Along the back edge of each of the two pieces of cloth fold ¼" of the material toward the wrong side. Crease carefully along a thread or follow a design motif to insure neat work. Hold this lapped edge in place with paste; use no more than absolutely necessary. Put an even coat of paste over the outside of the exposed cardboard. Butt the folded edge of the cloth up to the edge of the binding. Be sure the cover material extends equally over the top, side, and bottom edges. Rub out all air bubbles and wrinkles. Keep the warp threads of the fabric or the motifs of the design parallel to the edge of the book.

Repeat the process for the other side of the book. At this time the extra material just extends beyond the cover board on the outside edges.

When paper is used to cover the book, lap the paper over the back binding ¼″ instead of folding any of the paper toward the wrong side. A very light pencil mark placed on the binding material is a helpful guide when covering the surface of the cardboard with paste. It is essential to get plenty of paste along the edges. Any spot that has been neglected during pasting will cause an unpleasant bump on the cover later.

The pasting process is a much happier one if the work rests on a dozen or so loose sheets of an old magazine or newspaper. Then after every step the top paper can be pulled out from underneath the book quickly. Most paste leaves a stain that is not readily removed, and a paste-stained product is unsightly.

MITER THE CORNERS

Open the book cover and place it inside uppermost on the table.

Cut off each of the four corners of the cloth extending over the corners of the cardboard so that about ⅝″ or ¾″ of the cloth remains. This is cut at a 45° angle. Fold this narrower piece of material down over the corner of the cardboard. It will form a diagonal line across the inside of the cardboard. Paste into position. Always keep the material as close to the edge of the cover boards as possible. Now paste the material that as yet extends beyond the edges of the cover to the inside of the cover boards. If carefully done all the edges of the cardboard have been concealed.

Mitering paper corners is slightly different. Fold the top and bottom of the extending pieces of paper over the cardboard as tightly as possible. Crease. Be gentle; paper is sometimes so brittle that it cracks or punctures easily. Open these folds out again, and repeat the process for the side edge. Open it out again after the crease has been made. Now fold the top edge and the side edge over the cardboard at the *same time*. The corner of the paper sticks up in a shape not unlike a dog's-ear. Pinch the "ear," adjusting the two edges until the top and side pieces meet at a perfect right angle on top of the cardboard. With one hand hold these edges firmly in place; with the other fold the "dog's-ear" down first to the left, then to the right. When the edges are opened again, a diagonal crease has been made far enough away from the corner of the cardboard to insure full coverage. To be doubly sure, cut $\frac{1}{16}$" beyond this crease as one cuts off the corner triangles thus formed. Repeat for all four corners. Paste the top and bottom flaps onto the inside of the cover first. Put paste on the side flap, but before folding it down into place, tuck in the little projections at the top and bottom that were formed when the top and bottom flaps were pasted down, then when the side flap is in place all raw edges and cardboard have been concealed.

Line the Book

Paste in the center lining. This should always be cloth. Center it accurately. It should come to within $\frac{1}{8}$" of the top and bottom edges of the book. Hold a ruler firmly along one crack and close that cover. Repeat for the other cover. This is to prevent the lining from bulging or slipping out of place.

Line the front and back covers. Coat the wrong side of the lining papers with an even layer of paste. This piece, if measured accurately, should permit a $\frac{1}{8}$" margin of the cover paper to show beyond its edge at the top, bottom, and side when placed in position on the inside of the book. Usually the edge toward the center of the book then takes care of itself. It should come to ⅛" of the nearest center fold. The book will not close well, or the lining will wrinkle badly, if this piece of material overlaps the center fold at all. Repeat.

FASTEN THE TELEPHONE BOOK INTO THE COVER

Paste the narrowest piece of cardboard exactly in the center of the corresponding piece of lining material, miter the corners, and paste the extending parts to the wrong side. Cut three to five 36" lengths of cord, carpet warp, or leather thong. The length, of course, is determined by the size of the telephone book. They should be twice the length plus enough to make the tying of knots easy. Coat the wrong side of the cardboard just covered with a heavy coat of glue. Paste is not strong enough. Place the cords lengthwise upon this bed of glue at equal intervals, the long ends of the cords extending equally beyond the ends of the cardboard. Put another coating of glue over the center section of the book cover. Do not carry it to the edges; the cardboard to be placed there is smaller than the outside piece. Carefully place the cardboard in the book cover, sandwiching the cords between the two pieces of cardboard. Before going any farther place the completed cover, open, upon a smooth clean surface. Cover with a clean paper and weight down with a big pile of magazines, books, or other heavy material. Allow the book to remain under the weight until the glue has hardened.

To fasten the book into the cover, open the cover out flat, laying the cords out beyond the top and bottom. Place the telephone book, back binding down, upon the back binding of the cover, then open the book at the place indicated by the center cord

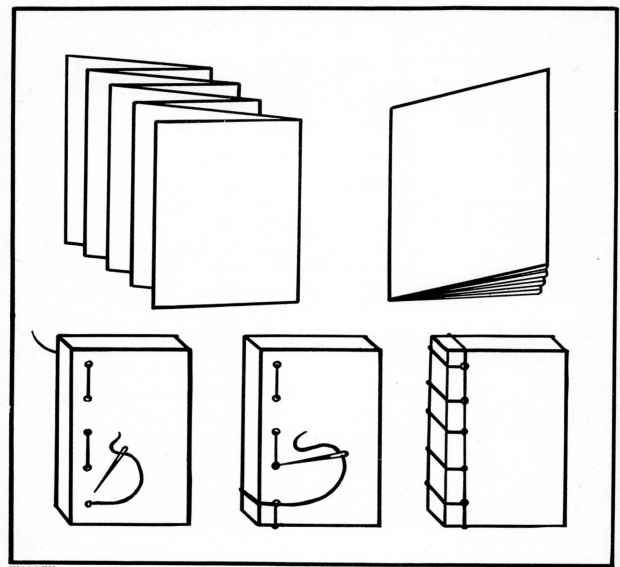

WARREN

JAPANESE BINDING

This method of binding is particularly suited to thin paper and is used where heavy cover boards are not needed. The booklet should not be too thick if it is to be flexible enough to open easily. Fold the paper as indicated in the first diagram. Each folded section should be as large as the page size desired and may contain as many folded pages as the paper size will permit. Gather the folded sections together with folded edges to the outside. Punch, drill, or pierce an uneven number of holes at the back edge of the gathered sections, spacing the holes evenly. For cover material, a folded piece of heavier paper should be used at the front and back. Sew together as indicated.

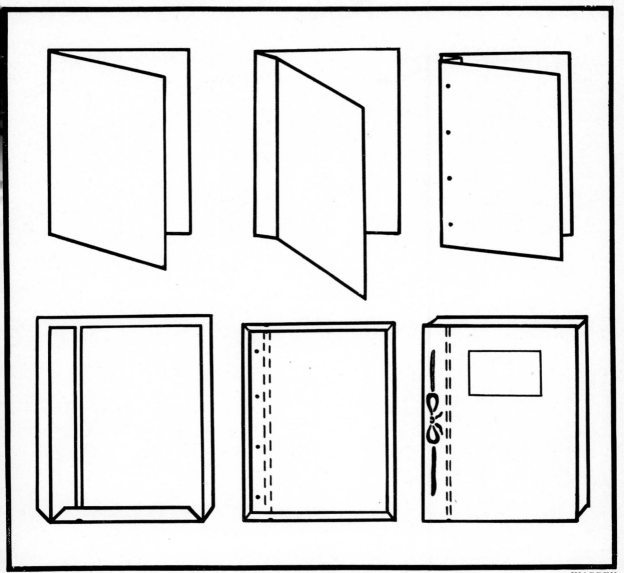

WARREN

STUB BOOKLET FOR PHOTOGRAPHS OR SCRAPBOOK

When a folio for mounting is desired, it is necessary that some form of stub be used in order to prevent it from springing open when the thickness of the mounted material is added to the original book. The above diagrams show how this may be achieved in simple fashion. At the same time the loose-leaf characteristic of this portfolio allows for the addition of more pages at will. The pages may be made of a fairly heavy paper—folded in the manner indicated to make the stub. Separate covers are made of cardboard sections covered and lined with fabric or bookbinder's linen. The booklet is fastened with cord strung through punched holes.

fastened to the cover. Tie the two ends up over the open book. Remember there will be a new directory some day, so use knots that will come open when one wishes them to, and leave ends long enough to use again. Tie the remaining cords inside the book in like manner, always opening the book above the cord first. If the cover feels the least bit damp slip wax paper between the cover one has made and the original cover of the book, then place under the weights until thoroughly dry. This is necessary to prevent the book from warping.

Chapter XV

Metal, Solder, and Acid

I F ONE HAS TIRED OF THE QUIETER CRAFTS THAT WE HAVE MEN-
tioned so far and would like to try a more exuberant technique,
metalwork will let one give vent to any excess of energy he may
have. It is not the kind of work that one can do in an apartment
building without losing all of his friendly neighbors, but if one
happens to live in his own home with an understanding and patient family, he may surprise them with a number of beautiful and
useful household accessories. (Perhaps surprise is the wrong word,
since this technique does not lend itself to secrets.)

The soft silver gray of pewter carries with it all of the qualities of gracious hospitality and blends beautifully with the subtle
colors of a well planned room.

Copper reflects a warm orange light and may be used to
brighten or accent a color scheme. Brass and the several new alloys
now on the market may be used to equal advantage alone or in
combination. The textures and colors of these metals combine
well, and decorative effects may be obtained by a simple well
planned use of two of any of these metals.

Perhaps to the novice the very contemplation of metalwork
is overwhelming. Actually simple things may be made with few
tools, a little time, and no previous training. We do not mean to
suggest that this is not a complicated technique; it is, but very

THOMAS

PEWTER HOUSEHOLD ACCESSORIES

by Dorothy Tillotson

It is important to choose pewter in a gauge consistent with the function of the object.

beautiful objects can be made by the beginner who may then graduate to the more difficult articles. There are many texts dealing with metalwork which give directions for objects requiring more skill and knowledge than those suggested in this chapter. Since this book is dedicated to the untrained beginner, we have selected the easier and more fundamental things that may be made. After skill has been acquired with the following of our suggestions, the interested person may obtain further directions for advanced metalwork in any library.

Among those things within the comprehension and skill of the beginner in this technique are plates, bowls, serving spoons, salad sets, candle holders of simple line, salt and pepper shakers, and napkin rings. Of these things listed, the plates and bowls which require pounding but not soldering are the most simple to make. Pewter may be obtained through dealers in art supplies or through companies dealing in artists' equipment and tools for craft work. These companies also handle the newer alloys that are becoming

[322]

THOMAS

PEWTER CANDLESTICKS
by Helen S. Petersen

Domes, discs, and cylinders of pewter were the simple units which were combined to produce so effective a result.

popular in metal craft work. Copper and brass may usually be purchased locally in shops using these metals or through one's hardware merchant. Of the metals mentioned, pewter is the softest, and therefore the easiest to manipulate. A simple first problem in this metal would be advisable in order that the technique be learned with as little difficulty as possible. The metal may be purchased in discs suitable for plates or bowls and cut to the diameter desired. The diameter of the disc determines the diameter of the finished bowl or plate. Pewter, as well as the other metals, comes in a number of thicknesses or gauges. A satisfactory gauge for ordinary use in bowls and plates is number 16. Lighter weights are numbered higher and heavier weights lower.

As already mentioned, the equipment needed for the first problems is relatively little. To form the hollow of the plate or

[323]

bowl, the metal is pounded with a suitable hammer. Mallets for metal pounding are usually made of wood, leather, or rubber, since these materials do not tend to nick the metal during the process. Rubber or wooden mallets may be obtained at auto supply stores. If a wooden mallet is used, care must be taken to prevent the wooden surface from becoming roughened during pounding, as it is apt to do. Sometimes this may be prevented by tacking a soft piece of leather over the head of the mallet. If this is done, the tacks must be placed at the sides of the wooden head so that they will not come in contact with the metal surface. If one does not have other leather suitable for this purpose, old glove leather will do. Careful observation as to the condition of the surface of the wood during the pounding process will lead one to discover any roughing of the wood before it becomes serious. The surface should be sanded with a very fine sandpaper immediately if such a condition becomes apparent. After sanding, the wood must be wiped carefully to remove any grains that may have become loosened from the sandpaper.

Vessels, Deep or Shallow

There are a number of ways of forming the depressed area in bowls or plates. The carved or turned wooden mold, shaped to the desired curve and depth, is perhaps the most satisfactory for the beginner. The first step is to secure a block of wood that is at least three-quarters of an inch thicker than the envisioned design of the plate or bowl, and one inch greater in diameter than the diameter of the plate, including both the rim and center area. If one is planning on making the mold himself, pine is the wood to choose. A carpenter, or someone having access to a lathe, can turn out a more perfect mold in a very short time, if those arrangements can be made. A hard wood, turned on the lathe, produces a well wearing mold.

Assuming that one is making the mold himself and has found a suitable piece of wood, the following directions should suffice:

1. Find and mark the center of the top surface of the block of wood.

2. Using the above mark as a guide, draw the circumference of the plate on the wood. Use a compass.

3. Using the same center mark, draw a line indicating the inside of the rim and the beginning of the sunken area of the plate.

4. With a wood chisel gently hollow out the center of the mold until it conforms to the desired depth and shape planned for the finished plate. While doing this keep in mind that the metal is to be pounded into this wooden form until the back of the plate fits perfectly into the lowest part of the mold. Any uneven portion or groove will be apparent on the finished product. Hence, chip out the excess wood carefully, just a small bit at a time, always working with the grain of the wood.

5. Sandpaper the carved portion to satinlike smoothness.

Any person who turns out the mold on a lathe will need a paper pattern to guide him in reproducing the design. Make a template of heavy paper or tag board that represents a cross section of the plate as it would be seen at the eye level. The back of the plate is the important part. The top may be left perfectly straight, since the pattern would be inserted into the area being hollowed out on the lathe or measured with calipers. That is why a fairly stiff paper should be used for the pattern. This method of checking the mold is likewise valuable to anyone hollowing out the mold with a chisel. It is so very easy to deviate from the original plan if some plan for control is not used.

It is not necessary to have any contrivance to guide the formation of the rim, since the disc of metal may be cut just to fit inside the first pencil line drawn on the wood to indicate the outside edge of the plate, then held there with the left hand while pounding the plate into shape. However, there are two ways of helping oneself make this easier. The entire area representing the rim may be lowered to the depth of one-eighth inch, then smoothed with sandpaper as before. The metal should then be of a size to just fit into this depressed circle easily.

More simply, the metal may be kept in place by pounding about six small nails part way into the wood, just beyond the pencil line indicating the outside of the plate, and deep enough to stay in place so that they will not be jarred out of position during the pounding process. The nails should be placed at equal distances from each other around the circumference of the plate.

Another way of guiding the formation of the lowered part of a plate—it is not satisfactory for bowls—is by the use of two pieces of smooth, hard wood. They should exceed in length the diameter of the entire plate by a number of inches, be at least an inch wider than the rim, and be thick enough to permit a desired depth to be attained to form the center of the plate. To use this method the two sticks are clamped, or nailed, to an old table; they should be parallel to one another and the space between the two inside edges of the boards should be the same as the diameter of the lowered part of the plate to be made. To keep the metal disc in place, nails

PLATE AND BOWL MOLDS—TURNING PLATE EDGE

WARREN

are pounded into the wood to form an arc that keeps the plate from slipping as it is being worked upon. If a portable mold is desired, the two sticks can be nailed to a board of the necessary size.

The actual making of the plate is simple. The first directions given apply to the "two-stick" mold.

Place the disc of pewter inside the nails forming the confining arcs. Hold the metal steady with one hand and tap the center of the plate firmly with the mallet. Direct the blows of the mallet so that they fall just to the inside of one of the sticks at the point where the stick is tangent to the circle indicating that portion of the plate to be depressed. In order that this be a fixed spot, mark the board plainly where it extends beyond the rim of the plate to indicate the place where the mallet strokes should be directed. Do not exert great force when pounding. The weight of the mallet alone, under a steady series of beats, lowers the metal more evenly than hard, sharp blows. As the metal is pounded, keep turning the metal disc so that each blow falls within an area partially overlapping the area affected by the previous blow, but progressing slowly around the center of the plate. Remember that the mallet is directed at exactly the same spot in relation to the wood, but that the pewter is turned slowly. Continue pounding the metal until the center has been lowered to the depth planned.

When the hollow wooden mold is used, the pewter disc is placed over the scooped-out area, held firmly with one hand and pounded into shape with steady overlapping blows as before. With a complete mold beneath the metal to shape it, the pewter need not be turned, but the mallet blows should be worked evenly over the entire surface, until it has been lowered to conform to the mold.

When pounding out plates or bowls, there is the danger of lowering the dish to too great a depth, causing the metal to stretch

[328]

to such a degree that it is paper thin or gives away entirely. Do not attempt to use 16 gauge pewter for a bowl that exceeds two inches in depth. Thicker metal, of course, would permit greater stretching without breaking.

To strengthen and finish the edge of the plate, the extreme outer edge of the plate may be rolled under. This is most easily accomplished in the following manner:

Hold the plate at an angle, top side up, against the sharp edge of a table or piece of hard wood that is stationary. The metal edge should not extend more than one-eighth inch over the edge of the wood. With a mallet, pound this extending edge over the wood, turning the plate during the process until the edge has been pounded back slightly all the way around. Care must be taken to maintain the same width for the rolled edge all around the plate or the circle is destroyed. After this edge has been pounded to almost an upright position around the plate, place the plate upside down on a flat surface and pound the edge back upon itself. Be sure that the top of the plate is protected from anything that might mar or dent its surface.

The size of the plate governs the finish required for the edge. A nine- or ten-inch plate needs a rolled edge; a larger plate frequently needs reinforcing by the addition of a wire placed inside the rolled edge, before it is pounded back on itself. Smaller plates are quite satisfactory if just filed smooth.

The surface of the plate requires some attention before it is ready for use. If there are any rough edges, these should be smoothed with a fine metal file and strips of very fine emery paper. The large surfaces of the plate are polished by first going over the entire plate with very fine emery paper, or number 3/0 steel wool. A rotary motion around the plate gives the best results. A further degree of satin smoothness is achieved by rubbing the plate with a soft cloth that has been dipped into oil and then powdered pumice. Maintain the rotary motion. The plate will look very smudged and black by this time, but a bath in warm, soapy water will remove the grime and expose the dull satiny surface. Pewter is at its best with a finish of this sort. It should not look like chromium.

Metal Etching

Sometimes it is desirable to etch a simple design upon the surface of a metal object. A border, a surface pattern, or a single centered motif are all suitable choices for the enrichment of a bowl or plate. The design should be worked out on paper very carefully, following the previously prescribed methods. Pewter does not lend itself to too fine or intricate a design, nor does the process of etching when done by the beginner. As one's skill develops, more intricate patterns may be attempted safely.

The design is traced on the metal by using carbon paper, strengthening the lines with pencil afterwards; or by pricking through the paper pattern with a sharp, pointed instrument such as a darning needle or a victrola needle set into a handle. After the paper pattern has been removed, the pricked dots may be connected with scratched lines. For a simple pattern made up of large areas the design may be cut out of paper and drawn around with a pencil, or more clearly with a needle.

The etching process involves the use of a resist and an acid capable of eating away the exposed parts. For the resist, asphaltum is used. This may be purchased at any hardware store or ten-cent store. It is a thick, viscous substance that hardens within twenty-four hours. It should be painted over any part of the metal that is to be protected from the action of the acid. This part of the design will stand out in relief on the finished plate. Besides protecting parts of the design, all undecorated parts of the plate should also be covered carefully with a coating of the asphaltum. This includes the back and edges. Try to avoid air bubbles forming in the asphaltum while painting with it. These permit the acid to reach the metal and give a pock marked effect over the surface. Allow the asphaltum to dry for at least twenty-four hours before the etching process is attempted.

For the etching process a container large enough to permit the complete immersion of the article to be etched is necessary. A glass dish, usually a glass pie pan or casserole, is adequate; but for very large articles, a piece of roofing paper folded up at the corners to produce a tray of sufficient size and depth is usable. Metal containers cannot be used, since they are susceptible to the action of the acid.

The acid most frequently used for etching pewter is nitric acid. A solution made of ten parts of water to one part of full strength nitric acid is usually strong enough. Put the water in the container first and then pour in the acid. Keep the face away from the fumes, and avoid splashing. Nitric acid burns one's skin. Immerse the prepared metal object in the acid bath. Very soon small bubbles will form on the surface of the metal exposed to the acid. If these are gently brushed away with a feather, the etching process will be hastened somewhat. When the metal appears to have been eaten away to the desired depth, remove from the acid bath and rinse in clear water. A spring clothes pin makes a good device for removing most pieces, or a piece of string may be placed under the plate so that the two ends hang out over the edge of the large acid container. These may be used to lift one side of the plate out of the

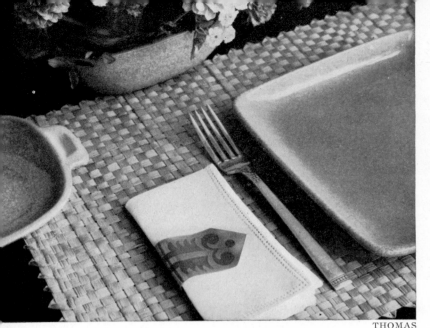

ETCHED NAPKIN CLIP

Pewter, pottery, and the coarser linens are harmonious.

acid. If the acid bath seems to be working too slowly, carefully add a small amount of acid and agitate the solution to mix thoroughly.

After the etched object has been removed, rinse very thoroughly in water to wash away any trace of acid. All of the asphaltum now has to be removed. This may prove to be tedious, but if it has been carefully applied in the beginning to form clean-cut edges, and a coating entirely devoid of air holes, there is great satisfaction in the emergence of a design free from the dark, unpleasant-looking puddle of asphaltum and kerosene. Kerosene or turpentine, generously applied to the asphaltum and rubbed with a soft cloth to speed up the process, is the most satisfactory for removing the acid resist.

The film of kerosene or turpentine should be washed off with warm water and soap. The surface of the metal will take on a more pleasant sheen if rubbed briskly with powdered pumice stone and oil. Water may be substituted for the oil. It works quite as well for this purpose. In case the edges of the plate are pock marked where the metal was not fully protected from the acid, a bit of filing or rubbing with fine emery paper will do much to restore the softly beveled or rolled edge that was originally produced. Another bath with warm water and soap and a final buffing with a soft cloth will complete the plate, making it ready for use.

There are many articles that lend themselves to decoration produced by etching. To mention only a few, one might consider: paper knives, napkin rings or markers, bracelets, clips for paper money, or clips to be worn with a suitable dress. Decorative pins for costume wear are easily made from any variety of shapes, and a quite satisfactory method of fastening can be provided by soldering a safety pin to the underside of the pin itself, after all decoration has been applied to the metal. Before soldering the safety pin, be sure to figure out the best way for the head of the pin to face. If it is put on in reverse, it would have to be opened and closed with the left hand. That is a little difficult for most people to manage. Buttons, either all pewter or made of a combination of pewter and copper, could also be etched. Copper etches very well. However, if the two metals are together, do not try to etch a design into both metals at one time. The speed of the action of the acid is not the same for each. One part of the object would be either underetched or overetched if this were attempted.

Serving Pieces

Sometimes a special serving spoon, useful for dressing, jellies or jams, salads, or nuts adds to the unusualness of the dish. These spoons should, of course, be designed to go well with the other silverware used during a meal, yet they may differ enough to supply a decorative effect to the table. The use to which they will be put will determine the general size and shape of the spoon—a wide, short-handled shape for nuts; long-handled and rather shallow but large shapes for salads.

The making of a spoon calls for some knowledge as to the properties of the metal which is being worked and involves somewhat more work and skill than that needed for pounding a simple bowl. It is not, however, a difficult problem and may be done by one with patience and some familiarity with the techniques.

A sketch should be made of the spoon showing the size and shape of the bowl and its relation to the length of the handle. This proportion should be planned so that the handle will balance the bowl of the spoon and at the same time allow for easy manipulation.

The handle of the spoon should be made of one or several lengths of pewter wire. This wire may be obtained through companies dealing in pewter and comes in various sizes and shapes. Square, round, and half-round are among the most common. Since the strength of the handle is determined by the size of the wire (pewter is a very soft metal) it is well to order a rather substantial size. It has been found that three-sixteenths to one-quarter inch square or round wire is very satisfactory. If the handle is not to be too long, one length of wire is sufficient. If a long-handled spoon or fork is being made, two lengths soldered together are more advisable.

The bowl of the spoon or fork is made from a small disc of pewter which may be of 16 gauge if the spoon is a small one or of 12 gauge if a large spoon such as a salad spoon is being made.

To make a pewter spoon, a few more supplies than those listed for the bowl or plate will be needed. This is a project which involves soldering, and an electric soldering iron is adequate and easy to use. One may purchase such an iron at any hardware store or at a five-and-ten-cent store. A metal file should also be bought at the same time to be used for keeping the point of the iron clean at all times. A small bottle of glycerin will serve as flux for the soldering process, and one or two small screw clamps will aid in holding the pewter in place during the soldering. Soft pewter solder may be obtained from the company that handles the pewter. This comes in lengths of wire and may be cut into small pieces for use.

To make a suitable mold for pounding the bowl of the spoon, follow the directions given for making a bowl mold in the preceding chapter. Sometimes the lower part of a larger bowl mold will have enough of a curved surface to make it a satisfactory spoon mold. In general, a serving spoon or ladle does not need to have a deeply curved surface. Follow the directions given for pounding a pewter bowl when shaping the spoon. Actually the problem is the same except for size.

The next step in the making of the spoon is forming the handle. The wire should be cut to the length planned, with an added amount of about three-fourths of an inch to permit soldering to the bowl of the spoon. If any decoration is to be applied to the handle, this should be done before the two main pieces are soldered together since it is easier to work on them separately. The handle may be treated in many ways. Small pewter balls may be soldered to the sides of the wire; small file marks nicely spaced may be in-

PEWTER SOLDERING EQUIPMENT

Clamps, files, tweezers, pewter solder, a small bottle of glycerine, and the soldering iron.

THOMAS

PEWTER FORK AND SPOONS, BOWL AND HANDLE DESIGNS

cised along the length or at the end; the wire may be bent with pliers into a graceful scroll form at the end; or wire of smaller gauges may be wound or wrapped around the handle at points in keeping with the general proportions of the spoon.

When two lengths of wire are to be soldered together to form a handle, they should be absolutely straight so that the sides are flush, one with the other. Clasp the two pieces together firmly with the screw clamps. It is a good idea to put folded bits of paper between the clamps and the metal to prevent marring the pewter surface. Brush the surface to be soldered with glycerin. A medicine dropper may be used instead of a brush. Some bottles come equipped with stopper of this type. Along the line between the two wires place small pieces of pewter solder. Apply the heated soldering iron to the solder. It will be necessary to hold the iron against the solder until the metal beneath it becomes well heated, since the solder will not melt and flow between the pewter pieces until they are heated to the melting point of the solder. Solder flows over a heated surface but not over a cool surface. When the solder reaches the melting point, it will turn shiny and liquid and will flow down between the pewter. It is well to remember that the pewter melts at a temperature only slightly above that of the solder so care must be taken not to keep the soldering iron on the metal any longer than is necessary. Perhaps it would be wise to practice with a few extra lengths of wire before attempting the finished product. Decoration that must be soldered onto the spoon is handled in the same way, clamping the various pieces to the handle and soldering them. This method of soldering is bound to leave some excess solder on the surface of the metal itself. Any extra solder may be filed off easily; but in planning the original design, one should remember to keep it simple enough so that its parts may be reached with a file. Such a design is most satisfactory from every standpoint. Flat pieces of decoration may be sweated onto the wire in the same method as suggested for pewter buttons as described under dress accessories.

The part of the handle which is to be soldered to the bowl of the spoon should be filed into a tapered wedge-shaped point. All filing should be on the back of the wire handle and should be done on about the last three-quarters of the handle. This tapered length should be bent with pliers to match the outer curve of the spoon bowl. Again, with the protected clamps, fasten the handle to the bowl of the spoon. Brush or apply glycerin along the edges of the parts to be soldered and place the solder along these same crevices. Solder as before, taking care not to overheat the metal. File off any excess solder and smooth down all the rough edges of the pewter. Bend the handle of the spoon to the desired curve. This can usually be done by hand; but if pliers are needed, pad the jaws to prevent marring the metal. Polish the metal in the same way as suggested for finishing the bowl or plate.

If a salad fork is being made to pair with the spoon, the tines of the fork may be sawed into the disc with a jeweler's saw, or if very simple in design, cut with metal shears. This should not be done until after the shaped pewter disc has been soldered to the handle.

Pretty and Practical

Further projects involving the use of soldering equipment will suggest themselves once this new technique has been mastered. Aside from the many possibilities of costume jewelry, which any ingenious person can work out for himself, household accessories may be easily made. Simple salt and pepper shakers may be made in a

PEWTER HOLDER FOR
A LARGE CANDLE

by Doris Cox

The candle was made from an accumulation of short ends of candles.

THOMAS

variety of forms which will fit into the accouterments of the table. The soldering may be done with an iron as suggested for the pewter spoons. These utensils should be made from flat lengths of pewter bent and soldered into the desired forms. A cylindrical form may be made by bending a strip of pewter around a piece of doweling of the desired diameter, a broomstick, or around a cylindrical iron stake such as used for more advanced pewter work (see catalogues of companies handling craft equipment). To the top of this rounded piece of pewter, a dome-shaped disc with holes of a suitable size drilled into it may be soldered; and to the bottom, a disc rounded upward slightly. The bottom disc should have a hole drilled into it which would be large enough to permit pouring in salt or pepper. A cork may be used as a stopper or a small piece of adhesive tape may be placed over the opening. The fact that the bottom disc has been rounded upward slightly will permit the shaker to stand even though a cork is used to fill the opening. The dome-shaped pieces are made in the same way as the bowls of spoons. There are other variations

[339]

of shapes which might be experimented with. A flat disc might be soldered to the bottom of the cylinder and a foot, made from a narrow strip of pewter bent into a slightly smaller cylinder, soldered to the disc. The top disc might also be flat instead of domed. The salt or pepper shakers need not be round; a square or even somewhat rectangular shape could be equally attractive.

After the beginner has become familiar with the qualities and some of the possibilities of the metal, new problems will suggest themselves in rapid succession. We have mentioned jewelry only briefly. Some of the articles which are easily made are: bracelets, etched, or decorated with pierced designs done with a saw and drills, or soldered decoration; buckles and buttons; brooches and bar-pins; necklaces or decorative pendants; and clips.

Among the more easily made household accessories other than those described in greater detail are: bookends, pierced, etched or decorated with solder-work; candle holders of simple design; decorative boxes, such as trinket, cigarette, or match boxes; plant stands, etched or pierced and fastened to a piece of wood; napkin rings or clips; coasters; and many other articles.

It is hoped that the illustrations in this chapter will be used as a source of stimulation rather than as something to copy. Pewter provides a wonderful outlet for the craftsman. As with any new material, it is first necessary to learn what pewter will do. It should never be forced beyond its potentiality. The soft glow of the surface of pewter is most consistent with an easy flow of line in the structural design, decorated simply and sparingly.

After one has decided upon a design suitable for pewter work, consider which soldering method is the most adaptable. When one *layer* of metal is placed upon another, sweating the two pieces together is expedient. There is less likelihood of any excess solder

THOMAS

PEWTER BOWL, LADLE, AND SALT AND PEPPER SHAKERS
by Dorothy and Alexander Tillotson

THOMAS

PEWTER AND COPPER NAPKIN RINGS
Designed by Helen S. Petersen and executed by the Minneapolis WPA
Handicraft Project

NAPKIN RING IN USE

An appropriate table setting
for the use of pewter.

remaining upon the surface. This method is described in detail in the discussion of pewter buttons. It would be recommended for the napkin rings and clips. All the soldering is done before the metal is bent into its final form. The use of the soldering iron is the better method whenever two *edges* are to be joined, such as two wires for a spoon handle, or a dome to the top of a cylinder as might be needed for a salt shaker or a candlestick.

No matter what the craft, neglect of finishing details is quite apt to result in an unsatisfactory product. Time spent thus is never wasted.

Chapter XVI

Festive Ways

PERHAPS THE FOLLOWING THINGS THAT WE ARE SUGGESTING DO not properly come under the heading of crafts since they are of a temporary and, in some cases, perishable nature. We do feel, however, that they offer fields for the application of design which involve techniques that may be experimented with inexpensively. At the same time, these articles will do a great deal toward making some holiday or special occasion a more gala affair and are projects in which the whole family enjoys taking an active part. The danger of loss is not great, and the products resulting from such round-table effort may be startlingly attractive.

These simple techniques are also suitable for the solution of the rainy-day entertainment problem when children are most apt to become annoyances rather than pleasures. And too, some of these articles may be demonstrated to the convalescent child or even to the adult who is yearning for something with which to pass the time.

To Anyone's Heart

Many, many times during the year, fancy or unusual cookies are in demand. This is especially true when a children's party is being given, or at Christmas time. We have experimented with the old-fashioned gingerbread cooky with favorable results. These cook-

GLORIFIED GINGER-BREAD

Confectioners' sugar sprinkled through the cut out parts of a paper "snowflake" gives a plain cake a festive air.

THOMAS

ies have been well received by every child who has seen or eaten them and have been equally enjoyed by the parents as well. May we pass on our two best experiments? Remember, these are not just cookies—they are works of art!

If Johnny or sister Sue have ever delighted in a handful of modeling clay, especially of the plasticine variety, the following gingerbread cookies will meet with great enthusiasm. The recipe given for the more traditional cooky is also used for the modeled cooky. Any ginger cooky recipe that is short enough to retain its shape and not puff up in baking would be suitable, but a small piece of the dough, pricked or shaped in some fashion, should be tested by baking to determine whether it really will hold its original form.

The process of forming the cooky is most elementary. First, a piece of dough is patted or rolled flat to form a sheet slightly larger than the visualized finished cooky will be. This is best when about one-eighth inch thick. The very smallest amount of flour should be used on the top surface of the dough for that would pre-

MODELED GINGER-BREAD COOKIES

Photograph from the Photographic Laboratory, University of Minnesota.)

vent the next layer from adhering to this foundation. Then by rolling up small cylinders of dough, or small pellets, that in some cases might be flattened out to form discs, a design is made on the first piece of dough.

An active imagination is about all one needs, for the more naïve the approach, the more entertaining the result. Imagine a girl-cooky made by putting long strings of the dough side by side to form wavy tresses, or little pellets placed side by side to form curls; raisin eyes; dough pellets, small cylinders, or a raisin for a mouth; pieces of blanched almonds for a necklace; buttons of raisins, almonds, or dough; red cinnamon candies are useful for decorative notes too. The bottom of her skirt could have dough braid, ruffles or pleats; eyelet embroidery of raisins or any other decoration one's fancy might dictate. Interesting textures or designs can be made with the tines of a fork, toothpick or any other gadget found in the kitchen that would leave an interesting impression when pressed into the dough.

MEXICAN BREAD

Little rolls of the dough and nodules made by pricking the surface of the loaf furnished a most satisfactory outlet for a Mexican baker's strong feeling for design.

THOMAS

Gingerbread men or women aren't the only things to make. All sorts of animals, birds, and fish can be concocted, and decorative flowers bloom in great profusion once the knack of using dough, almonds, raisins, and cinnamon candies for the various parts of a flower is developed. It takes about one trial to start one off. After the decorations have been applied or pricked or pressed into the basic dough, the excess is cut away, leaving just the planned shape ready to be baked. In order to facilitate moving these "masterpieces" on to a pan, the work may be done on a sheet of wax paper which is removed after the cooky has been baked. Ideas for the designs will probably be largely governed by the season of the year during which they are made.

The counterparts of these modeled cookies can be found in almost any well illustrated book on European peasant crafts. The cookies, or cakes, as they are called, are frequently very elaborate, and at a casual glance might be mistaken for wood carvings. Reproductions of them are usually found on the same pages upon which one finds carved butter molds.

[346]

A SWEET COUPLE

A cardboard pattern, cookie dough, frosting, and imagination.

THOMAS

Everyone is quite familiar with the gingerbread men that depend upon frosting for decoration. These, too, are of European origin. What joy it must have been to receive one as a gift. The bakers let imagination have full sway.

This recipe has been tested for these cookies:

MOLASSES COOKIES

⅞ c. shortening		⅔ t. allspice	
⅔ c. sugar		⅔ t. ginger	
4 c. flour		⅔ t. cinnamon	
1⅓ t. soda		⅔ c. dark molasses	
⅔ t. salt		⅔ c. cold coffee	

Cream the shortening and sugar together well. Sift the dry ingredients together, and add to the creamed ingredients alternately with the coffee and molasses, which have been mixed together. Chill the dough thoroughly. Roll out one-quarter inch thick and cut. Bake in a hot oven (400° F.) for fifteen minutes. This recipe makes about five dozen cookies of ordinary size.

[347]

PLAIN FROSTING

¾ c. confectioners' sugar
½ t. vanilla, or ½ t. lemon juice
Enough light corn syrup to produce the proper consistency

Put the sugar through a sieve to remove all lumps. Add the flavoring and corn syrup. For this purpose, the frosting needs to be fairly firm but still thin enough to be used in a pastry bag.

The special tool needed for this craft is a pastry bag. Many households have canvas ones on hand, but a paper one will serve the purpose admirably.

Use thin, tough paper (writing paper or fresh, clean wrapping paper) in sheets eight and one-half by eleven inches. Cut the sheets in half diagonally. Each piece will make a separate pastry bag. Wrap around to make a cornucopia with a very sharp point. This point should come in the middle of the longest side.

The three corners of the triangular piece of paper should come together at the open end, where they can be turned in several times so that the cornucopia will hold together firmly. The points may be cut in one of the three ways shown in the diagram. The plain tube opening is the one most used for gingerbread men.

For elaborate work small brass tubes with different-shaped openings are for sale at kitchen furnishing stores. These metal tubes may be used in the paper cornets or in the cloth pastry bag. When using the paper cornet, cut off three-quarters of an inch at the pointed end and drop the metal tube into it, letting it project through the opening at the end. Then put the frosting inside the paper cornucopia. These paper bags are most convenient when using frosting of several different colors. When only one color is being used, as in decorating a wedding cake, a cloth bag with a metal end

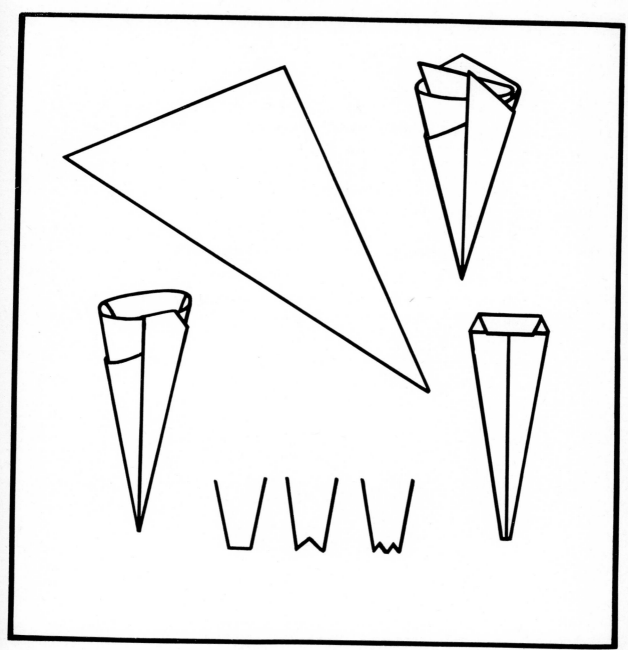

HOW TO MAKE A PASTRY BAG OF PAPER

to which the tubes may be screwed will be found more convenient, as the paper bags soften and break with much usage.

Put the frosting into the bag, filling it not more than one-third full. Bring the edges of the open top together, turn down the right hand corner, then the left hand corner; then fold over twice and continue to fold the paper tube down to the frosting. If using a cloth bag, twist the bag just above the frosting. This is done in order that all the frosting may be forced out through the tube at the lower end of the bag and also to prevent any of the frosting coming out at the top.

The consistency of the frosting will be a matter of experimentation for any person mixing it. It should be soft enough to go through the tube easily, and firm enough to hold its shape at the same time. If the frosting is too stiff, it will harden rapidly and crack off the cooky very soon. A plain frosting of water and confectioners' sugar or a fudge frosting cannot be forced through a tube as it becomes hard and dry.

The principles of correct use of color values stressed in earlier parts of the book apply here. The dough becomes a rich golden brown while baking, the frosting is light; bitter chocolate melted over hot water and painted onto the cookies with a small, clean brush adds the dark value needed. The chocolate effects rare and costly velvet for skirts, boleros, or breeches. Try a villain with a chocolate moustache!

Eggs in One Basket

The mention of holidays brings to mind the fun that a session of decorating Easter eggs can provide. The batik process is a good one to use. The simplest method is to gather up all the onion

UKRAINIAN EASTER EGG

THOMAS

skins one can find and put a layer of them in the bottom of a kettle large enough to hold all the eggs one wishes to boil.

A design, simple or elaborate, is then painted with hot wax on the shell of the raw eggs. The eggs should be at room temperature. Use an old brush because it won't be usable for paints after this. Place the eggs in the kettle, adding onion skins at the same time; add water and boil the required length of time. The eggs emerge a beautiful brown with the designs showing up in the creamy eggshell color. Do not stir the contents of the kettle with a spoon while the eggs are boiling. The edges of the spoon mar the design.

Another simple method is to put the design on boiled eggs with white or colored wax crayons. It is more simple to control the crayon than a brushful of hot wax. Wax all portions to remain the lightest color, dip into a dye bath, wax everything that is to appear this color, dip into the next dye bath and so on until all the desired colors have been used. So thin a coating of wax is used by this

[351]

CZECHOSLOVAKIAN EASTER EGG

THOMAS

crayon method that it is not necessary to remove it. If hot wax is applied, *warm* the eggs in a very *slow* oven until the wax has melted and run off. Wipe with a warm soft cloth.

The beautiful peasant-designed Easter eggs so often brought to this country are done on raw eggs which are never cooked, but are put away in a dry place for months until the contents of the shell dry up. They are given as tokens of friendship, not as food.

If the eggs are to be eaten, only vegetable dyes should be used. Eggs to be used for decorative purposes only may be dyed with wool, silk, or leather dyes. Some of the gayest colors are obtainable by soaking the color out of crepe paper. Some of the Ukrainian people who design many exquisite gift eggs each spring use this source for their dye supply. The resulting dye is not to be used on eggs to be eaten.

[352]

Craftsmen who are skilled in this waxing and dyeing technique, which is known as batik, use a *tjanting* to help them apply the wax more easily and accurately. Tjantings come in a number of forms, but all are designed for the same function: to hold melted wax. The most elaborate form is a small copper cup having one or more extremely small metal spouts, the simplest an inch-long piece of fine copper or brass tubing. These tiny reservoirs need to be fastened with wire to a convenient handle, such as a meat skewer or a lollipop stick. The tjanting is dipped first into a cup of melted wax, then kept at the right temperature during the waxing process by being passed through a candle flame now and then.

The people of Java and Bali, as well as those from some of the other Oriental countries, use the batik process on cloth for both wearing apparel and house furnishings. Cotton, such as fine nainsook, is very suitable for this technique. Silk produces a more brilliant color. Whatever the fabric used, all sizing must be washed from the fibers before the work is begun.

Designs made up of small geometric figures or of very decorative and conventionalized animals, birds, flowers, and fish are usually most successful for this technique.

The designs are traced upon the cloth with a pencil just dark enough to be seen during the first light dye baths. The cloth should then be tacked to a wooden frame to hold it taut during the waxing. Only the lightest color value of the design is waxed at first. Since this will be, in the completed piece, the color of the cloth itself it may be necessary to pre-dye the fabric to this color. If the wax has not completely penetrated the cloth, wax must be applied from the back of the fabric as well as the front. The tjanting is used to draw lines or to make small dots, a brush is more expedient for larger areas.

Beeswax, since it is more pliable than paraffin, is preferred for the batik process.

Batik dyes may be purchased at art supply houses. However, ordinary household dye prepared for the fabric being used is quite satisfactory. For batik work, the dye bath must be *cool* or the wax will melt and the work be ruined. Wet the waxed fabric completely, then immerse in the dye bath until the correct value has been obtained. Do not forget that the color will be lighter as it dries. Rinse in clear water and dry away from heat. Repeat the waxing and dyeing processes until all areas have been dyed to the colors desired. Never squeeze the material or the wax will crack and allow the dye to penetrate to the cloth.

The color plan for simple batiks must be one of *related* colors. However, one may use as many values of each of those colors as one wishes. The lightest values are dyed first, then the successively darker values are dyed. The effect of one color over another should be considered since the two colors will blend to produce a third. Small areas of colors or colors of contrasting hue may be painted in with a brush. When this is done, the dye should be kept in place with a waxed outline and then the colored area protected from later dye baths by being completely covered with wax.

When the dyeing is completed, it is necessary to remove the wax from the fabric. Large amounts of wax can be removed by placing the material between newspapers while it is ironed. The last traces of the wax can be removed only with a grease solvent. Naphtha will do this, but the fluid is extremely dangerous to use. It is wiser to use one of the noninflammable cleaning fluids which are on the market or to send the work to the dry cleaners where the wax may be removed by professional methods.

[354]

Batiked paper for gift wrapping is fun to make and is a fine method for trying out this old and once very popular craft. The methods used are similar to those given above, but it is unnecessary to subject the paper to the final cleaning process.

Each season will suggest new uses of any talent or skill developed by previous craft experiences. The person who doubts his ability might start his hobby during this time since fewer materials and less time would be needed. At whatever end of the game one begins, a fascinating time awaits the person willing to make the effort.

GINGERBREAD BIRD

Christmas tree ornament decorated with pleated paper wings, frosting, and colored sugar.

Now You Know

IF YOU HAVE NOT READ THIS BOOK FROM COVER TO COVER AT ONE sitting, but instead have read small portions of it at a time and have digested these bits thoroughly, you should be well equipped for more technical exploration in the crafts field. Perhaps you have made most of the articles described herein; perhaps you have made only a few. In any case, no doubt you have found that certain things have been more interesting to you. If this is true, then follow that branch of craft work to its very end; become an accomplished technician in that phase of art production. Much is being said today about the value of a hobby as a leisure time occupation or to mitigate emotional strain. If this book has led you to discover some interesting hobby, your life will be the richer for it. Do not allow your new interests to lag, but let them grow and develop into something of which you can be justly proud.

Of the many suggestions included in this book, some will be especially suited for use in the home, others to the enhancement of the wardrobe, many to camp or school. None of them call for an outlay of equipment beyond the means of most readers, and a large number of the articles can be made with little or almost no equipment. The directions for the construction and decoration of the various objects have been kept simple, keyed in as far as was possible to the novice. This was done by intent, since the book was planned to encourage, rather than to discourage, the beginner. Naturally, successful results are stimulating to anyone, but we would like to emphasize the fact that one or two failures do not indicate lack of ability. Patience rather than talent is of prime importance to the completion of a good craft product.

It is of utmost importance that the first few chapters dealing with taste, design, and color be understood thoroughly before even the simplest project is undertaken. This cannot be stressed too much, because the ultimate effect of the finished piece of work depends on a sound knowledge of the principles involved in its making. Constant reference to these chapters during the craft process itself will be insurance against possible failure. These first chapters are condensed and simplified, but if more information is desired, the library shelves may be referred to. We do feel that our information is complete, however, in so far as is necessary to the projects outlined in the rest of the text.

Bibliography

IT IS HOPED THAT A LIST OF BOOKS SUCH AS THIS WILL PROVE helpful in several ways to the reader. This is not an exhaustive list nor do all libraries have upon their shelves the very books mentioned, but these titles may give clues to appropriate substitutes. Often, too, one tends to narrow down source material to only those references dealing with the actual article about to be made. This practice handicaps one at the outset. There is always the possibility that new interests may be aroused by related material. If a personal clipping file is subdivided in the main as is suggested by the headings used for this bibliography, and then used thoughtfully, it will provide a rich source of stimulating ideas for years to come.

GOOD TASTE

ART AND LIFE, by Hannah Priebsch Closs, New York, Frederick A. Stokes Company, about 1938.

> Aims at pointing out that "art is inextricably interwoven with all aspects of life." Though it is a scholarly text, it is not pedantic. Excellent selection of illustrative material.

ART FOR YOUNG AMERICA, by F. W. Nicholas, M. B. Trilling, M. Lee, and E. A. Stephan, Peoria, Illinois, The Manual Arts Press, 1946.

> This book was written on the now popular theme of art for all. The approach is somewhat different, however, since it was intended as a text for beginning high school students and attempts to keep to their level of appreciation. Theoretical and technical application of the problems discussed are presented at the end of each chapter.

ART IN EVERYDAY LIFE, by Harriet and Vetta Goldstein, New York, The Macmillan Company, 1940.

> This book provides a sound standard upon which to build an ever-growing appreciation of both the aesthetic and the practical forms of art encountered in daily living.

[359]

ART TODAY, AN INTRODUCTION TO THE FINE AND FUNCTIONAL ARTS, by Ray Faulkner, Edwin Ziegfeld, and Gerald Hill, New York, Henry Holt and Company, 1941.

> This is an interesting book for those whose aim it is to understand the arts. It was written by three people who are well qualified to express their opinions as to the various phases of the allied branches of artistic endeavor.

GOOD DESIGN IS YOUR BUSINESS, by R. M. Bennett, Edward S. Evans, Jr., and Walter Dorwin Teague, Buffalo, New York, The Buffalo Fine Arts Academy, Albright Art Gallery, not dated.

> An excellent statement of design as found in daily living. Text brief and to the point. Many superior illustrations.

THE GRASS ROOTS OF ART, by Herbert Read, London, England, Lindsay Drummond, Limited, 1947.

> An outstandingly good discussion of taste. Read says that "skill should be taught as a basic education of the senses from infancy, not as an isolated habit learned at the end of the educational process."

THE PRACTICE OF DESIGN, compilation (with an introduction by Herbert Read), London, England, Lund Humphries and Company, 1946.

> This book should be read. It is important to one desiring to broaden his understanding of design in industry and its effect upon the products he buys.

THE STORY OF MODERN APPLIED ART, by Rudolph Rosenthal and Helena L. Ratzka, New York, Harper and Brothers, 1948.

> A book which enlightens the reader on the development of style in handicrafts and industrial arts. The fight for quality is not easy, and the struggle is being carried on by leaders in all countries. All the contributing factors of a period in a country are well discussed in this text.

DESIGN METHODS

THE ART OF COLOR AND DESIGN, by Maitland Graves, New York and London, McGraw-Hill Book Company, Inc., 1941.

> A logical and simple presentation of all the basic principles of two-dimensional design.

leum engravings, silk screen process, bookbinding, and booklets. These are prepared with clear instructions for amateurs.

LINO-CUTS, by Claude Flight, R.B.A., New York, Dodd, Mead and Company, 1928.

LINO CUTTING AND PRINTING, by Claude Flight, R.B.A., London, B. T. Batsford, Ltd., 1934.
> These are both good books on the subject. The contemporary approach of the latter is especially pleasing.

CARD WEAVING

BRIKVAEVNING (Card weaving), by Margrethe Hald, Forlag, Kobenhavn, Gyldendalske Boghandel-Nordisk, MCMXXXII.
> Although printed in Danish, this book is so well illustrated that it is fairly comprehensible to anyone with some knowledge of basic card weaving principles. It shows advanced techniques, many variations. The color plates are good.

CARD WEAVING, by Mary M. Atwater, New York, The Universal School of Handicrafts, 1931.
> Not only are directions and patterns for weaving this braid given, but uses for the finished product are suggested as well.

References to be found in the periodical THE WEAVER:
> NEW IDEAS FOR TABLET WOVEN RUGS, by Beatrice A. Shephard, Vol. 1, No. 3, July 1936.
>
> "STUNTING" ON THE CARDS, by Mary M. Atwater, Vol. 2, No. 1, Jan. 1937.
>
> CARD WEAVING TECHNIQUE, by Clara M. Youse, Vol. 6, No. 1, Jan.-Feb. 1941.
>
> DRAWING DOWN CARD WEAVING DRAFTS, by Mrs. W. F. McNulty, Vol. 6, No. 1, Jan.-Feb. 1941.

WEAVING WITH SMALL APPLIANCES, BOOK II, TABLET WEAVING, by Luther Hooper, London, Sir Isaac Pitman and Sons, Ltd., 1923.

FINGER WEAVING, BRAIDING, ETC.

BRAIDING AND KNOTTING FOR AMATEURS, by Constantine A. Belash, Boston, The Beacon Press, Inc., 1936.
> Good for techniques—valuable for anyone interested in making novelty belts or unusual cords for accessories.

References to be found in the periodical THE WEAVER:

THE "OSAGE" BRAID, by Mary M. Atwater, Vol. 4, No. 2, April 1939.

A FEW SIMPLE BRAIDS, by Mary M. Atwater, Vol. 7, No. 1, Jan.-Feb. 1942.

THE FINISH OF EDGES, by Mary M. Atwater, Vol. 7, No. 2, July 1942.

METALWORK

ART METALWORK, A Manual for Amateurs, by Emil F. Kronquist, New York, London, McGraw-Hill Book Company, Inc., 1942.

METAL WORK, by R. D. and M. E. Snively, Brattleboro, Stephen Daye Press, 1940.

> This book confines itself to simple problems; well illustrated with photographs.

PEWTER, Spun, Wrought, and Cast, by B. N. Osburn and G. O. Wilber, Scranton, International Textbook Company, 1938.

> This treatise leads to very advanced problems, but fundamental processes are well presented.

SIMPLE METALWORK, by E. Kronquist and A. G. Pelikan, New York, The Studio Publications, Inc., 1940.

> Both the Kronquist books are prepared very much as manuals. All the steps of the processes are very well illustrated with drawings and photographs.

NEEDLEWORK

ADVENTURES IN EMBROIDERY, by Ernest Thesiger, New York, The Studio Publications, Inc., 1941.

> Accessories for the home are described. The author realizes that all embroidery is not art—but may be merely patience and the ability to handle a needle. Elaborate historic and contemporary examples of the art of needlework are shown, but Mr. Thesiger understands that most needleworkers have at most only an hour or two each day at their disposal, and makes his suggestions accordingly. He insists that the work be done for a specific purpose.

APPLIQUÉ DESIGN AND METHOD, by Kathleen Mann, London, A. and C. Black, Ltd., 1937.

> The author recommends a very playful, free approach to the problem of design.

DICTIONARY OF EMBROIDERY STITCHES, by Mary Thomas, New York, William Morrow and Company, 1936.
    Just what the title implies. Excellent.

EMBROIDERY DESIGN, by Molly Booker, New York, The Studio Publications, Inc., 1935.
    Stresses an original approach to the problem of design.

ENCYCLOPEDIA OF NEEDLEWORK, by Therese de Dillmont, Alsace, Dornach, 1890.
    This book is from the D. M. C. Library. It is very old but very useful.

HOOKED RUGS, and How To Make Them, by Anna M. L. Phillips, New York, The Macmillan Company, 1925.

THE HOOKED RUG, by William Winthrop Kent, New York, Dodd, Mead and Company, 1930.
    A record of the origin and development of the hooked rug. Methods of making and suitable sources for design are included.

MODERN DESIGN IN EMBROIDERY, by Rebecca Crompton, London, B. T. Batsford, Ltd., 1936.
    A very imaginative approach. Some of the less-known stitches are used effectively. Well illustrated.

MODERN EMBROIDERY, by Mary Hogarth, Garden City, Garden City Publishing Company, Inc., 1933.
    Presents examples of the work of many well known embroiderers. This is a good source for motifs, use of materials, and ideas for household and costume accessories.

NEEDLEPOINT AS A HOBBY, by Geneva D. Lent, New York and London, Harper and Brothers, 1942.
    This book contains a historical development of needlepoint with an extensive and diagrammatic set of instructions for carrying on every step in the creation of needlework tapestries.

OLD PATCHWORK QUILTS, by Ruth E. Finley, Philadelphia and London, Lippincott, 1929.
    This is a presentation of the history and directions for making patchwork quilts.

THE SAMPLER BOOK OF DECORATIVE NEEDLEWORK, by Louisa E. E. Judd-Morris, Leicester, The Dryad Press, 1942.
    There are many useful diagrams in this book.

RARE HOOKED RUGS, by William Winthrop Kent, Springfield, The Pond-Ekberg Company, 1941.

A very interesting book to peruse before designing a rug.

QUILTS, THEIR STORY AND HOW TO MAKE THEM, by Marie D. Webster, New York, Tudor Publishing Company, 1948.

TOOLS AND TOYS OF STITCHERY, by Gertrude Whiting, New York, Columbia University Press, 1928.

Presents uses and development of the many implements used in making laces and needlework. Fine illustrations. Text presented imaginatively.

LEATHERWORK

GENERAL LEATHERCRAFT, by Raymond Cherry, Bloomington, Illinois, McKnight and McKnight, 1946.

Good history of leather, long list of supply houses, methods well explained and illustrated, wide variety of projects.

LEATHER CRAFT, by William H. Johnson and Louis V. Newkirk, St. Paul, Minnesota, The Hobbycraft Series, The Webb Publishing Company, 1945.

Good discussion on the preparation of hides; good drawings of tools, equipment, and processes. The articles to make are useful. Designs are above the average found in craft books except when they become too pictorial.

LEATHERCRAFT AS A HOBBY, by Clifford Pyle, New York, Harper and Brothers, 1940.

This is a good reference for techniques.

THE LEATHERCRAFTSMAN, by W. E. Snyder, Worcester, Mass., Grayton and Knight, 1936.

Good historic and technical section. Clear instructions and photographs. A good text.

LEATHER GOODS MANUFACTURE, by G. C. Moseley, London, England, Sir Isaac Pitman and Sons, Ltd., 1939.

A practical guide to modern methods and processes. The book is intended for the trade but has a great deal of information which will be valuable to the home craftsman.

LEATHER IN LIFE AND INDUSTRY, by John W. Waterer, London, England, Faber and Faber, Limited, no date.

> A very interesting book. Beautiful photographs. Discusses use of leather from historic times and into the future. No directions for processes but gives many suggestions for research.

LEATHERWORK, by I. P. Roseaman, Peoria, Illinois, The Manual Arts Press, no date.

> Uses British terminology. Excellent on manipulating leather. Author not much taken with tooled leather. Finished tailored pieces unusually good. Fine examples of stamping.

STENCILING

EARLY AMERICAN STENCILS on Walls and Furniture, by Janet Waring, New York, William P. Scott, 1937.

> Interesting historically.

HANDS AT WORK, by Emmy Zweybrück, Springfield, Massachusetts, The Holden Publishing Company, 1942. (Distributed by The American Crayon Company, Sandusky, Ohio.)

> A number of crafts are discussed, but stenciling is stressed. The illustrations are stimulating and informal in character.

THE SECOND STENCIL BOOK, by Frau Emmy Zweybrück, Sandusky, Ohio, The American Crayon Company, 1940.

> This book shows examples of work done with chalk and crayons, as well as with paint.

THIS AND THAT

DECORATIVE IDEAS, by Ivy Penelope Roseaman, Leicester, The Dryad Press, 1937.

HOME DECORATION WITH FABRIC AND THREAD, by Ruth W. Spears, New York, M. Barrows and Company, 1940.

101 HOME FURNISHINGS AND HOW TO MAKE THEM, by Lucina Wakefield, New York and London, Harper and Brothers, 1942.

LET'S DECORATE OUR HOME, edited by Anne Means, New York, Robert M. McBride and Company, 1941.

> There are many usable ideas in the four books mentioned above which might furnish ideas for articles that would lend themselves well to decorative design applied in any of the craft media.

DESIGN TECHNICS, by Felix Payant, Syracuse, Keramic Studio Publishing Company, 1934.

A presentation of the methods employed when handling various media used for the execution of designs.

THE ENCYCLOPAEDIA BRITANNICA

This is always a good reference to use. Techniques for many of the crafts are discussed here.

SOURCE MATERIAL

ANIMAL FORM

LES ANIMAUX, by Armand Dayot, Paris, Charles Moreau, no date. There are five volumes in this series.

A collection of drawings, photographs, and reproductions of sculpture. All excellent examples—they range from sensitive, realistic representations to advanced stylizations.

AUDUBON PRINTS

DESIGN IN NATURE, drawings prepared by the School of the Art Institute, Chicago, Field Museum of Natural History.

MUSEUM, Natural History Department.

For individual research.

NATIONAL GEOGRAPHIC MAGAZINE

NATURE MAGAZINE

ZOÖLOGICAL BOOKS

A thorough understanding of the anatomy of animals is a prerequisite to good drawing. Visit the zoo and draw!

PLANT FORM

ART FORMS IN NATURE, by Professor Karl Blossfeldt, New York, E. Weyhe, 1929.

Examples from the plant world photographed direct from nature. Every page is a challenge. About all that the designer need do is to combine forms. The photographs are exceptional.

BOTANY BOOKS AND SEED CATALOGUES

BOUQUETS ET FRONDAISONS, by E. A. Seguy, Paris, Massin, no date.

ÉTUDE DE LA PLANTE, by M. P. Verneuil, Paris, Librairie Centrale des Beaux-Arts, no date.

> Each plant form is analyzed carefully for structure and shape. The finished interpretations of these studies belong to a period of art now past, but the studies themselves will never be outmoded. The plans given for units, borders, and allover designs are very useful.

FLORÉAL, by E. A. Seguy, Paris, A. Calavas, no date.

> The designs appear to have been done with a very free brush technique. The style is splashy and far from being conservative. Unusual color combinations have been used. Designs of this kind would adapt themselves well to the technique of contemporary stenciling or screen printing.

FORMEN DES LEBENS, Botanische Lichtbildstudien, by Dr. Paul Wolff, Leipzig, Karl Robert Longewiesche, 1933.

> One hundred and twenty photographs of plant forms, every one beautiful in composition. The depiction of texture and detail is outstanding.

LA PLANTE EXOTIQUE, by Methurin Méheut, Paris, C. Massin and Company, 1931.

> The freedom of the brush strokes and the delightful color will certainly prove inspirational. This same artist has prepared other portfolios of drawings of animals.

NATURE'S AID TO DESIGN, by E. S. D. Owen and Louise W. Bunce, New York, John Lane Company, 1907.

> More photographs of flower and leaf form.

UNABRIDGED (OR ANY GOOD) DICTIONARY

> For leaf, root, and flower forms.

MOTIFS FOR ADAPTATION

GENERAL

DEKORATIVE VORBILDER, a yearbook of decorative design, edited by Armand Guérinet, Paris, 25 volumes, 1894-1928.

KUNSTGEWERBLICHE, Schmuckformen für die Fläche, no date.

> The designs in this collection are very abstract and somewhat bizarre.

ORNAMENTATION AND TEXTILE DESIGN, by Alfred F. Barker, London, Methuen and Company, Ltd., 1930.

> A book well supplied with photographs and drawings dealing with inspirational material ranging from architecture to nature forms.

PAPIERS, PEINTS, ET TENTURES MODERNES, by H. Clouzet, Paris, C. Massin and Company, no date.

> Good material to study with reference to space filling when making allovers. There are examples of interesting combinations of units, texture effects, and color combinations.

CONTEMPORARY

APPLIED ART IN FINLAND, World's Fair, New York, 1939-40.

L'ARREDAMENTO MODERNO, by Roberto Aloi, Milan, U. Holpli, 1934.

DECORATIVE ART, annual issues of the Studio Year Book, New York, The Studio Publications, Inc.

> Any book or magazine which records trends in design will help to keep one abreast of the times.

DECORATIVE ARTS OF SWEDEN, by Iona Plath, New York, Charles Scribner's Sons, 1948.

> A rich source for inspirational material especially from the standpoint of design.

DEUTSCHES HANDSWERKSGUT, by Walter Dexel, Berlin, 1939.

HEMSLÖJDENS HANDARBETEN, by Majn Lundbäck, Gertrud Ingers, and Mattis Hörlén, Stockholm, Lantbruksförbundets Tidskriftsaktiebulag, 1944.

> Excellent use of decorative stitching. Modern adaptations. Many simple motifs as well as more elaborate designs. Well illustrated. Swedish text.

NEW IDEAS FOR SURFACE DECORATION, Philadelphia, H. C. Perleberg, Publisher, no date.

HISTORIC

ARCHEOLOGY, any well illustrated text in this field.

DECORATIVE PATTERNS OF THE ANCIENT WORLD, by Flinders Petrie, London, University College, 1930.

> This is in the nature of a scrapbook in which have been collected hundreds of motifs.

THE EVOLUTION OF DECORATIVE ART, by Henry Balfour, New York, The Macmillan Company, 1893.
> Interesting for historical background.

PRIMITIVE ART SERIES, by Doris Rosenthal, New York, Brown-Robertson Company, no date.
> These motifs have been freely drawn and are much larger than material usually found in collections of this nature.

ROMANCE OF DESIGN, by Garnet Warren, Garden City, Doubleday Page Company, 1926.

NATIVE

ART AND LIFE IN NEW GUINEA, by Raymond Firth, New York, The Studio Publications, Inc., 1936.
> The illustrations demonstrate character in line and space division.

BRODERIES DES PAYSANNES DE SMOLENSK, by Princess Marie Ténichev, Paris, Libraire Centrale des Beaux-Arts, no date.
> Especially interesting color combinations.

DESIGN FROM PEASANT ART, by Kathleen Mann, London, A. and C. Black, 1939.
> This book shows motifs selected from various sources; then they are combined in a modern way so that they are suitable for present-day craftwork.

FOLK ART OF RURAL PENNSYLVANIA, by Frances Lichten, New York, Charles Scribner's Sons, 1946.
> Photographs, line drawings, color reproductions.

INDIAN DESIGN AND CRAFTS, a series of publications of the United States Indian Service which can be ordered from the Haskell Institute, Lawrence, Kansas.

JAPANESE WOODCUTS
> These are fine for color and allover patterns.

JAVANESE BATIK DESIGNS FROM METAL STAMPS, by Albert Buell Lewis, Chicago, Field Museum of Natural History, 1924.
> This author has other books, all of which are good references, on allied subjects.

LES TISSUS INDIENS DU VIEUX PEROU, by R. et M. d'Harcourt, Paris, Editions Albert Morance, 1924.
> The book is useful for source material of Peruvian motifs. Of greater importance is the lesson it teaches on the use of muted

color. Rich tones are tastefully combined. It points to the importance of color value and to the possibilities of a limited color palette.

MÖNSTERTECKNING, FÖR FOLK-AND FORTSÄTTNING-SSKOLAN, by John Sjösvärd, Stockholm, Albert Bonniers Förlag, 1924.

A portfolio of design plates in color prepared especially as inspirational material. The designs have been selected from articles of clothing and household goods. All are simple and well chosen accessories. Swedish text.

NORWEGIAN DESIGN IN WISCONSIN, a portfolio of Serigraphs (silk screen prints), by Elaine Smedal and Anne Tressler, Madison, Wisconsin, Campus Publishing Company, 1946.

Limited edition. Very useful for adaptations, the purpose for which the portfolio was originally designed.

PARACAS EMBROIDERIES, A Study of Repeated Patterns, by Cora E. Stafford, New York, J. J. Augustin, Publisher, 1941.

These are especially valuable for study of the importance of color value in design.

PEASANT ART IN EUROPE, by H. Th. Bossert, New York, E. Weyhe, 1927.

Large portfolio of plates in color. Excellent source for design.

PEASANT ART IN ITALY, edited by Charles Holme, London, Paris, New York, The Studio Ltd., MCMXI.

This is one of a series of books on European peasant art. All are good—excellent as design sources. Countries covered are Russia, Switzerland, Sweden, etc.

PENNSYLVANIA DUTCH, AMERICAN FOLK ART, by Henry Kauffman, New York and London, American Studio Books, 1946.

Line drawings, photographs, color reproductions.

PERSIAN TEXTILES, by N. A. Reath and E. B. Sachs, Pennsylvania Museum of Art, by Yale University Press, 1937.

PERIODICALS

CRAFT HORIZONS, a quarterly published by American Craftsmen's Coöperative Council, Inc., New York.

> Useful for keeping up to date on contemporary crafts.

WOMAN'S DAY, a periodical distributed by A & P Food Stores, New York, Stores Publishing Company.

> The needlework section of this magazine presents one of the most intelligent approaches to handicraft for the average woman now available.

RELATED FIELDS

ANCIENT EGYPTIAN, ASSYRIAN, AND PERSIAN COSTUMES AND DECORATIONS, by M. G. Houston and F. Hornblower, London, A. and C. Black, 1931.

ILLUSTRATED BALLET PROGRAMS

LEON BAKST, costume designs by Leon Bakst, Berlin, E. Wasmuth, no date.

PEASANT COSTUME OF THE BLACK FOREST, by Dora W. Pettigrew, London, A. and C. Black, 1937.

PEASANT COSTUME IN EUROPE, Vols. 1 and 2, by Kathleen Mann, London, A. and C. Black, 1931.

THE RUSSIAN BALLET in Western Europe 1909-1920, by W. A. Propert, New York, John Lane Company, 1921.

> Fine source material for the use of color. It is dramatic—with an abundance of vitality.

SCANDINAVIAN PEASANT COSTUME, by Kathleen Primmer, London, A. and C. Black, 1939.

> Abundant source material for headgear, as well as decorative notes for the entire wardrobe.

Index

Accessories, 81–342
  household, 234–342
    appliquéd or patchwork, 297–304
    batik, 350–355
    block-printed, 253–268
    embroidered, 280–293
    hooked rugs, 294–299
    portfolios, notebooks, 305–320
    stenciled, 269–279
    using leather, 191, 307
    using metal, 321–342
    using textiles, 251–304
    using wood, 234–250
  wardrobe, 81–233
    belt fob, illustration of, 191
    belts, 83–113
      leather, illustrations of, 186, 187, 188, 224, 226
    buttons, 116, 140–148, 224
    definition of, 82
    hat, leather mosaic, illustration of, 175
    hoods, 158–164
    mittens, 149–158
    purses, fabric, 117–139
      leather, illustrations of, 167, 170, 188, 219, 226, 228, 232
Adapting a design, 14–36, 125–132, 152–157
  illustrations of, 18–35, 152–157
  process of, 16–35

Adapting a design, to mittens, 152–157
  to tailored bag, 125–132
Allover designs, 66–74
  illustrations of, 26, 68–70, 72, 73
Antique finish for leather, 201
Appliqué, household accessories, illustrations of, 22, 23, 297–304
  technique, 300–304
  uses for, 300
  wardrobe, 108–111
    belt, 108–111
    leather, illustrations of, 174, 232

Bags, see Purses
Balance, in color, 44
  in design, 12
  in unit designs, 75–77
  kinds of, 12
Batik, 350–355
  eggs, 350–352
    illustrations of, 351, 352
  fabrics, equipment and materials for, 353, 354
    removing wax from, 354
    technique, 353–354
  paper, 355
Belt fob, illustration of, 191
Belts, 83–113
  card woven, 91–100
  embroidered, 20, 21, 100–113, 116

[375]

Belts, embroidered, designing of, 20, 21,
102, 103, 108, 110, 111
illustrations of, 20, 102, 103, 111
materials for, 102, 106, 108, 111, 112
fastenings for, 100, 101, 106–109
illustrations of, 30, 101, 109–111
finger woven, 81–91
finishing of, 112–113
leather, illustrations of, 186, 187, 188,
224, 226
Block printing, 253–268
borders, 264–267
corners, 264–267
diagrams for, 265
cutting the block, 255–258
equipment and materials for, 254, 259
illustrations of, 256, 257
methods of checking progress, 258
multicolor, 262–264
on leather, illustrations of, 182
preparation of block, 254, 255
printing, 258–267
illustrations of, 259–262
uses for, 253, 254
illustrations of, 26, 182, 252, 253,
255, 263, 266, 267, 268, 275
Book, leather bound, illustration of, 307
Booties, embroidered, illustration of, 116
Borders, 60–66, 264–267
block-printed, 264–267
corners, 65–66, 264–266
designing, 60–66
illustrations of, 24, 62
Bowls, metal, 322–330
equipment and materials for, 322–324
finishing surface of, 329, 330
illustrations of, 322, 341
molds for, 324–328
diagram of, 327
technique, 328, 329
wooden, 236–239
decoration and finishing of, 236–239
designing, 237, 238

Bowls, wooden, illustrations of, 237, 238
Boxes, leather, illustrations of, 191
wooden, illustrations of, 248–250
Braiding, four-strand, 101
Bread, Mexican, illustration of, 346
Buttons, 116, 140–148
cork, 143
embroidered, 116, 144
fabric, 143, 144
leather, 140, 141, 222–225
metal, 144–148
equipment for, 144, 145
illustration of, 147
wooden, 141–143
equipment for, 142, 143
illustration of, 141

Cake, decorated, illustration of, 344
Candle holders, illustrations of, 243, 322,
323, 339
Card case, leather, illustration of, 182
Card weaving, 91–100
belts, 91–100
designing for, 92, 97, 99
diagrams for, 94, 96, 99
equipment and materials for, 91, 92, 94
illustrations of, 92, 93, 97
technique, 97–100
Chair seat, needle point, illustration of, 293
Character in design, 45–52
Color, 37–44, 51, 52, 54, 71
harmonies, 41
schemes, 40–42
setting of, on cloth, 276
on paper, 278
source material, 42, 43
theory of, 37–42
use of, 43, 44
Cookies, gingerbread, 343–350
frosting recipe, 348
illustrations of, 345, 347, 355
modeled, 344–346
recipe for, 347

Corners, block-printed, 264–267
  border designs, 65, 66
  mitered, in borders, 265–267
    on portfolios, 313, 315, 316

Decorative design, 8, 18–35, 173
  on mittens, 5, 6, 153–157
  relation to structural design, 8–11, 173
  stitches, 104, 105
Design, 3–36, 45–80, 280–282
  abstract vs. realistic, 45–50, 79, 80
  adaptation of, 14–35, 154–157
    for mittens, 152–157
    for tailored bag, 125–132
    from one source, 18–35
  allover, 66–74
  border, 60–66
  character in, 45–52
  corner, 65, 66
  decorative, 8, 9, 18–35, 173
  definition of, 3
  evaluation of, 9, 45–55, 79, 80, 280–282
  factors of, 9–13
  methods, 60–80
  planning, 14
  source material, 53–55
  spirit of, 50
  structural, 3–8, 172
  suitability of, 50, 280–282
  surface, 66–74
  unit, 11, 74–80
Draperies, illustrations of, appliqué, 302
  block-printed, 252, 268
  stenciled, 269

Eggs, decorative, 350–352
  dyes for batik, 352
  illustrations of, 351, 352
Embossing leather, 190–193
  illustrations of, 191
Embroidery, decorative stitches, 104, 105
  for household accessories, 280–293
    designing, 280–283
    uses for, 289–293

Embroidery, for wardrobe accessories, 100–132, 149–164
  belts, 20, 100–112, 116
  booties, 116
  buttons, 116, 144
  dresses, 113, 114
  hat, 175
  hoods, 159–164
  jacket, 113
  leather, 174, 175, 232
  mittens, 6, 153
  purses, 125–132, 138, 232
  spectacle case, 174
  materials suitable for, 106, 114, 115
  scale, in combinations of material, 106
  source material, 282, 283
Emphasis, in color, 44
  in design, 13
Etching process, see Metalcraft

Finger weaving, 84–91
  diagrams, 87–89
  illustrations of, 84, 85
  materials for, 84
  technique, 85–91
    chevron pattern, 86–90
    diagonal stripe pattern, 89–91
Frosting recipe, 348
Function, effect upon design, 4–8, 172, 173
  factors determining, 4

Gingerbread men, see Cookies
Golden oblong, 11, 12
Good drawing, 45–51
Good taste, development of, 1, 2, 45–52, 82
Graining of leather, 172
Gussets for purses, see Purses

Harmony, of color, 11, 40–42, 52
  of consistent sizes, 11
  of idea, 10, 50, 67, 71
  of shape, 10, 13, 74, 80
  of texture, 10, 106, 332, 342

Hat, leather mosaic, illustration of, 175
Hoods, 158–164
    construction of, 160–163
    decoration of, 163, 164
    illustration of, 159
    pattern, cutting directions, 161–163
    source material, 158
Hooked rugs, 294–299
    appliance for making, 296, 299
    designing for, 298
    illustrations of, 294–296
    materials for, 298–299
Household accessories, *see* Accessories
Hue, of color, 37, 38

Incised leather, 193, 194
    illustrations of, 167, 187
Index of American Design, 15
Intensity of color, 39, 41

Jacket, embroidered, illustration of, 113
Japanese binding, 318

Keying stencils, 271–274

Lacing and stitching leather, *see* Leather-
    craft
Leather, antique finish for, 201
    appliqué, illustrations of, 174, 232
    bag, drawstring, illustration of, 170
    block-printed, illustration of, 182
    buttons, 140, 141
        illustration of, 224
    carved, place of, 166
    characteristics of, 169–171
    coloring or dyeing, 199–201
    cutting, 178
    embroidery on, illustrations of, 174, 175,
        232
    envelope purse, illustration of, 167, 228
    graining of, 172
    incised, illustrations of, 167, 187
    lacing and stitching, 206–223

Leather, mosaic hat, illustration of, 175
    protecting surface of, 201, 202, 231, 232
    purchasing of, 170–172
    quilted suède bag, illustration of, 219
    spectacle case, illustration of, 174
    tooled, illustrations of, belt closing, 30
        belt fob, 191
        belts, 186–188, 226
        book binding, 307
        box, 191
        buttons, 224
        card case, 182
        purses, 167, 188, 226
    transferring the design to, 179–181
    trimming and skiving, 202–204
Leathercraft, abuse of, 165, 166, 192, 199
    assembling parts, 229–231
    buckles, buttons and fasteners for, 222–
        225
    diagrams of, 222
    illustrations of, 167, 188, 191, 222,
        224, 226
    checking and planning, 204, 205
    coloring and dyeing process, 199–201
    cutting leather for, 178
    designing for, 172–176
    equipment and materials for, 176–184,
        193, 197–202, 205–207, 209, 210,
        216, 223, 227–229
    general suggestions, 196, 197
        for assembling parts, 229–231
        for handstitching, 220–223
        for surface care, 231, 232
    gluing and pasting, 205, 206
    gussets for purses, *see* Purses
    incising leather, 193–194
        illustrations of, 167, 187
    lacing and stitching, 206–223
        diagrams of, 212
        illustrations of, 208
        suggestions for, 220–223
    leathers for, 169–171
    lining, materials for, 228, 229

Leather, metal decorations for, 197–199
    illustrations of, 187, 188, 191, 224, 226
    Mexican Indian, illustration of, 226
    planning construction, 176–178
    reinforcement, materials for, 227, 228
    rye flour paste, recipe for, 205
    setting snap fasteners, 223–225
    skiving process, 202–204
    splicing thong, 210
        diagram of, 212
    surface finish for, 201, 202, 231, 232
    techniques, 184–195
        embossing, 190–193
            illustrations of, 191
        incising, 193, 194
            illustrations of, 167, 187
        modeling, 185–190
            illustrations of, 186–188
        stamping and texturing, 194, 195
            illustrations of, 182, 187, 226
        transferring the design, 179–181
        trimming and skiving, 202–204

Metalcraft, 144–148, 321–342
    bowls, see Bowls
    buttons, see Buttons
    candle holders, illustrations of, 322, 323,
        339
    etching process, 330–333
        designing for, 330
        illustration of, 332
        materials for, 330–332
        technique, 330–333
    molds for, 324–328
    napkin rings, illustrations of, 28, 332,
        341, 342
    plates, see Bowls
    salt and pepper shakers, 338–341
        illustration of, 341
    soldering, 145–147, 337–342
        illustrations of, 145, 335
    spoons and forks, see Spoons and forks
    surface finish, 147, 329, 330

Metalcraft, transferring design, 330
Methods of designing, 60–80
    allovers, 66–74
    borders, 60–66
    repeats, basic, 68–70
    unit designs, 74–80
Mitered corners, for borders, 265–267
    for portfolios, 313, 315, 316
Mittens, 5–7, 149–158
    adapting design for, 152–157
    construction of, 158
    illustrations of, 152–157
    materials for, 5, 150, 153
    pattern, cutting directions, 151
Modeling leather, 185–190
    illustrations of, 186–188
Molds for metal bowls, 324–328
Monograms, 282
"Morgue" or clipping file, 15, 118, 119

Napkin rings, illustrations of, 28, 332, 341,
    342
Needle point, 111, 112, 293
    illustrations of, 32, 103, 116, 293
Needlework, see Embroidery

Order, factors of, in design, 9, 13

Pastry bag, 348–350
    diagram for, 349
Patchwork, see Appliqué
Patterns, formal bag, 135
    hood, 160–162
    mittens, 151
    napkin ring, 29
    tailored bag, 121, 122
Pewter, see Metalcraft
Pillow top, appliqué, illustration of, 22,
    298
Place mats, illustrations of, 279, 290–292,
    297
Plates, metal, see Bowls
    wooden, 239–243

Plates, wooden, designing, 34, 241, 242
    finishing surface of, 236, 237, 243
    illustrations of, 34, 240–242
    materials and equipment for, 242, 243
Pompons, 164
Portfolios, 305–320
  adjustable, illustration of, 306
  Japanese binding, 318
  scrapbooks, illustration of, 309
  stub booklet, illustration of, 319
  telephone book cover, 305–320
    construction of, 310–320
      diagrams of, 313
    illustration of, 308
    materials for, 305–310
Proportion, Greek standard for, 11, 12
  in color, 43
  in design, 11
Purses, afternoon bags, 132–134
    illustration of, 32
  beach bag, illustration of, 119
  classification of, 117, 118
  fabric, 117–138
  fasteners for purses, diagrams of, 222
    illustrations of, 167, 188, 219, 226
  formal bag, 134–139
    construction of, 134–138
    decoration of, 138, 139
    illustration of, 135
    materials for, 135, 136
  gussets for, diagrams of, 222
    illustrations of, 167, 188
    sewing of, 221, 222, 230, 231
  handles or pulls for, 125, 222
  knitting bag, illustration of, 120
  leather, illustrations of, 167, 170, 188, 219, 226, 228, 232
  needle point bag, illustration of, 32
  quilted suède bag, illustration of, 219
  source material, 118, 119
  special purpose bags, 118
    illustrations of, 119, 120

Purses, tailored bag, 120–132
  adapting a design for, 126–132
  construction of, 121–125
    diagrams of, 123
  decoration of, 125–132
  illustration of, 121
  materials for, 121, 127

Quilts, illustrations of, 297, 299

Repeat patterns, basic, 68–70
Rhythm, in border design, 60–62
  in color, 44
  in design, 13
Rye flour paste, recipe for, 205

Salt and pepper shakers, 338–341
Scale, allover design, 67
  in combinations of materials, 106
  in design, 11
Screen, block-printed, illustration of, 252
Setting of color, on cloth, 276
  on paper, 278
  snap fasteners, 223, 225
Skiving leather, 202–204
Soldering, *see* Metalcraft
Source material, illustrations of, 18, 128, 154, 238, 239, 268, 281, 283, 290, 297, 301
  where to find, 15, 53–55, 158, 282
Spectacle case, illustration of, 174
Spoons and forks, 333–338, 341
  diagrams of, 336
  equipment and materials for, 334, 335
  illustration of, 341
  technique, 334–338
Splicing thong, 210
  diagram of, 212
Stamping and texturing leather, 194, 195
  illustrations of, 182, 187, 226
Stenciling, 269–279
  cutting the stencil, 271
  designing for, 270

Stenciling, equipment, materials for, 269–271, 277, 278
  keying the stencil, 271–274
    diagram of, 273
  large units, 276, 277
  on paper, 278
  setting color, on cloth, 276
    on paper, 278
  technique, 274–278
  uses for, 269
    illustrations of, 24, 119, 269, 274, 275, 277, 279
Stitching and lacing leather, *see* Leathercraft
Structural design, 3–8, 172
  control over decorative designs, 8, 9, 11
  function of object, 4–8, 28
Stub booklet, 319
Subordination in design, 13
Surface design, 66–74
Surface finishes, for leather, 201, 202, 231, 232
  for metal, 147, 329, 330
  for wood, 236, 237, 243, 246, 247, 250

Telephone book cover, *see* Portfolios
Tiles, wooden, 244–247
  coloring surface of, 245, 246
  construction of, 245–247
  decoration of, 246–247
  finishing of, 246–247

Tiles, illustration of, 59, 245
Tooled leather, *see* Leather
Tooling techniques, *see* Leathercraft
Transferring designs to fabrics, 102, 103, 132, 285
  to leather, 179–181
  to metal, 330
  to wood, 238
Trays, *see* Plates

Unit designs, 11, 74–80
  basic layouts, 75–77
  illustrations, 75–79

Value, in color schemes, 51, 52
  of color, 38, 39, 41

Wall hangings, appliqué, illustration of, 301
  block-printed, 251, 253
  embroidered, 284–289
    finishing of, 285, 286
    hanging of, 286–289
    illustration of, 287, 288
    materials for, 284, 285
  stenciled, illustrations of, 274, 275
Wallpaper, illustrations of use, 57–59
  materials used with, 56
Wardrobe accessories, *see* Accessories
Wood finishes, 236, 237, 243, 246, 247, 250